# DISEASES OF THE WILL
## Alcohol and the Dilemmas of Freedom

While associated with comfort and pleasure, alcohol
continues to be a 'problem' substance, both for medical
and political authorities and for many drinkers. In this
broad-ranging and innovative historical-sociological
investigation, Valverde explores the ways in which both
authorities and individual consumers have defined
and managed the pleasures and dangers of alcoholic
beverages. She explores the question of free will versus
determinism and how it has been challenged by ideas
about addiction, morality and psychology during the
last 150 years. Drawing on North American, British and
other sources, the book discusses topics including nineteenth century 'dipsomania', the history of inebriate
homes, Alcoholics Anonymous, fetal alcohol education
and liquor control. It will appeal to readers in legal
studies, criminology, sociology, psychology, social
theory and the history of medicine.

MARIANA VALVERDE is Professor of Criminology at the
University of Toronto. She has also lectured in the
Sociology and Women's Studies departments at the
University of Toronto. Her previous books include *The
Age of Light, Soap and Water* (1991) and *Sex, Power and
Pleasure* (1985). She has co-edited and contributed to
several other titles and published numerous articles in
journals such as *Social History, Economy and Society* and
*Studies in Political Economy.*

# CAMBRIDGE STUDIES IN LAW AND SOCIETY

The broad area of law and society has become a remarkably rich and dynamic field of study. At the same time, the social sciences have increasingly engaged with questions of law. In this process, the borders between legal scholarship and the social, political and cultural sciences have been transcended, and the result is a time of fundamental rethinking both within and about law. In this vital period, Cambridge Studies in Law and Society provides a significant new book series with an international focus and a concern with the global transformation of the legal arena. The series aims to publish the best scholarly work on legal discourse and practice in social context, combining theoretical insights and empirical research.

Anthony Woodiwiss *Globalization, Human Rights and Labour Law in Pacific Asia*
 0 521 62144 5 hardback    0 521 62883 0 paperback

*This book is dedicated
to the memory of
José-María Valverde, 1926–1996*

# DISEASES OF THE WILL

## Alcohol and the Dilemmas of Freedom

*Mariana Valverde*

CAMBRIDGE UNIVERSITY PRESS
Cambridge, New York, Melbourne, Madrid, Cape Town, Singapore, São Paulo

Cambridge University Press
The Edinburgh Building, Cambridge CB2 2RU, UK

Published in the United States of America by Cambridge University Press, New York

www.cambridge.org
Information on this title: www.cambridge.org/9780521623001

© Mariana Valverde 1998

First published 1998

*A catalogue record for this publication is available from the British Library*

*Library of Congress Cataloguing in Publication data*

Valverde, Mariana, 1955–
    Diseases of the Will: alcohol and the dilemmas of freedom/
Mariana Valverde.
        p.    cm. – (Cambridge studies in law and society)
    Includes bibliographical references and index.
    ISBN 0-521-62300-6 (hardcover: alk. paper).
    ISBN 0-521-64469-0 (pbk: alk. paper).
    1. Drinking of alcoholic beverages – History. 2. Alcoholism –
History. 3. Alcoholics – Rehabilitation – History. 4. Alcohol – Law
and legislation – History. 5. Free will and determinism. I. Title.
II. Series.
HV5020.V35 1998                                              98–7276
362.292´09–dc21

*National Library of Australia Cataloguing in Publication data*

Valverde, Mariana, 1955.
Diseases of the will: alcohol and the dilemmas of freedom.

Bibliography.
Includes index.
ISBN 0 521 62300 6.

1. Alcohol – History. 2. Drinking of alcoholic beverages.
3. Free will and determinism. I. Title. (Series:
Cambridge studies in law and society).

394.13

ISBN-13 978-0-521-62300-1 hardback
ISBN-10 0-521-62300-6 hardback

ISBN-13 978-0-521-64469-3 paperback
ISBN-10 0-521-64469-0 paperback

Transferred to digital printing 2005

# CONTENTS

CONTENTS

# ILLUSTRATIONS

# ACKNOWLEDGEMENTS

This book turned out to be a far more massive project than I had anticipated, both at the level of empirical research and at the level of analysis. It would not have been possible to complete it without the generous material and moral support provided by people and institutions too numerous to be named here. I would nevertheless like to publicly thank at least some friends, colleagues, and organizations for their time, goodwill, and expertise.

Material support was largely provided by the Social Sciences and Humanities Research Council and by the Centre of Criminology, University of Toronto. Among other things, the SSHRC three-year grant enabled me to use the highly skilled research assistance of Benedikt Fischer, Lachlan Story, Kimberley White-Mair, and Mary Lynn Young. The Centre of Criminology's staff, especially Rita Donelan and Gloria Cernivivo, efficiently administered the grant. The Centre also provided an inexhaustible supply of moral and intellectual support.

The librarians and staff at a number of institutions, most of which are working under severe constraints due to cutbacks, also provided crucial support. I would like to thank the Addiction Research Foundation, the British Library, the Wellcome Institute in London, and, at the University of Toronto, the Centre of Criminology Information Centre, the Robarts Library, and the Science and Medicine library.

Former and current doctoral students have been an important part of my life over the past few years. I would like to especially thank Ian Baird, Kelly Hannah-Moffatt, Janice Hill, Margaret Little, Lucy Luccisano, Paula Maurutto, Phil Mun, Anna Pratt, Lealle Ruhl, Jacinth Samuels, and William Walters.

The generous interest shown by the groups with whom I shared the research – often at embarrassingly early stages – was also crucial. I received a great deal of useful feedback from audiences at at the Addiction Research Foundation, Queen's University, Carleton University, the University of Victoria, Lancaster University, the London History of the Present research network, and the Toronto History of the Present group.

The women with whom I share responsibility for *Feminist Studies* are a constant source of inspiration in sustaining the paradoxical but historically necessary project to do and to encourage excellent work while not taking ourselves too seriously. Special thanks to Ellen Ross and Claire Moses.

About twenty members of Alcoholics Anonymous contributed greatly to this book by agreeing to be interviewed at some length, and a large number of AA members welcomed myself and my research assistant, Kimberley White-Mair, into open group meetings even though it was clear that we were not necessarily going to write a glowing account. Some AA members phoned out of the blue to volunteer to be interviewed; one man kindly sent me some material I would otherwise not have had. Their generosity with each other as well as with us made a significant dent in the cynicism that, like most researchers, I have cultivated.

Many people made this book possible by reading drafts of chapters, sharing their knowledge, patiently correcting mistakes, and offering much support and editorial advice. Paul Antze gave long and useful comments on several chapters and shared his own research on the recovery movement. Geoff Bunn, Kurt Danziger, and Alan Collins patiently tutored me in the history of psychology, and, in addition, Alan Collins read several chapters critically and carefully. Lynne Marks provided support from an early stage and shared materials from her own research on the history of insanity. Robert Campbell shared his knowledge of liquor control, and André Chamberlain gave me materials and ideas for the aboriginal prohibition section. Ricardo Campos Marin shared his work on the history of alcoholism in Spain. Jurgen Rehm and Benedikt Fischer facilitated my access to the resources of the Addiction Research Foundation and let me read very useful unpublished papers. Rosemary Gartner, Steve Katz, Nancy Hewitt, Sally Merry, Tom Osborne, Ellen Ross, Bill Simon, Muriel Vogel-Sprott, Chris Webster, and Lucia Zedner all read specific chapters with a generous spirit. Robin Room shared his knowledge of American alcohol science with me and gave me essential feedback. Ian Baird, Jim Tennyson, and Kimberley White-Mair used their own felicitous intuition to find appropriate illustrations.

Many friends cheerfully put up with a great deal of alcoholism talk at various points over the past years, read drafts (sometimes on the spot), and generally kept me going. I especially want to thank Allan Greer, Clifford Shearing, Carolyn Strange, and Lorna Weir for their support and excellent advice. On his part, Peter Fitzpatrick managed to single-handedly maintain my interest in deconstruction and legal theory, even as I was immersed in Foucaultian labours about which he must have had more reservations than he showed. And although she did not comment on drafts, Barbara Cruikshank probably did more than any other friend to get me to finish the book, since I had to finish it in order to begin a new, jointly authored one.

Pat O'Malley has generously supported me at every step of the way, acting as a model friend and a model editor. Talks with Pat on 'addiction' and on 'risk' taught me a great deal and shaped the book in decisive ways: indeed, it is likely that, without his support and help, this book would never have been written. He made important suggestions about the book's contents and facilitated its publication, putting his own work aside to deal with the practical details of revising the manuscript – details made more difficult by an inopportune postal strike into which a crucial diskette vanished.

Nikolas Rose has been a key source of inspiration for all of my work over the past five years. His comments on several of the chapters were invaluable. But, most importantly, he has been consistently willing to engage in a practice of friendship that includes disagreement and criticism alongside kindness and support. His criticisms and his enthusiasms have shaped the book much more than is apparent from the notes.

Intellectual work is not easily separable from one's life. My mother, Pilar-Hedy Gefaell, has always provided care and support, and my late father, José-María Valverde, was from the beginning of my writing career to the end of his life my most forgiving reader. A professor of aesthetics discontented with traditional philosophy, he was instrumental in my decision, made long ago but still visible in this book, to take up historical research projects. The last conversations I had with him before he died were about this book, and as I wrote it I often heard his voice in my mind.

My partner Maggi Redmonds and our son Nicolas have lived with this book and its author since its inception, and deserve more than thanks for supporting me through their love. I am particularly grateful to Maggi for being a constant reminder that the most interesting ideas are not necessarily those of scholars, for doing more than her share of the childcare as this book was being completed, and for sometimes forcing me to be more in touch with the ethical and political issues of our present. Nicky amazed me with his ability to muster genuine enthusiasm to repeatedly ask, "Which chapter are you working on now?". Finally, I take great pleasure in acknowledging here our beautiful new daughter Ming, who was given to us as this book was nearing completion. Her presence, though sometimes interfering with much-needed sleep, has been a constant source of happiness and hope in our household and for all our friends.

# INTRODUCTION

'Let's have a drink!' is a statement made in a large number of diverse situations. When we want to celebrate and when we need to commiserate; when we are pursuing a sexual interest and when we are getting over a romantic failure; when visiting with friends we like and when socializing with relatives we don't like; when the workday is over and when the boss is making us miserable; when a baby is born and when someone dies: all of these situations seem to most of us to lead naturally to drinking. And by a drink we of course mean an alcoholic drink, with other liquids being regarded as soft drinks, as substitutes, for no liquid other than alcohol is freighted with such diverse expectations, comforts, fears, and hopes.

If alcohol is a major part of our lives because of the multiplicity of situations and experiences which we feel call for a drink, it is nevertheless not an unproblematic aspect of our lives. Large numbers of people have come to regard themselves as having 'a drinking problem', and we often scrutinize other people's drinking behaviour for signs of potential alcoholism/addiction. Alcohol has been problematized for at least 150 years, not only at the level of individual consumption but also at the level of national populations. Taxes on alcoholic drinks have often constituted a major part of government revenue, the licencing of pubs and retail outlets selling liquor has taken up a considerable amount of governmental energy, and the regulation of the liquor traffic has been a major feature of the history of many states, giving rise, for instance, to the only amendment to the US Constitution geared to governing consumption.

Why has alcohol been so important in everyday life, as a substance evoking strong feelings of both pleasure and danger,[1] and so

1

problematic from the point of view of the authorities governing both individuals and populations?

DISEASES OF THE WILL

One of the earliest writers on what would later be classified under alcoholism, the American physician Benjamin Rush, noted that, although people begin drinking of their own free will (which in the 1780s meant drinking hard liquor – wine and beer were not regarded as alcoholic), the habit of drinking eventually leads to the disappearance of the very willpower that had been deployed by the drinker to seek the drink. Dr Rush – whose silhouette graces the logo of the American Psychiatric Association, and who was one of the signers of the US Constitution – argued that habitual drunkenness should be regarded not as a bad habit but as a disease, a "palsy of the will".[2]

The question of the will's ability or inability to flex itself was central to theological debates in the seventeenth and eighteenth centuries; in Rush's country, for instance, it had been the key bone of contention in the battle between determinist Calvinists and the free will Arminians. The question of will and determination was also central to European philosophy from Descartes to Kant, and lost its interest only when moral philosophy as a whole went out of fashion. In the nineteenth century, the question of the will was taken up by the new sciences of physiology and neurology: brain localization studies unsuccessfully attempted to translate the theological debates about the freedom of the will into the somatic paradigm of brain areas and functions. In the courts, the medico-legal construct of moral insanity (in France, monomania) pursued Rush's notion of the palsy of the will in arguments regarding the diminished responsibility of criminals who were not suffering from a disease of the mind (and were hence not legal lunatics) but who were perhaps diseased in that capacity linking mind and body, the will. The drink monomania diagnosis was not especially successful, however, since despite many efforts to medicalize habitual drunkenness or alcoholism, the courts and the general public believed that heavy drinkers, if they really tried, could indeed flex their will and stop their destructive drinking. In the present day, drunkenness, even if psychiatrically classified as rooted in a prior condition (dependence), is rarely thought to excuse crimes, although it may serve to mitigate the sentence. And, as discussed in chapter 8, a recent high-profile Canadian case, in which the Supreme Court decided to allow an extremely drunk offender to claim automatism and hence be potentially freed from responsibility, led to great public agitation, a re-assertion of the old Christian notion that drunks are morally responsible even if they don't really know what they are doing, and a quick legislative move to remove the automatism defense for drink-related offenses.

The failure of the project to extend the moral insanity/ monomania/psychopathy model to drinking is one aspect of the long decline of the project to construct a science rather than a philosophy of the will. Despite the efforts of some scientific writers and clinicians at the turn of the century, most notably the British physicians who founded the Society for the Scientific Study of Inebriety, science and medicine had by 1900 decided to operate on a model in which the only two real entities were the mind and the body. Diseases were henceforth either physical or mental, or a mixture of both. They had to locate themselves somewhere on a spectrum that only included the mind and the body, not the will. The project to construct a third, hybrid category, named by the French scientist Theodule Ribot *maladies de la volonté*, diseases of the will, did not prosper. Toward the end of the nineteenth century, as psychology differentiated itself from neurology on the one hand and from philosophy on the other, the question of the will was largely abandoned.[3] The will was henceforth dismissed as a meta-physical notion whose only place in scientific psychology was as a straw figure to be refuted in the development of behaviourism and other forms of anti-humanist objectivism.

If psychology abandoned the will, that did not mean it was reclaimed by philosophy. As a philosophy undergraduate, in the mid-1970s, I was once involved in a conversation at the student pub about free will vs. determinism. The one member of faculty who happened to be present opined that the question of free will was the sort of thing that ordinary people thought philosophers dealt with, but was in fact of no interest to real philosophers. This was and remains true. Philosophers now tend to either reject or, more commonly, to simply ignore, the legacy of nor-mative ethical philosophy within which 'the will' had been located. Nevertheless, the fact that we eager and naive undergraduates were fruitlessly wondering if philosophy had any insights to offer on the question of individual freedom appears to me now as highly significant. Eve Sedgwick has perceptively pointed out that, whatever philosophers might opine, in publications or in pubs, since the 1970s we have been collectively experiencing an "epidemic" of free will: an intense valuation of personal freedom, an inescapable imperative that "the idea of free will be propagated".[4] Reflecting on the proliferation of addiction-recovery groups loosely based on the twelve steps of Alcoholics Anonymous, Sedgwick has noted that large numbers of people have become avid consumers of advice on how to prevent and cure the paralyses of the free will that afflict us as we go about the business of shaping ourselves through consumption – the consumption not only of problem liquids and solids, such as alcohol and drugs, but of all manner of commodities, pleasures, and behaviours.

On the World Wide Web, dozens of self-help groups concerned with questions of the will and its palsies can be accessed if one looks up www.netwizards.net/recovery/. Alcoholics Anonymous and other alcohol-focussed groups can be accessed through an on-line recovery network that has mushroomed thanks to the happy coincidence that the Internet, like lay mutual-help organizations, is decentralized, non-hierarchical, non-professionalized, and can easily accommodate participants who want to remain anonymous. Although AA remains by far the largest organization and the prototype of these proliferating groups, drink is not the sole or even main preoccupation of this network. There is a page for "Workaholics Anonymous", one for "Overeaters Anonymous", one for "Nicotine Anonymous", and one entitled "Recovery from debt home page" that usefully reminds us that credit cards can be a dangerous site of addiction. What is perhaps most interesting about the proliferation of sites for diagnosing oneself as an addict in need of recovery is that even the activities usually associated with health and recovery have themselves become suspect. Alcoholics are often told to take up daily exercise as a healthy replacement for drinking habits, and addicts of all varieties are often counselled to pay more attention to their intimate relationships. But exercise too can now be an addiction, as can sex, and even love: "Emotions Anonymous" is one of the self-help groups listed on "Recovery Online". Sedgwick shows that freedom-seeking projects can suddenly turn into their opposite and come to be experienced as yet another slavery, another addiction; "as each assertion of will has made voluntarity itself appear problematical in a new area, the assertion of will itself has come to appear addictive".[5]

From Benjamin Rush's "palsy of the will", through nineteenth century monomania, to the proliferation of addiction-recovery programmes, one can see a clear line of continuity. This line does not resemble an evolutionary diagram, however. Unlike those dealing with illnesses of the mind or of the body, those who have struggled with questions of the will have rarely known that there is a long history of ruined projects to seize and maximize the will's freedom. In tracing the connections linking palsy of the will, monomania, inebriety, alcoholism, and addiction, I did not discover a previously unknown straight evolutionary line, but rather something like a compulsion to repeat the same dilemmas and re-enact the same paradoxes of recovery highlighted by Sedgwick. Is the will free? If even people who are not insane sometimes feel an overwhelming compulsion, say to have another drink, is this a sign that we are not free? But given that some people do kick the drink habit, does this mean that individuals have the power to overcome social and biological determinations? If addictions are diseases of the will, how can anyone flex that diseased will with sufficient force to 'kick the habit'?

Alcohol has been a problematic substance for modern European societies because questions of addiction have been and continue to be important sites upon which the complex dialectic of personal freedom and control/self-control has worked itself out historically. The working out, however, has not been a linear process, nor a neatly dialectical one. The Freudian metaphor of 'the compulsion to repeat one's traumas' is a more appropriate descriptor of the history of addiction/recovery than any teleological framework.[6] The fact that the history outlined in chapters 1 through 5 is full of unwitting repetitions of old dilemmas is particularly ironic given that addiction-recovery programmes all share an assumption that addiction is bad precisely because it is felt as a compulsion, a "slavery from within".[7]

But if the paradoxes plaguing the technologies of the self available today for overcoming compulsions are what this book is ultimately attempting to understand, why focus on alcohol? Answering this query will take some time, since it requires a quick tour through the complex interaction between the history of drugs and the history of alcohol.

DRUGS AND ALCOHOL: AN UNEASY RELATIONSHIP

Today's addiction framework arose through the combination of two different sets of concerns and practical problems. One set of concerns was located within the field of illicit drugs. Throughout the nineteenth century, opium, morphine, and cocaine were regarded as mildly problematic substances of marginal interest to projects of social and moral regulation. In the first decade of the twentieth century, a number of circumstances combined to generate an international panic about the opium traffic, and this was followed, in the 1920s, by a more generalized panic about the figure of the drug fiend. Opium derivatives, morphine, and cocaine, came to be regarded both by experts and by the general public as highly dangerous substances that would immediately cause addiction in virtually anyone. Because their medical use was increasingly restricted, law enforcement agencies gradually assumed jurisdiction over the drug field. Drugs were linked to crime, and drug issues were kept separate from questions arising from the consumption of legal substances such as tranquillizers or, for that matter, alcohol. It bears reiterating that this was not because of new pharmacological knowledge, but simply because illicit drugs were governed through a different set of institutions than either legal drugs or alcohol. But the paradigm of addiction did not grow exclusively out

CRAZED BY DRINK.

" God's rational offspring . . . become a brute."

Temperance campaigns in the nineteenth century suggested that alcohol
was inherently addictive, in contrast to mid-twentieth century theories of
'the alcoholic personality'. (Left: from T.S. Arthur, *Grappling with the
Monster*, New York, American Publishing Co., 1887; right: from Rev W.H.
Daniels, *The Temperance Reform*, New York, Nelson & Phillips, 1877; both
courtesy of the Seagram Collection, University of Waterloo, Ontario.)

THE WAY OF TRANSGRESSORS IS HARD.

of the international struggle to suppress illicit drugs. Another stream that merged with the addiction that had already been constructed through the criminalization of certain drugs was the question of drinking. This became possible only because, by the 1950s, the drinking 'problem' had come to be regarded in most advanced industrial nations as fundamentally a question of that minority of deviants, the alcoholics.

In the 1940s and 1950s, experts located in American universities had largely convinced the English-speaking educated public in the United States and elsewhere that the drink problem was really a problem of the deviant tendencies of a small minority of drinkers. Almost as soon as this view succeeded, however, it was increasingly challenged. This happened partly because nobody managed to offer a clinical definition of alcoholism as a disease that gained general acceptance, and partly because developments within medicine and science brought about a displacement of the alcoholism paradigm by epidemiologists and public health people who did not treat individuals but who instead worried about the increasing levels of *aggregate* alcohol consumption. In the 1960s and 1970s, experts located in the emerging alcoholism research institutions in Helsinki, in Toronto, at Rutgers University in the United States, and in the World Health Organization's European office began to disseminate a formulation that would drastically transform the alcohol field: 'alcohol and other drugs'. Much to the dismay of those American alcohologists who were struggling to make alcohol studies and alcoholism treatment respectable and fundable, the new formulation took alcohol out of the realm of normalcy, where it been placed since the repeal of Prohibition in 1933, and put it right next to the shadowy realm of illicit consumption, the underworld of the drug fiend.

Re-classifying alcohol as a drug shifted the spotlight away from the individual alcoholic and back toward the substance itself. This might have led to a renewed prohibition campaign – and, indeed, the Toronto experts who led the way in research on aggregate national levels of consumption were and still are known as neo-prohibitionists by those who want to discredit them. But even the most worried epidemiologists did not suggest that alcohol be actually governed like 'other drugs'. Criminalizing alcohol was not an option in the happy-consumer climate of the 1960s and 1970s. The alcohol-and-other-drugs campaign of the 1970s therefore had a different effect than the otherwise similar concern about the drug-like properties of alcohol of the 1890s. It encouraged governments to worry less about alcoholism treatment (which had never worried them excessively, even at the height of the alcoholism-as-disease model) and to instead prioritize issues such as liquor advertising, liquor prices and taxes, the age of drinking, and opening hours.

A general concept of addiction (later rephrased, with little sub-
stantive change, as dependence) was thus created, through the mixing
of the drug addict identity and the disease concept of alcoholism. This
concept, however, instantly became so capacious as to lose its power and
even its meaning, precisely because of its inclusion of virtually all
drinking and, very quickly, other socially accepted forms of consumption. If the executives who had a couple of martinis after a hard day's
work – or somewhat later, the secretaries who smoked on coffee breaks
– were now to be regarded as addicts, the stigmatizing power of the
term 'addict' was in danger of being dissipated to the point of extinc-
tion – which is, of course, what is happening with such developments as
the "Recovery from debt home page".

ALCOHOL AND GOVERNANCE

Because drinking has never been confined to a small minority, alcohol
is a more important site than illicit drugs for the governance of populations. And because drinking has rarely been criminalized, alcohol
provides an opportunity to examine the processes involved in governing *spaces* of consumption (bars and pubs, most often). The byzantine
systems of liquor control devised after the repeal of prohibition in both
Canada and the United States, for instance, which have no parallel in
the drug field, constitute a wonderful site upon which to study the ways
in which moral regulation, fiscal policy, and administrative law were
mixed and managed with very little public input.

That liquor control provides great opportunities for the study of the
interaction of a dizzying variety of governmental mechanisms and aims
is not my own insight. A 1936 US study funded by John Rockefeller
argued that alcohol control systems provide "a rich and accurate history
in public administration", because alcohol has the ability to preserve
administrative forms for social science as it preserves specimens in the
biologist's laboratory:

> In short, it may be said that there are few major problems of public
> administration which do not emerge in striking fashion in connection
> with the governmental effort to control the consumption of alcohol. In
> fact, alcohol is an unusually favourable medium in which to study many of
> these problems [of administrative law], even as it is a favourite medium
> for the preservation and study of natural forms in the museum or the
> laboratory.[8]

The consumption of alcoholic drinks allows us to study the complex
interactions between virtually all major modes of governance available
to authorities today – not because of any inherent chemical-sociological

properties, but rather because alcohol has in fact been considered simultaneously as socially problematic and socially acceptable in a multitude of ways. Drinking is a site of addiction: but wine is also consecrated as Christ's blood in Christian church services. Drinking is at one level subject to medical jurisdiction: but it is simultaneously governed by spiritual self-help groups, by religion, and by domestic interactions (marital and parental). Drinking is shaped and regulated by culturally specific habits and rituals that are neither legally enforced nor medicalized; by the apparatus of the criminal law; by the specific administrative machineries of on-site and off-site licencing, and by general administrative machineries such as tax collection and customs inspection. It is also regulated through marketplace mechanisms, including not only liquor advertising but also the marketing of alternatives to alcohol, such as the temperance/health drinks of the 1890s and the soft drinks of the twentieth century.

This complexity makes it, as I found out with some dismay, a very difficult topic to tackle in a single book. But the regulatory richness of the drinking question makes it an ideal topic through which to study the complex and unpredictable interactions and accommodations *among* different modes of governance.[9] Part of the theoretical impetus for this book was a certain discontent with studies of social and moral regulation that artificially isolate a single mode of governance, assuming that what is to be studied is medicalization, or professionalization, or the shift from disciplinary control to risk-based management.

The history of alcoholism is fundamentally characterized by the persistence of what one might call regulatory anarchy. Choosing one site somewhat at random, let us count the ways in which alcohol was regulated in an American urban hospital in the early 1960s. First, the staff cafeteria would likely be barred from selling beer, although a cocktail party for donors might be going on simultaneously in another room. The state machinery of liquor licencing would thus be visible even in the midst of a health apparatus. Meanwhile, some patients might find themselves being labelled as alcoholic personalities by psychiatric social workers, while some psychiatrists, regarding drinking as a superficial and not very significant symptom, diagnosed one aboriginal patient as having an innate incapacity to drink, while diagnosing a young middle-class white male drinker as suffering from repressed homosexuality. And at the same time, the hospital admitting staff might regularly call the police to take away skid-row men who had repeatedly used the hospital to recover from a bender. This not wholly fictional example shows about six quite contradictory ways in which alcohol is governed and is used to govern other things *at a single site.*

Although it evolved into a more general project to use the governance of alcohol as a site in which to analyze the ways in which our wills, our health, and our consumption patterns are governed, this book started out as a study of alcohol*ism*. Alcoholism interested me because, although certainly subject to medicalization, it is a field in which failures, contradictions, and refusals have been perhaps more common than in better studied related fields, such as the history of mental illness and the history of sexuality. It is a striking feature of the history of alcohol that psychiatrists in what was probably the golden age of psychiatric authority – the United States in the 1950s – openly refused to consider alcoholism as a proper object for their particular specialty. Homosexuals and depressed housewives were avidly taken up as objects of psychiatric expertise, but most psychiatrists – especially psycho-analysts – dismissed alcoholics as unsuitable and/or unworthy of their attentions. Today, although psychiatric tools are often used by social workers and therapists dealing with problem drinkers in all English-speaking countries, an overwhelming majority of North Americans consider AA to be a more appropriate referral for drinking problems than any medical institution.

Asking 'why was alcoholism not successfully medicalized?', I event-ually discovered that, although some diseases of the will – most notably, neurasthenia – were indeed medicalized, even if only temporarily, the management of individual alcohol consumption has generally deployed very eclectic combinations of methods, ranging from biodeterminist medical ideas to homey little techniques of auto-behaviour modifica-tion. It is not that medicalization failed: it is rather that alcoholism treatment has been and still is an explicitly hybrid project, borrowing bits from psychiatric science, clinical practice, Christian techniques of the self, high philosophy, New Age spirituality, self-help manuals on success and enterprise, and so forth. This finding has some theoretical significance: it may encourage the abandonment of the paradigm, popular among feminists and other critical scholars, of a linear process of medicalization that either succeeds or fails, in favour of a less abstract approach that pays close attention to the creativity and eclecticism of front-line work.

Precisely because the basic finding in regard to the medicalization of alcoholism was that the question was wrongly posed because it pre-supposed that there really is a linear process called medicalization, it became necessary to explore the hybridity and the practical com-plexities of the governance of alcohol(ism) in realms beyond those of diagnosis and treatment. Initially this was posed in Foucaultian terms: how does the governance of *populations* through alcohol connect with the governance of individuals and their relation of self to self in

11

alcoholism recovery? But in doing the research on the more impersonal projects for governing alcohol, I eventually realized that the available Foucaultian concepts – biopower, health maximization, discipline, security – were not sufficient. The liquor control systems studied in chapter 6 have rarely concerned themselves with either disciplining drinkers individually or maximizing the nation's health. Concerns about orderliness, public morals, and the non-corrupt running of the liquor business have predominated, rather than the rationalities documented by Foucaultian sociologists of health, medicine, sexuality, and crime. Most crucially, liquor control and licencing systems have not had as their direct and main targets either individuals or populations. The gaze of inspectors and liquor-board authorities has been trained upon *the establishment,* a particular space defined economically as well as physically. It is significant that the Liquor Control Board of Ontario has, since its inception, demanded a monthly "conduct report" not from drinkers but from each licenced establishment. Although disciplinary techniques familiar from other realms – for example, regular visits by inspectors – are deployed, the fact that it is the space designated by the legal/physical term 'establishment' that is being disciplined raises a number of issues regarding our understanding of the meaning and significance of the term 'discipline'. The analysis of liquor licencing and liquor control carried out in chapter 6 challenges, among other things, the prevalent assumption that governance in modern times has evolved from sovereignty to discipline to risk management.

Liquor control and licencing are powerful state apparatuses, but the state does not have the monopoly on alcohol regulation (even in so-called 'monopoly' states, such as the province of Ontario, where I live). Chapter 7 thus presents a brief overview of non-state programmes for controlling liquor consumption. The first set of such programmes, generally carried out through existing therapeutic channels but sometimes also through specialized addiction-recovery networks, consists of programmes designed around the rationalities of risk reduction, harm reduction, and harm minimization. These programmes, widely available in other contexts – for example, needle exchange programmes are harm reduction programmes in the field of HIV transmission – present themselves, particularly outside the United States, as post-moralistic, as leaving it to the drinker him/herself to set goals. But as we shall see, although there are indeed programmes that seek to empower drinkers to better regulate and control their drinking and thus avoid harm to themselves, a good number of harm-oriented programmes are more concerned with harm to 'society' or to non-drinkers, and to that extent have a strong disciplinary bent that is rather in tension with the logic of harm reduction. The most successful of these programmes to reduce harm *to others*, in North America at least, concerns drinking by pregnant women.

But state officials and therapeutic professionals are not the only authorities governing the consumption of alcohol at the level of either the whole population or specific problem subpopulations. Chapter 7 follows up the discussion of biomedical risk reduction by a brief discussion of the regulation of drinking by market forces, focussing particularly on the case of the Coca-Cola company, which has been a huge success story partly because its product was marketed both as a temperance drink and as a mixer. This study of Coca-Cola's successful project to make a non-alcoholic drink as full of pleasure and hedonism as alcoholic drinks suggests, more generally, that the sphere of commercial consumption (which is usually studied with cultural-studies rather than Foucaultian tools) cannot be left out of any thorough analysis of governance.

These two chapters, featuring state bureaucracies, therapeutic establishments, and commercial interests, might on their own create the misleading impression that if the disease model of alcoholism failed, it was because governing individuals has become increasingly irrelevant in the governance of alcohol as measures to govern risks have come to the fore. The final chapter thus analyzes one site – the criminal law, in Canada and parts of the United States – in which the Victorian notion of the free individual with a sovereign will is being reasserted with tremendous force, with extremely drunk offenders now being held accountable for all the consequences of their actions. This phenomenon, which is facilitated by the rise of certain neoconservative moralities that combine very uneasily with neoliberal techniques for governing impersonally, fits very well with Eve Sedgwick's brilliant insight into the propaganda for the free will that characterizes our present.

While the history of alcoholism diagnoses and treatments, and to a lesser extent the workings of Alcoholics Anonymous, have been studied by some (few) scholars, the topics covered in chapters 6–8 are largely unexplored, and deserve to be studied in much more detail than can be done here. Those chapters are therefore presented not as exhaustive specialist studies but rather as tentative sketches of the alcohol terrain, the terrain within which alcohol*ism* is but a small part. In beginning to sketch that terrain, I have for the sake of coherence emphasized the ways in which various formal and informal mechanisms for managing and shaping the consumption of alcohol have laboured under the shadow of Benjamin Rush's palsy of the will – the spectre of alcoholism. Even the explicitly modernizing and pleasure-positive projects aimed at normalizing drinking and removing the outdated controls that proliferated in the English-speaking world from the 1960s to the 1980s were driven by the fear of excess and haunted by the figure of the alcoholic, albeit the emphasis was now on the self-regulating capacity of the many rather than on the propensity to excess of the few. One such modernizing project, the British Columbia Commission on the liquor laws of 1969, eloquently denounced the "rigid rules, regulations, and strictures now in effect, interpreted and implemented by an authoritarian Board"; but the denunciation of old-fashioned moralism was followed, as if inevitably, by a ringing conclusion calling on governments "to alleviate the tragedy of alcoholism".[10]

## CONTINUITY AND CHANGE IN THE GENEALOGY OF FREEDOM

In some fields, historicity is such that the questions we ask are today completely different from those asked a generation or two ago. In the sphere of sexuality, the questions asked by both experts and consumers have changed radically over the past 150 years. The Victorians, Freud, the conservative psychoanalysts of the 1950s, the advocates of homosexual equality of the 1960s, and the queer nation activists of the 1980s and 1990s did not simply have different views: more radically, they did not think about sexuality with the same tools and did not ask the same questions. In the field of alcohol, by contrast, if we confine ourselves to European and North American societies, there is a remarkable continuity in the basic questions that have been asked by very heterogeneous actors in completely different settings.

The striking tendency of concerns about the free will to unknowingly repeat the past is borne out by turning from the Internet recovery network to an eighteenth century tract by the great New England Calvinist theologian Jonathan Edwards, entitled *Freedom of the will*.[11] Edwards, who wanted to supplement John Locke's influential science of the understanding with his own "science of the will", regarded the habit of excessive drinking as a perfect example of how the Christian dogma of the moral responsibility (freedom) of the individual could be reconciled with the specifically Calvinist doctrine of the determination of the will. Edwards argued that the will is never free in the sense of being undetermined, since there are always motives and causes for everything we do, but that nevertheless, although our will is always freighted with causation, each one of our *actions* is free in the sense that we might have done otherwise. For Edwards, the Calvinist doctrine of determination and the scientific study of the causes of human behaviour are not in the least incompatible with the attribution of moral responsibility to such people as habitual drunkards:

> A drunkard, who continues in his drunkenness, being under the power of a love, and violent appetite to strong drink and without any love to virtue;

but being also extremely covetous and close, and very much exercised and grieved at the diminution of his estate, and prospect of poverty, may in a sort desire the virtue of temperance; and though his present will is to gratify his extravagant appetite, yet he may wish he had a heart to forbear future acts of intemperance . . . but still he goes on with his drunkenness; such a man has no proper, direct, sincere willingness to forsake this vice . . . for he acts voluntarily in continuing to drink to excess . . .[12]

Edwards concludes that, although particular actions may not be consciously chosen but may be direct offshoots of a particular habit, nevertheless habits are themselves produced through the accretion of chosen actions and, to that extent, we are responsible for our own habits.

The theory of the relation between habits and freedom developed by Jonathan Edwards in the 1750s is essentially that of Alcoholics Anonymous. In AA, people are encouraged to define themselves as a particular sort of person – an alcoholic – whose essential nature it is to drink to excess. Some people *are* alcoholics; they are a distinct group, characterized by the inability to drink casually and in moderation. But, unlike most psy identities, AA's alcoholic identity is not meant to excuse drunken behaviour as the actions of a poor soul who can't help what he does because his nature ineluctably determines his actions. For AA, as for Edwards, determination/causality is the true ground of freedom. The superior moral state that AA calls sobriety can only be achieved by those who have successfully struggled against their own determinations, against the demons or the genes that drive them to drink. Members of AA sometimes express heartfelt thankfulness that nature or God or their parents made them into alcoholics, because only as alcoholics were they able to find AA and achieve sobriety – statements implying that the sobriety of recovering alcoholics is a higher spiritual state than the everyday consciousness of the moderate drinker.

This dialectic of freedom and necessity was also constitutive of what the foremost British expert on addiction of the late nineteenth century, Dr Norman Kerr, called inebriety. Inebriety was not drunkenness: it was a condition characterized by losing control over one's consumption, whether of alcohol, coffee, morphine, or of any other substance. And although Dr Kerr accepted most of the tenets of the late nineteenth century deterministic fatalism of degeneration theory, nevertheless he found it in himself to sing the praises of those who, despite being burdened with "the inebriate diathesis" (i.e. an inborn tendency to consume uncontrollably), managed to fight against it, in a valiant battle of the free will against its own determinations. In a tribute that would never have been sung in praise of other degenerates – the feeble-minded immigrant, the hysterical woman – Dr Kerr waxed eloquent about "the continuous and victorious struggle of such heroic souls with their hereditary enemy – an enemy the more powerful because ever leading its treacherous life within their breasts . . .".[13]

The contemporary genre of addiction-recovery literature, which significantly overlaps a great deal with the abuse survivor literature, by and large presents a similar, thoroughly Protestant view of the dialectic of freedom and determination. Despite the prevalence of genetic and familial determinism in contemporary explanations of behaviour, most of us do expect ourselves and others to flex the will and do battle against whatever inner slavery would otherwise be our destiny. Not all streams within the addiction/abuse recovery movement are agreed on the precise balance of freedom and determination. Adult Children of Alcoholics (ACOA), for instance, is different from AA in that it stresses determination – particularly the influence of early family life – much more than personal moral responsibility. Whereas AA meetings are often relentlessly cheerful, ACOA meetings are often full of tragedy, melodrama, and self-pity.[14] But although AA and ACOA choose to emphasize opposite sides of the dialectic of freedom and determination, they share the view that one is not born free: one becomes free by individually struggling against external and internal determinations.

We shall see in chapter 3 how this dialectic of freedom and determination could be deployed just as easily to sing the praises of some recovering alcoholics as to coerce other alcoholics into locked asylums so that, losing their freedom, they would be given the opportunity to regain it. A typical argument in favour of compulsory committal to state inebriate asylums was made in 1862 by an Anglican professor of theology who was also a physician, Toronto's Dr James Bovell. In a manner reminiscent of Jonathan Edwards, Bovell argued that "whoever asserts that there be no such thing as government, if man is a free being, places himself in direct opposition to common forms of speech", adding that

> . . . herein is discovered the true and proper meaning of the words *government* and *obedience*. These words, in their proper acceptation, imply the liberty of the subject . . . And it is to enable the slave of intemperance to escape unto *the perfect law of Liberty*, which he is under obligation imposed by his nature to obey, that we desire to remove him from the dominion of passion . . .[15]

Having transmuted freedom into coercion and back into freedom twice in these few lines, Bovell concluded, less dialectically and more categorically: "Man is a slave in desire and passion, he is free only in will. The will is enslaved when under the dominion of desire."[16] That the will is enslaved by the dominion of desire is at one level a typically Victorian statement;[17] but, at another level, it is not so far from the claims made in

Overeaters Anonymous and Sex Addicts Anonymous, and it is certainly a common theme in alcoholism treatments across time and place. And Bovell's claim that drinking alcohol increases the risks of becoming enslaved to one's own passions converges with the post-Christian, consumer-focussed project to market a whole series of drinks (from Ovaltine to Coca-Cola) as liquids that increase one's mental and spiritual health, one's freedom, as well as one's physical health.

The centrality of the concern for freedom – a freedom defined largely as self-control, as the will's power to manage desires – in alcoholism treatments means that a study of the patched-together, often unsuccessful, semi-medical programmes of addiction recovery, harm reduction, and provision of alternative drinks is of importance not only to those interested in drinking, in consumption, or in the history of the will (if there are such people), but to anyone pursuing Foucault's insights about the ways in which our desire for freedom and the requirements of the authorities have become increasingly aligned in recent times. The work of Nikolas Rose is perhaps most relevant to those of us interested in a genealogy of modern freedom. Against the sort of libertarian discourse that was popular in both lay and expert progressive circles in the 1960s, Rose has persuasively argued that freedom is by no means the opposite of control or regulation: freedom has become, in the mass democracies of the twentieth century, the primary programme of governance. We are governed not against but *through* our freedom. Psychologists provide non-directive counselling and help us to choose our own priorities; teachers avoid direct moral regulation and teach small children to choose X or Y for themselves with knowledge of the consequences; and the dismantling of social security programmes for the elderly is justified with the argument that we are not truly free if we depend on the state, and that therefore we must save and scrimp and plan in the name of freedom. Individual freedom, then, is not a utopian force threatening the status quo, as the existentialists and the hippies thought, but is rather the means through which the status quo perpetuates itself in our very souls. The questions for today's social analysts are therefore not about how to minimize alienation and maximize freedom, but rather: "How have we come to define and act toward ourselves in terms of a certain notion of freedom? How has freedom provided the rationale for all manner of coercive interventions into the mad, the risky, or those at risk?"[18]

At one level, we all know that we are governed through our freedom. Children are not fooled by the fake choices given to them by parents and teachers, and television viewers are not deceived by the images that boost bank profits by promising us freedom. And yet this everyday skepticism is rarely taken seriously and used to challenge our own assumptions and habits of thought. Irony and skepticism tend to be pushed to the margins. People in the North American recovery movement, for example, tend to think that their historically specific experiences of seeking freedom by battling the habits and compulsions of the alcoholic or the codependent identity are valuable and worth recording not because they provide an opportunity to understand our particular present, but rather because our individual anxieties about freedom are timeless examples of the universally recognizable human quest for freedom as such. The specific experience of alcoholism/ addiction is thus not analyzed historically, but rather instantly subsumed under the ahistorical abstractions about personal growth, journeys of self-discovery, and so on, that are everywhere propagated by the marketers of fake-leather classics for the popular bookshelf.[19]

And, with a few exceptions, the scholarly literature on alcoholism and addiction in turn tends to repeat this ahistorical and ethnocentric perspective. The present book does not attempt cross-cultural analyses of how what we call the will works in non-European societies. But it is possible to study one's own culture without reproducing ethnocentric myths about the inherently fascinating and world-historical character of the inner dilemmas and spiritual struggles of one's own peers and ancestors.

The ethnocentrism of alcoholism studies has been occasionally flagged within the literature itself, perhaps most starkly in a thoughtful article by Robin Room, arguably the world's leading authority on alcoholism. Despite his location at the very centre of the policy-oriented world of addiction research, Room manages to defamiliarize his own context, remarking that some cultures do not even make a major distinction between feeling and thinking and that, without this distinction, it is impossible to construct a cross-culturally valid set of diagnostic criteria for addiction or dependence. He goes on to note that, if the experience of alcoholism as loss of control is culturally specific, it is because the values and beliefs that underlie the concerns with alcohol documented in this book are themselves historically specific.[20] Room's analysis needs to be pushed only slightly to arrive at the conclusion that, if alcoholism is culturally specific, it is because the very thought that the pursuit of self-control and the maximization of the will's freedom are tremendously important human endeavours is itself culturally specific. The pursuit of the ever-elusive free will, though perhaps a common denominator for most of the history of the West, is always enacted in specific sites, using historically specific technologies: although early Christian mystics sought a kind of personal freedom that was dialectically linked to self-subjection, they would not have defined sinful behaviour as addictive.

Therefore, despite the fact that the dilemmas of freedom documented in this book show striking continuities across time, the analysis of the workings of the will and its freedom is historical through and through (hence the frequent use of case studies). And although the emphasis of this book is on the persistence of the question of self-control as freedom, important historical shifts are nevertheless documented in the way in which people have set out to govern their souls by governing their drinking and that of others. Although many of these shifts are traced in the course of the first four chapters, it is appropriate to make some general remarks here about differences between then and now.

One major difference between the alcoholism treatment programmes that existed prior to World War I and those that have been popular since the invention of Alcoholics Anonymous is rooted not in the forward march of science (as alcohol experts tend to believe) but rather in the rather uneven march of what one might call everyday democracy, to distinguish it from the often undemocratic political practices of electoral politics. A century ago, the personal care dispensed by private physicians to their middle-class clients and by nuns or Salvation Army officers to their poorer clients was traditional "pastoral" care in that, even when some of the shepherds were ex-sheep, it was very clear in any given situation who were the sheep and who were the shepherds. Michel Foucault's insightful analysis of pastoralism fits these practices very well;[21] but, because of its specific historical orientation, Foucault's analysis neglected the ways in which the pastoral care of the souls of the flock changed in the twentieth century with the rise of mutual-help groups. Self-help is not particularly new; the self-help literature of today has very clear roots in the genre of spiritual improvement booklets used by Christians for many a century. But *mutual* help, as a set of practices that are not as likely to be mediated through individual reading and examination of conscience as through face-to-face group meetings generally including only those who define themselves as sheep, is perhaps more novel. It is not completely new, since some Protestant sects, such as the Quakers, developed techniques for a horizontal and decentralized care of souls in the eighteenth century. But the watershed in the dissemination of mutual help, as the gathering of a flock that refuses to be shepherded except by other sheep, the event that can be taken (somewhat but not completely arbitrarily) as marking the democratization of pastoralism is the founding of AA. Whether or not it works to cure alcoholism, AA has certainly succeeded in developing a whole array of non-professionalized, low-cultural capital techniques for acting on oneself that have profoundly shaped our present. In the same way that even people who do not know or believe in Freud's work still use

19

the notion of the unconscious on occasion, so too have AA terms – for example, 'being in denial' – come to form part of the general stock of contemporary language, and therefore deserve more serious analysis than they have thus far commanded.

There is one more discontinuity that I would like to highlight, again comparing the situations covered by chapters 2 and 3 with the development of addiction recovery since AA, although for the purposes of this distinction AA belongs to the old rather than to the new. This discontinuity can best be explained by comparing the melodramatic narratives of sin, despair, and joyous salvation offered by the Salvation Army to drunkards with the resolutely ironic and postmodern language used in at least some of today's mutual-help and self-help groups. The Internet (which has of course given rise to medical worries about the propensity of youth to become addicted to surfing)[22] has developed its own reflexive and ironic discourse of addiction. A take-off on AA's twelve steps, replacing AA's Higher Power with the almighty Webmaster and the soul with the hard drive, has been sent out on e-mail by "Interneters Anonymous"

1. We admitted we were powerless over the Internet and online services – that our computers and modems were overused.
2. Came to believe that the almighty Webmaster could restore us to sanity.
3. Made a decision to turn our will, lives and mousepads over to the almighty Webmaster.
4. Made a searching and fearless inventory of our hard drives . . .[23]

Interneters Anonymous is an explicitly ironic concept, given that telling Internet addicts to log onto recovery chat lines is like telling recovering alcoholics they can only meet in bars. But the ambiguity of the e-mail message (are the writers aware of the paradox? is the message somewhat serious? does it matter?) is not unique to the Internet situation. Although people in AA tend to be earnest about their organization, and to that extent belong with the 'old' rather than with the postmodern, parodic new, nevertheless there are plenty of situations in which even the most zealous AA member will poke fun at his/her own earnestness. In most situations, the reflexive irony is confined to moments of self-deprecating humour in which people say, "Oh well, it may be bullshit, but some of it works for me". This stance has many parallels, from the radical professor who nevertheless conscientiously ranks her students in a hierarchy, to the anti-psychiatry activist who nevertheless takes Prozac, because it works.

This typically postmodern pragmatism – the willingness to live with sharp contradictions between the intelligence and the will, as Gramsci famously put it – does not mean that the postmodern thinkers are correct in pronouncing ideology in general to be dead. The recovery movement that AA has spawned in the past decade or so is more ideological than AA: there is a whole theory of the inner child that people who have had various misfortunes have to believe in before they can be healed. As Slavoj Zizek has insightfully pointed out, the condition of postmodernity has not in fact brought about a cosmopolitan and enlightened skepticism, at least not in most locations. Rather, although we are wary and wise consumers of ideological discourses, including our own, nevertheless we generally find it impossible to do without them. Zizek puts this in Lacanian terms: "The Power, in its functioning, relies on this very split between our conscious knowledge of the Power's impotence, our ironical distance toward it, and our unconscious belief in its omnipotence."[24] In other words, we believe in what we know is unbelievable. We know deep down that freedom is just another word used by the authorities to govern us, to sell us things, to persuade us to accept coercion of all kinds; but we nevertheless find it impossible to do without the belief in freedom. Being postmodern enough to question all truths, including our own, we are still not sufficiently postmodern to make do without truths. The ironical stance, therefore, tends to be confined to moments of humour.

It is, nevertheless, the potential for that ironical displacement not of this or that theory of addiction but of the very idea of a quest for personal freedom that distinguishes today's epidemics of the will from those of earlier times. If this book can contribute to deepening and grounding that irony, to making us question not only how we have been governed but even the values in whose name we think we have challenged convention and defied the authorities, then it will have fulfilled the author's hopes. My hopes are not defined in terms of freedom; but, mixing Hegelian and Foucaultian terms, they can perhaps be defined as the desire to understand just what we, in our specific historical moment, are doing.

BOYHOOD.
The First Step.

YOUTH.
The Second Step.

MANHOOD.
A Confirmed Drunkard.

OLD AGE.
A Total Wreck.

Narratives about alcoholism have often been intertwined with other, usually gender-specific, narratives of the stages of moral development and moral failure. (From T.S. Arthur, *Grappling with the Monster*, New York, American Publishing Co., 1887; courtesy of the Seagram Collection, University of Waterloo, Ontario.)

# CHAPTER 1

# DISEASE OR HABIT? ALCOHOLISM AND THE EXERCISE OF FREEDOM

This chapter presents an overview of and a theoretical reflection upon the arguments about alcoholism treatments, alcohol regulation, and the question of the will that are elaborated in subsequent chapters. It first analyzes current medical and popular definitions and criteria of alcoholism and alcohol dependence, and then turns to a consideration of the proliferation in our present of the most successful addiction treatment technique ever invented, the twelve steps of Alcoholics Anonymous. The paradoxical use of the twelve steps by groups and self-help books that seek to maximize the individual power of codependents gives rise to a more general reflection on the contradictions of projects aimed at the free will. The work of William James and John Dewey on the importance of habit is briefly recalled in order to suggest that many of the dilemmas and *aporias* of the free will in our own time could perhaps have been circumvented if the twentieth century, rather than re-enacting the nineteenth century battles about free will and determinism, had followed through the pragmatists' interest in every-day *habits*. An official expert committee of the World Health Organization on addiction decided in the 1950s that alcohol was somewhere between a vice and a disease, a hybrid of habit and addiction. The contradictory WHO statement can stand as a reminder that, even at the height of the medicalization project, lack of control over drinking could not be easily classed as a deviant identity. Vice and habit continually interrupted the project to construct a deviant medicalized identity for alcoholics. Not coincidentally, the sharp binary opposition between freely willed and determined acts presupposed by most alcoholism literature has also been continually undermined by the repeated return of that intermediate category, habit.

DRINKING AND THE SOUL

Although the term 'alcoholism' is no longer found in medical classifications of diseases, it continues to be used both in ordinary speech and in
many expert discourses. It is probably most widely circulated in the in-
between, quasi-expert zone occupied by advice columns, television talk
shows, and magazine articles. The US National Council on Alcoholism
and Drug Dependency has put together a self-administered questionnaire to help people decide whether or not they are alcoholics that is
typical of the way in which this liminal zone, from which so many people
obtain information and advice, arranges the issue of alcoholism. The
first question asks: "Do you occasionally drink heavily after a dis-
appointment, a quarrel, or when the boss gives you a hard time?" After
exploring the feelings one has about drinking and the feelings that lead
to drinking, the test moves into the classic terrain of the tragedy of
alcoholism: through secret drinking, to the experience of regret for
things done while drunk, to blackouts, morning-after shakes, suicidal
thoughts, and, finally, hallucinations.[1]

The twenty-six question quiz on drinking experience will here stand
for the generalized project to provide, outside of the contexts of clinical
advice and referral, easy-to-use tools to enable ordinary people to make
their own diagnoses. In common with similar questionnaires on other
issues ('Is your teenager a drug addict?' 'Are you a compulsive shop-
per?'), this test turns a heterogeneous collection of situations into an
implicit 'slippery slope' leading inexorably from the ordinary behaviour of question 1 to the extreme problems described in the last few
questions. The diverse and not obviously related experiences evoked in
the questions are unified by being distributed as elements in a single
narrative of tragic downfall.[2] This tragic script – a very common form of
problematization in the sphere of social problems – is reinforced at the
end of the test with the suggestion that *any* drinking that is connected to
feelings of either guilt, regret, or plain unhappiness is potentially
alcoholic: the Council tells us that if we answer 'yes' to any of the twenty-
six questions, we "may" be alcoholics.

What is most striking about this typically overinclusive definition of
alcoholism (or, more accurately, of the vaguer condition of being at risk
of alcoholism) is that at least five of the twenty-six questions make no
mention of either drinking or sobriety. Three of them are: "Do more
people seem to be treating you unfairly without good reason?"; "Are you
having an increasing number of financial and work problems?"; "Do
you sometimes feel very depressed and wonder if life is worth living?" If
you drink without worrying, then, it would appear that you are not –
short of seriously injuring yourself physically – at risk of alcoholism; but

if you experience guilt either before or after drinking, then you are in trouble.

The centrality of feelings is remarkable historically: it is only in the twentieth century that we have come to regard drinking or other behaviours as problematic insofar as they are linked to unhealthy or otherwise questionable feelings. As Foucault pointed out, Christianity regarded the pleasures of consumption as problematic only if linked to sinful desires; feelings were not very important. The Greeks in turn emphasized neither desires nor feelings, focussing rather on the aesthetic proportions of the conduct in question: excessive indulgence in eating, drinking and sex was for them problematic if connected to lack of harmony and balance.[3] But today one cannot defend oneself against the accusation of alcoholism by claiming that one's drinking is done in the best of taste or with a pure heart: it is the connection between drinking and feelings – of inadequacy, of pride, of sadness – that has come to be the source of alcohol's problem status.

The alcoholism test quoted above is not an inquiry into drinking as much as a test of the soul's relation to itself. Do you feel free and happy? or do you feel constrained, depressed, and guilty about the very behaviour that you engage in to relieve depression and guilt? Is drinking just something you do, or is it implicated in a negative, viciously circular relation of self to self?

People familiar with medical discussions of drinking and addiction might object that this particular test of one's ability to care for one's own soul is not representative of current expert knowledge on alcoholism. But if we turn away from semi-popular clinical advice and to the pages of medical classifications, we will find the same striking emphasis on the subjectivity and emotional state of the patient, rather than on objective 'facts'. What is perhaps the most famous text in the history of alcoholism in English-speaking countries, E.M. Jellinek's 1960 *The disease concept of alcoholism* (still widely cited today), has a number of different ways of defining alcoholism, but the main criterion distinguishing those people who drink heavily but are not "addicted" from those who are truly diseased is that the latter group suffers from "loss of control".[4] Jellinek states that there are several types of alcoholics who drink as much as the worst addict, even to the point of suffering from cirrhosis of the liver; but they drink because they want to, not because they feel compelled to do so. Since they do not suffer from "loss of control" they are therefore not diseased, even though they are alcoholic.

In the nineteenth century, scientific studies of loss of control tended to assume that volition and its dysfunctions were to be accessed strictly through the gazes of physiology, clinical medicine, and/or psychiatry. In the twentieth century, by contrast, the will lost its privileged relation with medicine and psychiatry. The will came to be measured and objectivized through casework and questionnaires, techniques requiring the active involvement of the patient him/herself. Unlike symptoms, feelings cannot be directly observed: they have to be reported and at least partially interpreted by the patient.

The mid-twentieth century project of documenting the feelings and hence probing the will came under attack in the 1960s, as some social scientists decided to pursue the strategy of measuring and evaluating not the will of individual drinkers but the collective health of the nation. Today's experts – many of whom have carefully read Jellinek's reasoning and pronounced it contorted and arbitrary – claim that they are not attempting to measure self-control or spiritual health. Heavily influenced by the discourse and the data gathering techniques of epidemiology, they believe they are mapping the 'harm' and/or the 'risk of harm' posed by drinking or drug taking. They see themselves as measuring consequences, not willpower, and offering neutral disease maps that can be used by health professionals, governments, and health consumers themselves to evaluate risks and make informed decisions, without any need for moralizing or psychologizing.[5] But the search for objective measures is in this area stymied by the fact that what is or is not a harm, in the context of drinking, is itself subjective. What appears to some as a normal Saturday night might be regarded by others as dysfunctional, harmful, and therefore pathological behaviour. Physicians consulting the American bible of psychiatric medicine, the *Diagnostic and Statistical Manual* IV (DSM-IV), are told:

> Substance-related Disorders are distinguished from nonpathological substance use (e.g. 'social drinking') and from the use of medications for appropriate medical purposes by the presence of tolerance, withdrawal, compulsive use, or substance-related problems (e.g. medical complications, disruption in social and family relationships, vocational or financial difficulties, legal problems).[6]

The DSM-IV admits that, unlike other drugs, alcohol does not necessarily cause physical withdrawal symptoms in many people, even with extremely heavy use. If one takes out physical withdrawal from the list just quoted, what is left is the fuzzily defined, non-medical, primarily social terrain of collateral damage – legal problems, disruptions in relationships, and so on.

The supposedly objective category of harm thus cannot do the work that is assigned to it in the new paradigm of dependence that has been installed (in scientific circles only) as an unsatisfactory replacement for the admittedly moralizing and difficult to operationalize category, addiction.[7] Having to resort to such extra-medical criteria as whether one has been arrested for drunk and disorderly conduct indicates that physicians have not succeeded in defining the boundary between the normal and the pathological in *medical* terms.

The socially relative nature of the DSM-IV diagnostic criteria is evident from the fact that much emphasis is placed on the ways in which the drinker's occupational and family life is disrupted by alcohol use. These criteria tend to assume certain norms of social respectability. If one is a bartender or a prostitute, for instance, heavy drinking may facilitate rather than hinder "occupational functioning" and "usual social activities". Extremely heavy drinking among such people would not be considered indicative of either abuse or dependence, unless they passed out on the job or irreparably damaged their liver. This suggests that "disorders" such as alcohol dependence depend to some extent on one's occupation (as well as on owning a car, since traffic accidents figure largely among the symptoms).[8] Renaming alcoholism under the supposedly neutral banner of "substance-related disorders" has not sufficed to eliminate the morally and culturally specific values that have always been integral to the process of distinguishing excessive drinking.

Along with social criteria, such as arrests and problems with one's family, the DSM-IV also lists a series of questions about the state of the drinker's soul in its diagnostic advice to physicians. Attempting to define dependence – which is a less severe condition than abuse – American psychiatry uses the subjectivity of the drinker as a major criterion of pathology. Differing quite sharply from European approaches, which in general make no reference to the intentions or the feelings of the drinker/drug user, the DSM-IV states:

> The following items describe the pattern of compulsive substance use that is characteristic of Dependence. The individual may take the substance in larger amounts or over a longer period than was *originally intended* (e.g. continuing to drink until severely intoxicated despite having set a limit of only one drink). The individual may express *a persistent desire* to cut down or regulate substance use. Often, there have been many unsuccessful efforts to decrease or discontinue use . . .[9]

The drinker's feelings of shame and worry about drinking are thus taken out of the sphere of ethics/morality and lifted into medicine to help fill out the diagnostic criteria for a disorder that is no longer known as alcoholism, but which bears all the marks of the history of alcoholism as a history of the struggles of and over the will. The inclusion of emotional and ethical criteria has a peculiar effect: people who drink extremely heavily without ever trying to cut down will be less likely to be pathologized than those individuals who for one reason or another worry more about their drinking.

In the DSM-IV and in recent medical literature, therefore, the soul and its disturbances – now known as feelings – have by no means been replaced by the logic of consequences and harm.[10] It is thus apparent that the effort to objectivize and scientize what was first called alcoholism and then addiction has been and remains a "congenitally failing operation".[11] Despite the work that has been done to make 'psychoactive substance abuse/dependence' a more scientific category than its predecessors, we are left with a psychological disorder that waxes and wanes depending on one's moral scruples, one's occupation, the moral standards of one's spouse, and whether or not one owns a car. What is perhaps most remarkable is that the most obvious objective measure, namely the quantity of alcohol consumed over a set amount of time, is never mentioned. Among the dozens of conflicting psychological, biological, spiritual, and commonsense definitions of alcoholism that I have collected over the past years, *none* made any reference to the *amount* of alcohol ingested.[12]

'Alcoholism' and its successor terms refer to the relation of the soul to itself, not to any objective state of affairs. Despite what might be suggested by the fact that alcoholism is now no longer a specific disease but one of a number of "*substance*-related disorders", one of this book's key arguments is that the governance of alcoholism and addiction are not characterized by the government of *substances* as much as by the attempt to use substances (and, more recently, addictive behaviours) to govern the realm of freedom.

The evolution of various ways of governing the soul's relation to itself – a relation that has for a couple of centuries emphasized the absolute worth of what we call freedom – could be traced through a close study of medical discourses on inebriety, alcoholism, addiction, and so forth. But such a study would have a tendency to assume that medical textbooks, journal articles, and dictionaries are the prime tools for governing alcoholics, an assumption which is patently false, for medicine generally but especially in the quasi-medical or para-medical field of alcoholism. Thus, the method chosen for this book is an approach that privileges the *technologies* of recovery, since it is those that are crucial in the government of alcoholics. The systematic discourses that are largely aimed at governing physicians will be discussed to some extent, especially in chapter 2, but the emphasis of this book is not on the history of medicine: the history of medicine is only one of the strands, and not always the most significant one, of the history of alcoholism.

Among the technologies of alcoholism treatment and recovery, pride of place undoubtedly goes to the 'twelve steps' developed in the 1930s by Alcoholics Anonymous and now used as the main or even the exclusive tool, not just among the two million or so members of AA worldwide but in most North American treatment programmes, whether run by physicians, by social workers, or by religious staff.

THE DISSEMINATION OF THE TWELVE STEPS

The twelve steps, a technique that is unique in having successfully colonized many medical sites without having even the slightest medical credentials, is a text with very humble origins. They were written down in the late 1930s to record the practical wisdom accumulated by the first 100 members of AA as they struggled to help each other stop drinking and to devise organizational forms to enable sobriety. In the manner of an agenda for a business meeting (most early AA members were white middle-class males, many in business), the text was not a book or even a pamphlet, but rather a series of twelve points. The points were written down by Bill Wilson, the main founder of AA; but the text went through a committee-like process of refinement and revision before it was published, for the first of innumerable times, in the collective 'Big Book' entitled *Alcoholics Anonymous*.[13] In the process of finalizing the text of the steps, fights emerged between those AA members who wanted a clearly Christian content and those agnostics who argued for "a psychological book".[14] The document was therefore not the systematic work of a single author or a single perspective, but rather a text generated through political compromise, a text – similar to the declarations of UN conferences – that simultaneously reflects and papers over the irreconcilable differences that nobody thinks will ever be resolved. (The full text of AA's twelve steps can be found in the Appendix.)

More will be said about the twelve steps' complex relation to both religion and medicine in chapter 5, in the context of a study of Alcoholics Anonymous. For now, however, we will take a brief look at the dissemination of this little text sixty years later, in our own time. The approach to this mini-study of the twelve steps, an approach that begins with asking what work the text does rather than with content analysis, befits AA, an explicitly pragmatist organization that is always asking 'what does it do?' rather than 'what does it mean?'[15] Be that as it may, if one is interested in techniques of recovery, the twelve steps are key not only because of their central role in alcoholism treatment but also because they provide the switchpoint through which alcoholism treatment techniques were extended to a wide range of other behaviours. The twelve steps – which can be put to any use by any organization since the copyright on them lapsed in 1989 – are the basis, the common denominator, for today's broad-ranging recovery movement.[16]

In the North America of the 1980s and 1990s, the twelve steps (along with other techniques developed by AA) have given rise to a new disease known as codependence.[17] A disease entity born out of the Adult Children of Alcoholics organization, codependence is perhaps the most significant endpoint of the history of the will and its addictions that is traced in this book. What is most striking about codependence is that what was previously considered to be a morally superior position of forbearance and support – the position of the sober wife and the long-suffering teenage son or daughter of an alcoholic – has been turned into a disease in its own right, a disease characterized precisely by a tendency to 'love too much' to the neglect of the care of self. Whereas the alcoholic in AA considers him/herself to suffer from too much pride and a misguided feeling that he/she can control drinking, the codependent suffers from the opposite disease of the will – a feeling of worthlessness and low self-esteem.

Codependence arose not among alcoholics but among the wives and children of alcoholics – especially the "adult children", who in the United States came to form a diffuse but powerful network. Family members had by no means been excluded from the AA project, since at a fairly early stage the spouses of AA members organized themselves into the Al-Anon network of support groups, and later on Ala-Teen was built to provide mutual support for the children of alcoholics, whether or not their parents were in AA. Neither spouses nor children of alcoholics are regarded as candidates for *treatment* in the AA paradigm, however, since it was taken for granted that it was the alcoholic or addict who needed help, not the 'normal' relatives. But in the late 1970s and early 1980s, scholarly psy experts and writers of pop psychology began to propagate the idea, now regarded as commonsense truth by most North Americans, that the "children of alcoholics are highly prone to learning disabilities, eating disorders, stress-related medical problems and compulsive behaviours".[18]

In their attempt to define a new psychotherapy market among the millions of young adults who had experienced alcoholism in their family of origin, the discoverers of the new condition expressed astonishment that "until just a few years ago, co-dependency was unknown in the alcoholism field". They stated as a fact known to every up-to-date therapist that "co-dependency is a *primary* disease and a disease within every member of an alcoholic family".[19] The term 'primary' is important. While the emphasis was initially on the ways in which those close to alcoholics, particularly wives and children, acquire dysfunctional behaviour patterns as a result of constantly lying to, about, and on behalf of alcoholics, the logic of the disease model soon took over, making the former noble victims of others' pathology into pathologized subjects. As John Steadman Rice explains in an insightful study, "codependency, the advocates asserted, is the cause of all addictions, rather than – as earlier thinking had held – the *product* of intimacy with an addicted person".[20]

The self-appointed advocates of the disease model of codependence, not content with the large potential field provided by families of alcoholics, moved to pathologize and offer treatment for virtually anything. Even if you were not married to an alcoholic, you might be suffering from codependence, for you might be engaged in the same covering-up behaviour typical of wives of alcoholics. Or you might be overworking yourself at the office and mopping up after your boss' mistakes . . . the symptoms of codependence are everywhere. What is perhaps most notable for our purposes, since it presents a stark contrast with the socially conformist assumptions of the vast majority of alcoholism treatment programmes, is the new pathologization of behaviours that had hitherto been regarded as healthy and functional, such as caring for one's wayward husband or worrying about one's children. The codependence network, meeting in 1989, came up with the following definition of codependence: "A pattern of painful dependence on compulsive behaviours and on approval from others in an attempt to find safety, self-worth, and identity."[21]

This project could not have been undertaken without the widespread dissemination of vaguely feminist ideas about assertiveness and self-worth throughout American society; and indeed, the codependence project, which is implicitly feminized in the same quiet way that the AA programme was masculinized, can be regarded as one of the unexpected results of the mainstreaming of feminism.[22] But once assertiveness has been valorized, it is difficult to put limits to it. The new networks of codependents legitimize assertiveness on the part of the feminized codependents to the point of encouraging behaviour that would usually be called selfish and irresponsible. Exemption from ethical judgement is obtained by claiming that the behaviour that might seem selfish to others has an important therapeutic function.[23]

If a homeless drunk, an incest survivor, and a responsible well-off mother without a single trauma to her name can all think about their present situation as the direct outcome of a psychological condition of codependence, it is because codependence is simultaneously real and not real. It is easy to see the ways in which codependence is a fiction, the latest and vaguest in a long series of illnesses constructed in obviously instrumental ways by experts looking for clients. The existing critical commentaries show in painstaking detail that codependence covers so much ground and can have so many uses that it means nothing in particular, and that its success shows only that even conduct generally regarded as socially appropriate can be pathologized. But, to paraphrase Foucault on madness, if codependence does not exist, that does not mean that it is *nothing*. Codependence, as the name for a loose assemblage of books, organizations, therapy groups, and etiological models that have built specific networks and businesses and have disseminated beyond those specific networks, is indeed something. It may not be real, but it has real effects. The capaciousness of the notion of codependence allows the effects to be quite varied depending on the actors and the context. But there is a lowest common denominator linking the multifarious personal and professional projects going on today under the banner of codependence, and that is the project to maximize a specifically neoliberal freedom that, in the literature of the movement, is presented as freedom *as such.*

In the self-help technologies of edifying videos, self-esteem workbooks, and codependence support groups, freedom is both the end of recovery and the means. It is the supreme value for the sake of which we work on the self and it is simultaneously the technology through which we act on the not-yet-free self. The codependence text authored by the founding president of the American organization Adult Children of Alcoholics, entitled *Choicemaking: for co-dependents, adult children, and spirituality seekers*, has the following back cover blurb:

> Freedom and recovery. In CHOICEMAKING, the author explains that 'freedom from' and 'freedom to' are essential elements of recovery – how freedom from our pain and our past gives us the freedom to choose our life's path in recovery. She uses her own experiences to show us how to become free and how to enjoy being free to make choices. She also discusses some of the pitfalls we might encounter.
>
> An outline of the journey toward spiritual self-satisfaction and wholeness – the freedom of choice – is provided in this eloquent work. CHOICEMAKING is necessary reading for anyone who has lived with addictive relationships, whether the addiction was to a drug or to another person.[24]

This text, like most for-profit non-medical psychotherapy, assumes that people are already free, and need training only in exercising that freedom wisely. Other sources, less optimistic and consumeristic, point out that clients are not already free, and that the purpose of treatment is the difficult task of building up their very capacity for freedom. Most of the alcoholism treatment programmes and projects for regulating alcohol consumption discussed in this book assume the latter rather than the former – that is, they regard freedom as something to be worked on, built up, and maximized, not as an existing capacity that merely needs to be exercised in the right direction.

But whether freedom is thought to be inborn or whether it is regarded as the hard-earned product of a long and difficult process of self-formation and training, freedom is what alcoholism, addiction, and alcoholism's strange offspring, codependence, are all about. And that part of the self/soul that Western culture regards as the seat of freedom – not only now but for some centuries – is the will, often called 'willpower' today. From alcoholism through drug addiction through codependence, diseases or dysfunctions of the will have generally been thought of as caused by too little willpower. As a Finnish analyst of the cultural contradictions of alcoholism puts it, alcoholism, as a construct and as an experience, is rooted in the perceived opposition between one's willpower and one's desires or inner urges. Alcoholics are those whose willpower is too weak to say no to the next drink: "Alcoholism and other addictions can be seen as reflections of this generally conceived tension between desire and will."[25]

Most discussions of alcoholism assume that, if the ratio between desire and will is not satisfactory, the solution is not to suppress desire (as might be suggested by Christian and Buddhist ascetics) but rather to strengthen the will so that it can better control desire. And yet it is also part of the commonsense wisdom on alcoholism that, if alcohol in general acts to weaken the will and disinhibit desire, alcoholics are characterized by having a weak will to begin with. The problem is then how to build up the will's capacity in a population whose wills are weaker than average.

In general, alcoholism treatments have been based on the assumption that weak wills can only be strengthened by their own action, not by any outside intervention. Just as muscles that have degenerated through inactivity can only be built up by their own action, not by medicine, so too the cure for the diseases of the will has always been thought to lie in exercising the will itself in a sort of moral physiotherapy. Although drugs, vitamins, and hypnosis have all been tried, the consensus has been that none of these external treatments work in the absence of a valiant effort of the diseased will to overcome its disease. Or, to put it differently, freedom cannot be instilled into people by force or through medication: the will's capacity for freedom can only be built up by freely exercising that very will, however diseased or out of shape it might be. On occasion, addiction treatment programmes have distinguished between the bad will – the self-will or wilfulness of Victorian ethics and Victorian medicine – and the good will, the willpower that one uses to stop drinking. But more commonly the two contradictory functions of the will have not been sharply distinguished, even when the paradox created by using the term 'will' to encompass both desire and its regulation is noted.

As shall be seen in some detail in chapters 2 and 3, nineteenth century physicians pursued their inquiries into the relation between will, desire, and the consumption of problematic substances by classifying conditions such as kleptomania and alcoholism as lesions of the will whose treatments overlapped with the nerve cures offered for such conditions as neurasthenia – rest, beef tea, and various other measures to enable the will's strength to recover. In AA's twelve steps, however, the problem of the will does not present itself as it did for the physicians of neurasthenia, kleptomania, and inebriety. Taking a Calvinist view of the will, the twelve steps proclaim that the essence of alcoholism is the mistaken feeling that we do have willpower, that we do have control; and they go on to suggest that the solution to problems of dependence is not asserting one's willpower even more but rather acknowledging one's profound weakness, one's powerlessness.

The tremendous success of AA and its offshoots in the present day is remarkable among other reasons because the Calvinist doctrine of the essential fallenness and frailty of human nature is at odds with the neoliberal belief in the ability of every individual to empower him/herself to any extent that they choose.[26] Codependence is the neoliberal mutation of the Protestant ethic and the spirit of capitalism, whereas AA represents classic Weberian capitalism, in which the Protestant ethic had more to do with self-control than with self-fulfilment. The stereotype of a codependent that is generated in the literature is the ever-reliable, hard-working, somewhat dour person who is always organizing other people, showing his/her superior abilities to do what is useful and necessary, and ending up vaguely disappointed in everyone and in him/herself. Such a person would have been considered admirable in former times. But today, in the age of feelings, stiff upper lips and well-organized desks are more likely to be regarded as ethical liabilities than as assets.[27]

The problem of codependence is thus not one of absolute lack of will: the codependent is not at all like the listless, ineffective neurasthenic, and not very much like the daydreaming, self-deluded alcoholic. Codependence is not characterized by a deficiency, or an excess, in the *amount* of willpower: it is rather characterized by a willpower's twisted development. Codependents go around obsessively organizing workplaces, seeking perfection, and caring for others – to the neglect of the care of self. Their willpower needs to be folded inward rather than outward.

The codependent is simultaneously more free and more determined than the alcoholic. She is more free because, while AA members are told that they will be forever unable to control drinking, and hence forever linked to the fellowship of AA, codependents are told that a few books supplemented by some group therapy will suffice to take their spiritual health into a state of better than well. But at the same time, although the promise of codependence recovery is much bigger than that made by AA, the anxiety is correspondingly greater. The AA member can boast about not having had a single drink in fifteen years; but who among us could boast that we have consistently looked after our souls properly every day for fifteen years? Who can definitely say that we went to work in the morning because we truly chose to work, as opposed to going out of a desire to please others, due to coercion, or out of mere habit?

Codependence, then, takes the quest for individual freedom to its extreme, where it turns into its opposite. We are promised a boundless freedom not only to choose among existing things but even to transform the self that does the choosing. But at the same time, the dangers are no longer confined to bottles or pills. All substances are potentially addictive if addiction is an attitude, a relation of self to self; and even when not consuming substances, such innocent behaviours as taking care of a sick child could be a symptom of codependence. Thus, with codependence, we are freer than ever and less free than ever. Such is the paradoxical condition that has been facilitated by the prolife-ration of the twelve steps.

## DECONSTRUCTING THE OPPOSITION OF FREEDOM AND NECESSITY: HABIT

The only philosophical forefather openly acknowledged by AA's founders (and still read in today's recovery circles) is the American philosopher William James. James' *Varieties of religious experience*, with its pragmatic encouragement to readers to define anything that they found spiritually healing as religion, helped the fledgling organization to maintain its uneasy balance between the agnostics, who favoured a psychological, scientific, secular approach to drinking and drunken-ness, and those who believed in Christian remedies for the soul.[28]

James, like most thinkers of his time, believed in the will. However, James does not reproduce the traditional dualism that underlies most of the addiction-recovery programmes that have been popular in European societies. In the framework of American pragmatism devel-oped by James, Charles Pierce, and John Dewey, the mind–body dualism of Christian philosophy is not only avoided, but is explicitly deconstructed. The theorization of habit plays a crucial role in this deconstructive project.

Habits are fundamentally conservative, tending to keep us in our place and to preserve the social status quo:

> Habit is thus the enormous fly-wheel of society, its most precious conservative agent. It alone is what keeps us all within the bounds of ordinance, and saves the children of fortune from the envious uprisings

of the poor. It alone prevents the hardest and most repulsive walks of life from being deserted by those brought up to tread therein . . . it protects us from invasion by the natives of the desert and of the frozen zone. It dooms us all to fight out the battle for life upon the lines of our nurture and our early choice.[29]

Habits tend to perform conservatism, then; but habits are not automatic or unchangeable. They are not subsumed under what James calls "reflex", the realm of unfree natural motion. The whole apparatus of habit formation and re-formation, William James tells us, is an essential precondition of freedom, modernity, and creativity, since society needs a centripetal force to keep it together even as the force of invention pushes it forward. So, although habit is dull, conservative, and freedom-denying, it is nevertheless highly functional for freedom.

Given the fact that human conduct is largely habitual, and that it needs to stay habitual if the more fortunate inhabitants of the United States are not to be invaded by Africans and Eskimos, the task is therefore not to fight habit in general but to reform the habits. Habits are like chores, in that they are the essential precondition for the existence of a higher sphere of action and thought; but they are also themselves the site for the constitution of freedom.

Habits appear as mere habits, as the realm of natural necessity, only if one believes in the undetermined moral autonomy of moral philosophy. For pragmatism, however, the idea that there is a sphere of moral freedom that is quite opposed to the world of natural necessity is a fiction generated by the bad habit of thinking abstractly.

Quitting drinking is one of the examples given by James to prove that the binary opposition between the freedom of the will and the necessity of nature is fundamentally misconceived. In the chapter of *The principles of psychology* entitled "Habit", James argues that changing one's habits is not a matter of sheer willpower, for although "many, perhaps most, human habits were once voluntary actions, no action, as we shall see in a later chapter, can be primarily such". Habitual action, such as drinking too much or taking opium, is thus best reformed not by attempting to suddenly flex one's will by mental effort, but rather by physically stopping the chain of behaviours and neural connections that have been set up and worn into a groove by previous repetitions. "It is surprising how soon a desire will die of inanition if it is never fed," he writes, reflecting on the generalized opinion that the best treatment for habitual drinkers was complete abstinence.[30] Virtue is the product of everyday little habits, those semi-conscious patterned acts that are neither fully willed nor completely automatic. Good and bad habits, which for James are equivalent to virtue and vice itself, inhabit the hybrid zone, often known as second nature, that has always been neglected by theology and philosophy.

John Dewey continued James' reflection on habit. Developing James' critique of the binary opposition between will and desire by showing how this opposition is rooted in the fundamental binaries of Western culture – mind vs. body, freedom vs. necessity – Dewey argued that the purest will, the most heroic flexing of the moral muscle, cannot exist for more than a second unless it quickly becomes rooted in ordinary habits. "Thought which does not exist within ordinary habits of action lacks means of execution." Dewey continues James' deconstruction of the opposition between habits and freedom as follows: "We think that by feeling strongly enough about something, by wishing hard enough, we can get a desirable result, such as virtuous execution of a good resolve . . . We slur over the necessity of the cooperative action of objective conditions . . ." He goes on to add that, if one undertakes to reform a personal habit such as excessive drinking, the way to succeed is not to flex one's moral muscle but to reorganize one's surroundings:

> The hard drinker who keeps thinking of not drinking is doing what he can to initiate the acts which lead to drinking. He is starting with the stimulus to his habit. To succeed he must find some positive interest or line of action which will inhibit the drinking series and which by instituting another course of action will bring him to his desired end . . . The discovery of this other series is at once his means and his end. Until one takes intermediate acts seriously enough to treat them as ends, one wastes one's time in any effort at change of habits.

Dewey took the deconstruction of the Victorian binaries of will vs. impulse, freedom vs. necessity, human vs. animal, further than James, by challenging James' original assumption that habit and volition have opposing ethical and political effects: the former conservative, the latter progressive. The formal effect of habit may be to conserve energy and set up a chain of repetitions by transforming a once impulsive or willed action into second nature; but, nevertheless, the *content* of one's habits may well tend to maximize rather than minimize originality and personal freedom. Education, Dewey famously argued, should involve the development of children's habits of freedom, rather than, as was the practice of the time, training children to repeat the conventional wisdom of their elders and re-enact their past habits.

> Even liberal thinkers have treated habit as essentially conservative. In fact, only in a society dominated by modes of belief and admiration fixed by past custom is habit more conservative than it is progressive. It all depends on its quality.

37

The neglect of and contempt for the realm of the habitual that has dominated both theology and philosophy, Dewey notes, is rooted in the myth of the transcendental subject. Foreshadowing Foucault's analysis of subjectification, Dewey notes that "the doctrine of a single, simple and indissoluble soul was the cause and the effect of the failure to recognize that concrete habits are the means of knowledge and thought". In fact, however, "concrete habits do all the perceiving, recognizing, imagining, recalling, judging, conceiving and reasoning that is done".[31]

The self-described philosophy of habit developed by American pragmatist thinkers was not taken up by the major post-World War I European philosophers. From Heidegger to phenomenology and existentialism, European philosophy remained engaged in a pursuit of what pragmatists would describe as the abstract freedom of the transcendental subject. By contrast, the *science* of habit was taken up by American scientific psychology: in the 1930s and 1940s, behaviourism attempted to find once and for all the mechanical foundations of habit, in rat-laboratory studies devised to measure behaviour change, quantifying it in the units that psychologist Clark Hull baptized as "habs".[32] But the measurement of rat behaviour in "habs" in the hope that this would lay the basis for a science of the human soul was a deployment of habit that learned nothing from pragmatism. Behaviourism reproduced the binary opposition between the will and necessity, the mind/spirit and the body, that Dewey and James had already deconstructed. The project pursued by Hull, and behaviourism generally, was precisely to reduce human behaviour to natural necessity. In the meantime, European philosophy pursued the opposite abstraction, the project of a human freedom conceived of as *against* the necessity of the natural sciences.[33]

The study of habit was thus appropriated by the advocates of natural determinism, a move that did not do justice to the rich possibilities of the pragmatist approach. But at the level of everyday knowledge and everyday practices of the self, habit formation continued to play a key role. From the inebriate homes that sought to reform habit by removing drinkers from their haunts and placing them in rural retreats, to AA's project to cobble together techniques for living one day at a time, the actual business of replacing the habits of heavy drinking with habits of health has continued to use and create techniques for personal reform that rely neither on theory nor on preaching, but on modest rearrangements of one's living space, one's daily routines, one's trivial little habits of the soul. These practices for reforming the soul have gone largely unnoticed by psy experts and have been totally ignored by philosophers. And yet, while the history of technologies of habit reform has not been acknowledged as significant in theoretical discourse,[34] habit has not remained at the subterranean level. It has continued to reappear, like a pesky mosquito that refuses to be shooed away, in both expert and lay discussions of the etiology and the treatment of alcoholism and addiction.

In the context of alcoholism, habit often appears not as the other of freedom and volition, as it did in William James' work, but as the other of *disease*. Is habitual drinking merely a bad habit, Dr Benjamin Rush asked in the 1750s, or is it a disease? This question has re-occurred in virtually every site studied in this book. In the nineteenth century, alienists asked: is drinking too much a moral vice, a bad habit, or a mental disease? Many protestations were made at scientific meetings that the subject at hand was "the disease of inebriety, not the vice of drunkenness",[35] but vicious habits were regarded by most physicians as the content of the disease of inebriety: persisting in a bad vice/habit would eventually produce disease.[36] In the 1930s, AA argued that alcoholism should be classified as a disease, which for them meant *not* as a habit. And so forth, until 1996, when cigarette companies defending themselves from lawsuits in the United States attempted to argue – unsuccessfully – that smoking is not an addiction but is merely a matter of habit.

While William James' opposition of habit to volition and intelligence tended to align habit with necessity and determination – as in the phrase 'the *force* of habit' – contrasting it with disease performs the opposite manoeuvre. The habit vs. disease contrast aligns habit with the freedom of the will. Anything that is managed as a disease is something we have little or no control over; by contrast, a habit, even if, like heavy drinking, it has become second nature, is nevertheless subject to some degree of personal control.

The debate concerning the status of alcohol in respect to "habit forming drugs" that took place in the World Health Organization in the early 1950s provides a rare glimpse into the difficulties caused by the attempt to theoretically separate mere habit from addiction/ disease. In the 1940s, the WHO had an expert committee on "habit forming drugs", focussed mostly on opium derivatives and morphine. The committee's name was changed to "Committee on drugs liable to produce addiction" to better reflect popular and medical usage, since the old language of the opium habit had, by around the 1950s, given way to the language of opium addiction.[37] So far, so good. But the problems came when the committee considered alcohol. E.M. Jellinek, one of the members of the expert committee, explains that heroin and morphine were easily classified as "addictive", with no dissenting opinions; and there was a consensus that these drugs, defined as drugs that had an inherent addictive effect regardless of the person taking them, required international controls. There was also agreement that there should be a category of less dangerous, not addictive drugs – now to be called "habit forming" – and that these drugs, which form only "psychological habits", not physical dependence, could be left to the jurisdiction of individual nations, without standardized or coordinated international controls. There seems to have been general agreement on which drugs to place in this category. Disagreement, however, surrounded the question of where to place alcohol. Was alcohol an addictive drug, or merely a habit-forming drug? After a number of impassioned presentations, the experts ended up avoiding the issue: they created a third, hybrid category, "intermediate between addiction producing drugs and habit forming drugs", and put alcohol in it. The WHO committee, attempting to give its political compromise on alcohol a veneer of science, wrote:

> Alcohol must be considered a drug whose pharmacological action is intermediate in kind and degree between addiction-producing and habit-forming drugs . . . Damage to the individual may develop, but does so in only a minority of users. The social damage that arises extends, however, beyond these individuals themselves.[38]

Whether habit or addiction or a unique hybrid of the two, alcoholism was bad because of its social effects. By 'socializing' alcohol, the WHO experts were able to create a consensus that alcohol needed to be regulated without entering into debates about the pathological effects of wine subsidies or liquor-licencing policies. The socialization of alcoholism in the 1940s and 1950s will be analyzed in detail in chapter 4; for present purposes, it suffices to point out that even the experts who drew a line between addiction and habit in regard to drugs were defeated by alcohol, declaring it to be a peculiarly hybrid substance.

One of the reasons why habit has been ignored by both psy experts and by philosophy (with the exception of pragmatism) is the historical fact that, while in Aristotle's time theorizing habit was the fundamental business of professional ethical philosophers, in our own time habit has been demoted in the hierarchy of knowledge institutions. As Dewey pointed out, philosophers tend to be more interested in the transcendental subject than in the phenomenal realm of habit. Psy scientists, from nineteenth century monomania experts to Freudian analysts of the 1950s, have been similarly uninterested in habits for their own sake: habits are of interest to science only as symptoms of underlying pathological conditions or as useful tools for replacing one behaviour with another. While diseases are the entities upon which medical and psy expertise has been built, habits – at least the habits of actually existing humans, as opposed to the habits of Dr Hull's laboratory rats – have generally been left to the authority of low-level experts, such as writers of manuals on how to get your child to sleep through the night.

The persistence of habit, its tendency to constantly haunt and upset both the philosophers of freedom and the scientists of necessity, is thus connected to the persistence of that realm of knowledges that, while not science-free, are definitely considered, even by their practitioners, as marginal and of low status. Habits are the material upon which kindergarten teachers and speech therapists work. They do not form a lay or everyday realm that can be kept sharply separate from professional expertise; but there is nevertheless a distinction between the often atheoretical or resolutely eclectic pursuit of habit reform and the pursuit of scientific knowledge. These two projects do of course coexist: speech pathology and childrearing manuals do have some scientific content, and, at the everyday level, our own attempts to reform habits such as drinking, eating, and exercising are shot through with bits of medical knowledge. But analytically, the realm of habit formation has had a logic of its own.

As Eve Sedgwick points out in her analysis of the fetishization of the free will performed in the literature of recovery, it may be useful for those interested in a genealogy of the will and its compulsions to look at the realm of habit.

> I'll just suggest briefly that the best luck I've had so far in reconstructing an 'otherwise' for addiction attribution has been through a tradition that is not opposed to it or explanatory of it but rather one step to the side of it. That is the tradition of reflecting on *habit*, a version of repeated action that moves, not toward metaphysical absolutes, but toward interrelations of the action – and the self acting – with the bodily habitus, the sheltering habitation, everything that marks the traces of that habit on a world that the metaphysical absolutes would have left a vacuum ... [T]he worldly concept of habit has dropped out of theorized use with the supervention in this century of addiction and the other glamorized paradigms oriented around absolutes of compulsion/voluntarity.[39]

Although I am obviously in agreement with Sedgwick in regard to the fruitfulness of inquiring into habits rather than addictions, which is why I have written about James and Dewey here, nevertheless it is important to avoid creating a new binary or suggesting that American pragmatism has all the answers. The reflections on habit produced both by thinkers such as Dewey and by the unsung individuals who have devised non-medicalized alcoholism treatments, do not, unfortunately, amount to a solution to the practical troubles and theoretical impasses connected with alcoholism. The highlighting of habit is not used here to wave a flag and tell everyone: "Ah, here's the solution to all our problems, this hitherto neglected approach is the true one, etc." Any systematic inquiry into habit would likely reveal a set of problems that would turn out to be the mirror images of the better-known problems of medicalization and addiction. In any case, in our time, there is no autonomous field of habit, no everyday world that is in fact separate from the disciplinary apparatuses built up by scientists and professionals. The point of the reflection on habit begun in this chapter and continued sporadically throughout this book is not to provide a solution but simply to demonstrate that the medicalization of alcoholism was not inevitable, and that it was neither complete nor consistent even when it did take place. Habit is here used, therefore, not to construct a new mechanism for research and treatment but, more humbly, to highlight – by contrast – an outline of the archeology of addiction and, ultimately, of a genealogy of the free will.

CHAPTER 2

# REPAIRING DISEASED WILLS: VICTORIAN SCIENCE AND PASTORAL MEDICINE BEFORE ALCOHOLISM

*The will is at the root of human conduct. It is the basis of moral*
*action. It is the foundation of wisdom. It is the controller of impulse.*
*Without it duty cannot be done . . . Without it in some strength no*
*civilized, moral and permanent form of human society could exist.*
*If it be true that this most authoritative faculty of man is in any way*
*lessened by alcohol, that substance would seem to need no other*
*condemnation.*                                    Sir Thomas Clouston, MD[1]

For about 150 years, 'alcoholism' has been found in some medical dictionaries but not in others. Even when officially recognized, it has often been defined as the *effects* of long years of heavy drinking on the body, rather than as a disease entity that leads people to drink too much. Today alcoholism is often included under the larger category of addiction or under the term that has replaced it in scientific discourse, dependence. But medical experts cannot agree on whether the substance is physically addictive, or whether the problem of alcoholism lies rather in an identifiable psychological predisposition. Psychiatrists, on their part, seem unable to agree on whether alcoholism is a disease or a symptom, and if a symptom, a symptom of what.[2]

Disagreement and debate about medical matters is of course not unique to alcohol. But debates about other conditions tend to assume that, if something is a disease at all, it is therefore a *medical* entity, to be defined and treated and cured by medical practitioners. The most striking and distinctive feature of the history of scientific and medical discourses on alcohol is found in statements to the effect that, even if alcoholism is a disease, it is not a medical entity, but rather a mixed medical–moral entity best left to the jurisdiction of religion, social work, and/or self-help groups.

The influential alcohol scientist Selden Bacon, reflecting in 1976 on the thirty-year project by US social and medical science to devise a scientific explanation for alcoholism, was honest enough to admit that "the 'disease' notion was an alien view to the [medical] profession. It was 'inserted' or 'foisted upon' or 'sold to' the medical profession chiefly by outsiders."[3] These outsiders – first, the scientific temperance activists of the early twentieth century, and, after the 1930s, Alcoholics

Anonymous – used the term 'disease' not to hand over control of alcohol questions to medicine, but simply to de-stigmatize the population which they sought to reach and reform. Robert Straus, another leading member of postwar alcohol science circles, shared Bacon's view about the tactical use of the term 'disease':

> A medical model was initially promoted in the 1940s and has been advocated since then by many persons especially interested in alcohol problems including the fellowship of AA. As I have suggested earlier, its promotion was a form of deliberate social policy aimed at reducing the public stigma, altering moralistic connotations, and . . . [stimulating] a greater sense of public responsibility reflected through governmental programs of research, treatment, and prevention.[4]

As Bacon put it: " 'Alcoholism is a disease' was a slogan that worked. But was it 'true'?"[5] Thus, even in the 1960s, when science and medicine had not yet been challenged by movements that ranged from anti-psychiatry to New Age self-help, American alcohol scientists admitted that the disease model had been paradoxically most successfully deployed by groups that refused medical leadership.

Alcoholism was dropped from the International Classification of Diseases in the late 1970s. It is also no longer found in the US classification of diseases, the *Diagnostic and Statistical Manual* (DSM-IV), although a physician who wants to justify health insurance coverage of treatment for an 'alcoholic' patient can use the broad category of psychoactive substance dependence as diagnosis.

Although I began work on this book with the aim of documenting the increasing medicalization of the 'vice' of drinking, the research showed that alcoholism does not fit the model of uneven but increasingly successful medicalization that has been developed by scholars in studies of psychiatry, sexology, and other sciences. This is not to say, however, that science and medicine have neglected the study of alcohol and alcohol consumption. Precisely because of the preponderance of success stories about medicalization, it may be useful to engage in a close study of a process that does not fit the 'onward march of medical science' model.

In the twentieth century, the most sustained project to subsume alcohol under a scientific paradigm took place in American universities in the post-World War II period. In the nineteenth century (which for the purposes of this book we will take as not ending until 1914), a number of different schools, without ever seeking to create a special field of alcohol studies, nevertheless used alcohol/ism as an important site upon which to deepen and extend the reach of biomedicine. This chapter will analyze the work of some of these schools, focussing on

British medicine and science but including some reference to American and French developments. This documentation of the fragmented and little-known prehistory of alcoholism raises some significant questions about standard historical sociological views of the power of Victorian medicine. We will see that the heterogeneous concerns gathered around what became known as alcoholism were deeply rooted in the old question, raised both by philosophy and by popular discussions about sin and vice, of the human will and its freedom. This chapter and the next demonstrate that, unlike other human capacities, such as memory,[6] the will was subsumed under science only briefly and largely unsuccessfully, during the heyday of degeneration theory. This chapter examines the question of the will's freedom in the context of the medical practices and discourses of the second half of the nineteenth century, while chapter 3 will examine the same question in the narrower context of the institutional treatments available around the turn of the twentieth century for those designated as inebriates.

## BETWEEN REASON AND MADNESS: MONOMANIA AND DIPSOMANIA

One of the recurring themes of Victorian culture was the ongoing war between science on the one hand, and religion and law on the other, regarding the nature and extent of individual human responsibility.[7] An important early battle in this war was waged by a group of Paris-based physicians led by the prominent alienist J.E.D. Esquirol.[8] Esquirol and his collaborators were interested in pursuing studies of that grey area between madness and reason conceptualized in the early nineteenth century as partial insanity. "Monomania" was the main term deployed in France, and to some extent elsewhere, to initially map and occupy that liminal zone. In the English-speaking world, a similar move was effected through the category of moral insanity. This was applied to people who committed violent crimes out of a derangement short of full-blown madness. British 'moral insanity', which like its French counterpart (monomania) was thought to involve not so much an alienation of reason as "lesions of the will", was a notion popularized during the 1840 trial of Edward Oxford for attempted injury of Queen Victoria.[9]

Monomania was a derivative of mania. "Mania", a common diagnosis made in nineteenth century asylums, was taken to indicate an alienation of the mind characterized by excitation, hyperactivity, and, in many cases, symptoms such as visions and delusions.[10] ("Furious mania" was a favourite term of asylum doctors or alienists.) Mania was opposed to melancholia (roughly similar to what we would now call major depression); and both were contrasted with dementia, a condition including many forms of cognitive dysfunction.[11] Esquirol and his Parisian

colleagues argued that the domain of the brand-new science of psychiatry ought not to be confined to mania, melancholy, and dementia, but
should extend to the shadowy zone between sanity and insanity
inhabited by, among others, those who would now be called alcoholics.

Using the traditional three-fold classification of the faculties of the
mind (intellect, emotions, will),[12] Esquirol and his circle proceeded to
divide monomania into three types: monomania of the intellect,
applying to people who were quite rational with the exception of one
subject or 'fixed idea'; monomania of the emotions, such as exaggerated
and inappropriate love; and monomania of the will, *monomanie
instinctive*. Alcoholics fell into the third category, and were discussed
under that heading at some length in Esquirol's magnum opus *Des
maladies mentales*.[13] In histories of psychiatry, the monomania of
drunkenness has always been overshadowed by the more famous
homicidal monomania appearing in both the courthouses and the
urban novels of the mid-nineteenth century. But just as the homicidal
monomania diagnosis provided a golden opportunity for the secular
sciences of the mind to challenge both the criminal law and religion by
arguing that one does not have to be constantly and completely insane in
order to be found not guilty by reason of insanity, so too the monomaniac drunk posed important questions about the extent and
character of moral and legal responsibility, since heavy drinking was,
unlike murder, an extremely common practice that could not be easily
'othered'.

Volitional monomanias, claimed Esquirol's disciple Georget, were
characterized by the irresistible impulses to act that were experienced
by people who were not necessarily mentally impaired.[14] Esquirol
himself was not wholly convinced that there could be a mental disease
affecting only the will: in his discussion of *monomanie instinctive* he
narrates many case studies in which the person who committed
impulsive acts eventually fell into full-blown madness, either mania or
dementia. But he does admit that apart from the familiar problem of
mental and physical deterioration caused by excessive drinking – the
toxic effects constituting alcoholism in its nineteenth century meaning
– there is at least in some drinkers a pre-existing condition that causes
them to drink uncontrollably. Pre-existing drink monomania can take
two very distinct forms, physical and moral. Physically, one can speak of
drink monomania when "the stomach is in a peculiar condition, which
causes the patient to suffer an excessively painful degree of physical
prostration. It is then that this organ demands strong drinks. It is a
disordered appetite; a real longing." But there was also monomania of a
non-physical, that is moral, origin. Here there is no gastric or other
physiological abnormality: rather, "the moral principle is prostrated, the

patient is destitute of energy, incapable of thinking or acting; is overwhelmed by a sense of weariness and irritability of temper, and drinks, at first to excite, then to divert the feelings . . .".[15]

Esquirol's typically careful description underlines an important genealogical point: contrary to the claim made in numerous studies of alcoholism to the effect that alcoholism was invented in the early or mid-nineteenth century, I am arguing that the twentieth century category of alcoholism should be traced back to the discovery of mono-mania and the associated notion of lesions of the will, not to what the nineteenth century called alcoholism. In the nineteenth century, the latter term referred strictly to the *effects* of long-term heavy drinking.[16]

How were monomanias of the will to be treated and cured? As is well known, Esquirol followed his predecessor Pinel in arguing that the moral treatment of lunatics had great medical value and ought to be used by physicians as well as by clergymen, nuns, and other non-medical personnel of asylums.[17] Moral treatment, devised originally as a set of practical measures to help the insane, consisted partly of environmental measures such as open and pleasant asylum architecture, large gardens, and rural vistas, but also included individual treatment measures such as advice and moral support. Although moral treatment was – more so in Britain than in France – originally associated with a critique of the evils of asylums and the failure of strictly medical cures, many physicians seem to have quickly adopted it not to displace drugs or other methods but as an additional treatment suitable for particular patients.[18] Esquirol ends his section on drink monomania suggesting that monomaniacs as well as maniacs need institutionalization, but this is followed by the rather non-medical suggestion that "instructions and religious precepts, the counsels of philosophy, the reading of treatises on temperance . . . will be auxiliaries to isolation".[19]

As we shall see shortly, turn-of-the-century physicians sometimes developed relations with alcoholics of their own class and gender that transcended the parameters of the clinical, spending much time and personal effort in seeing them through the dark night of the soul caused both by the drink and by withdrawal. This type of personalized pastoral–clinical care[20] was not usually practiced on lunatic asylum populations. The cultural gap between physicians and patients, the sheer size of most lunatic asylums, and the nature of the problems of most of the patients all worked to make individualized care unlikely. Despite the limitations of asylum clinical medicine, however, individu-alized moral support, albeit of a somewhat despotic character, was regarded by the monomania experts as crucial in treating all mono-manias, not only those specifically designated as belonging to the will. None other than the founder of the thoroughly deterministic school of degeneration theory, B.A. Morel, advocated such treatment for women suffering from what is now called post-partum depression. In her study of monomania, Jan Goldstein notes that Morel's text on "manie des femmes en couche" uses no less than three times a metaphor that wonderfully combines the individualized care of pastoralism with the despotism of asylum medicine. What is needed, Morel states, is a *"transfusion of the will of the physician into that of the patient* [emphasis added]".[21]

'Drink monomania' was not a term commonly used in English-speaking countries. But a very similar term invented by a German physician in 1819, 'dipsomania',[22] became very popular in medical circles. The great Parisian asylum physician and anatomist Valentin Magnan, who combined studies of the physiology of alcohol poisoning in dogs with highly individualized care for patients suffering from delirium tremens, stated in his 1874 magnum opus that "dipsomania" is "a particular form of volitional monomania [*monomanie instinctive*], commonly rooted in heredity".[23] In Britain, Dr Alexander Peddie suggested in the 1850s that dipsomaniacs (also known as oinomaniacs) should be subject to legal sanctions similar to those applicable to the insane. Complaining that the existing lunacy laws did not allow for "degrees" of lunacy (that is, for partial insanity), Peddie suggested that dipsomaniacs came under Prichard's category of "moral insanity",[24] which as noted earlier was thought to be a disease of the will. Several decades later, Dr Peddie was still advocating managing drinking problems through legal/social discipline. Advocating the institutionalization of inebriates by drawing a parallel with compulsory vaccination, Peddie wrote that "the liberty of the subject is indeed a precious trust; and that it should be jealously watched over and protected is the ruling glory of the British constitution; but the welfare of Society is still more sacred".[25]

Like so many other terms used to govern alcohol, 'dipsomania' was never very stable. The original meaning of the term seems to have been very broad, including much if not all of what later became alcoholism.[26] Later on, however, the term came to be restricted to occasional bouts of drunkenness, as distinguished from daily excessive drinking, and this usage is still occasionally found in medical dictionaries. But the term never caught on outside of biomedical circles, and was never consistently deployed. One medical dictionary from 1890 states that dipsomania is a degenerative nervous disease often rooted in family history and distinguishes it sharply from habitual drunkenness, described as a "vicious custom".[27] This potentially fruitful distinction did not catch on: a decade or so later, the British Inspector of Inebriate Asylums used "dipsomania" synonymously with the legal categories of habitual drunkard and habitual inebriate.[28]

It would be idle to speculate why dipsomania failed to catch on, but it may not be idle to point out that if dipsomania had triumphed, this label would have placed excessive drinkers firmly in the domain of psychiatry, along with nymphomaniacs and homicidal monomaniacs. Despite its proximity to what British physicians called 'the borderlands', the ambiguous zone between reason and insanity not yet populated by the neuroses, dipsomania was fundamentally an alienists' term, with all the frightening connotations inherent in the old term "furious mania". Dr Thomas Clouston, the prominent Scottish psychiatrist cited in the epigraph for this chapter, defined dipsomania as "a congenital weakness in the inhibitory qualities of the brain", and explicitly linked it to Jack the Ripper's homicidal mania.[29]

The repeated calls by Dr Peddie and Dr Clouston for state measures to deprive dipsomaniacs of their liberty were consistent with the mono-mania project of extending the discursive reach of psychiatry and the social/legal power of physicians into the liminal zone between madness and reason. But that was precisely the weakness of the dipsomania model. Although medical despotism did indeed prosper in the nineteenth century in respect to certain populations, alcoholics – many of whom were gentlemen of the same class as, or a higher class than, the physicians – were never successfully subjected to the despotic tendency of psychiatry so ably analyzed by Robert Castel.[30] The attempts made by Dr Thomas Crothers in the United States, and by Peddie and his collaborators in the United Kingdom, to manage alcoholics as if they were insane were notoriously unsuccessful. The model of alcoholic as lunatic was never seriously pursued in real life, as opposed to in the writings of a few specialized physicians. Dipsomania, while not dis-appearing completely the way that its synonym 'oinomania' did,[31] was displaced, very fitfully but very successfully, by the term 'alcoholism', invented in 1852 but not acquiring its contemporary psychological meaning until well into the twentieth century.[32]

However influential in certain circles, then, the promoters of the dipsomania diagnosis were not necessarily representative of the medical profession as a whole. Many nineteenth century asylum doctors, like many psychiatrists in the mid- to late twentieth century, did not consider excessive drinking as a properly psychiatric problem. Contrary to the narrative of relentless psychiatric imperialism popularized among other writers by Andrew Scull,[33] in the case of alcohol the tendency to extend the reach of the alienist or psychiatrist into the in-between zone appears to have been subject to a recurring counterforce, a sort of refusal to medicalize. The refusal did not necessarily imply an autocritique; it was often associated – as it still is today – with a sense that physicians should not waste their precious time on social misfits such as alcoholics. Along these lines, an American State Lunacy Commissioner argued in the asylum doctors' organ that, precisely in order to safeguard the integrity of insanity science, habitual drinkers should be excluded from its purview. Converging with the religious view of vice, from the opposite direction, John Ordronaux argued that drinking may be facilitated by disease but is not itself a disease:

> The problem of self-abasement or self-redemption is entirely within his control, provided he exercises a continuous determination of his will not to partake. The key to the riddle of this alleged disease lies in man's own will, and without this will-effort, no physician can cure or even relieve him; with this will effort, no physician is needed to cure him, for the distemper is always within his own control.[34]

### INEBRIETY: THE GENEALOGY OF ADDICTION

The failure of the dipsomania project did not result straightaway in the victory of alcoholism. A great effort was made, particularly in Britain, to popularize the term 'inebriety' at the end of the nineteenth century. Inebriety was initially conceived as an umbrella term whose primary associations were with heavy drinking but which could also cover the opium habit, morphinism, and other conditions that later came to be called addictions. The most influential proponent of this classification in the United Kingdom, Dr Norman Kerr, was also the leading figure in the British Society for the Scientific Study of Inebriety. As early as 1887, however, Dr Kerr himself complained that people were starting to use the term "alcoholic" to refer to the predisposing condition leading to excessive drinking, instead of reserving it for alcohol poisoning and focussing the scientific study of causes of drinking on the broader category of "inebriety".[35]

'Inebriety' in Kerr's broad sense did not take: alcohol questions were not successfully articulated with questions of illicit drug taking until many decades later, well after World War II, despite the heroic efforts of Kerr and his successors. Even his counterpart in the United States, Dr T.D. Crothers, defined "the inebriate constitution" exclusively in terms of factors causing excessive drinking, hence isolating drinking from the consumption of other substances.[36] 'Inebriate' became a polite euphemism for habitual drunkard or dipsomaniac: for example, the British legislation on "habitual drunkards" had its name changed in 1898 to "The Habitual Inebriates Act".

The British Society for the Scientific Study of Inebriety represented this ambiguity quite vividly in its proceedings (starting in the late 1880s) and in the journal that succeeded the proceedings, even though there was a token acknowledgement (probably led by Dr Kerr) of the similarities between alcohol use and the use of substances such as narcotics, coffee, and tobacco. In marked contrast to the process through which, in the 1970s, alcohol consumption began to be re-visualized as an addiction through an analogy to drug taking, in the 1880s drinking was the paradigm case of inebriety – in Aristotle's sense of paradigm, that is, the case providing the core meaning of a term that has analogical ripple effects.[37] In the 1880s, smoking and drug taking were classified under inebriety not through any scientific definition – the various substances did not share any chemical features – but through analogy. Thus, in the 1880s, morphine and tobacco consumption were problematized by being compared with drinking, whereas today excessive drinking is regarded as somehow *like* being addicted to drugs.

In the United States, where the discourse of alcohol consumption was dominated by the temperance movement, the broader meaning of inebriety seems to have been even less successful than in the United Kingdom. By the 1940s and 1950s, 'inebriate' was simply a somewhat obscure word for 'alcoholic',[38] and soon after that it faded from both popular and medical use.

## EVOLUTION AND DRINKING: MATERNAL DRINKING AND HEREDITY DEBATES

Discussions of the relation between alcohol and the will were given a new twist in the 1880s by the branch of evolutionary science known as degeneration theory. Degeneration theory, as is well known, translated old moral judgements about the mentally handicapped, about single mothers, and about vice, into the scientific language of evolution. B.A. Morel – the French alienist who spoke of "transfusions of the will" – had invented the term to refer to physiological processes of tissue degeneration, but the term acquired a much wider meaning late in the nineteenth century. While mid-Victorian interpretations of Darwin tended to assume that evolution was largely an onward-and-upward process, late Victorian commentators such as Max Nordau and Cesare Lombroso argued that human evolution was at risk of going backward through atavism or biological regression.[39] In the late Victorian paradigm of degeneration, one did not have to decide whether a condition was biological or moral: bodily features were moralized and moral vices were blamed for causing physical degeneration. This meant that heavy drinking, popularly and medically regarded as a hybrid object – part vice, part disease – was easily assimilated into the theories and schemes of degeneration writers.

Although some physicians maintained the old view that moderate amounts of alcohol could be harmless or even purifying and

51

therapeutic,[40] alcohol was regarded by most physicians in the United Kingdom, the United States, France and Germany as an important "racial poison".[41] The degeneration writers' view of alcohol as a racial poison merged imperceptibly with the increasing tendency of physicians to sympathize with temperance concerns, which were in turn often intertwined with and reinforced by scientific eugenic fears. A complete historical study of the central role of alcohol in degeneration discourse is beyond the scope of this study, but some original light can be shed on the well-known discussions of degeneration and vice by focussing on debates about parental drinking and its effects on offspring, debates which in the United Kingdom more than elsewhere ended up blaming working-class mothers (not drinking fathers) for the physical and moral failings of the nation.

Most degeneration writers who believed (with Lamarck) that one's physical and moral *conduct* could be inherited by offspring did not target mothers. If germ cells could be shaped by conduct, paternal conduct was as crucial for racial health and the transmission of the inebriate diathesis as that of mothers. In keeping with this version of the degeneration paradigm, Zola's best-selling novels describing the downward progression of degeneration across several generations of a French working-class family focus on alcoholic men as well as on degenerate women. It is not clear that willpower would ever suffice to reverse the degeneration process; but insofar as there was a role for individual moral resolve, men were targetted as well as women.[42]

This equal-opportunity degenerationism continued to be popularized in the early twentieth century in the discourse of North American social purity and temperance movements. A fairly typical example is a book entitled *Alcohol and the human race*, by an American ex-Navy officer active in temperance circles. This warns the readers about how "alcohol vitiates the ensuing chain of life and becomes a cause of degeneracy", but emphasizes that alcohol affects all "germ plasm", not just the woman's body. His tirade about alcohol and racial degeneration is thus aimed equally at men and women, "the fathers and mothers of the race".[43] Along the same lines, the popular view – reiterated by some scientific writers – that children conceived during a bout of drinking would be born defective tended to responsibilize fathers as well as mothers.

In sharp contrast to today's discourses on pregnancy and drink, degeneration theory's claim that the inebriate constitution was a cause of degeneration was sometimes gendered to women's advantage. The strong, women-led temperance movements in the United States and Canada often deployed eugenic concerns about race degeneration to exhort *men* to stop drinking and smoking, and reading impure books.

Degeneration theory was, as is well known, deployed against women in North America, particularly in the long moral panic about 'feeble-minded' single mothers; but alcoholism was, in every country other than Britain, gendered in the opposite direction, with men seen as the worst culprits. American physicians were significantly influenced by the view of the Women's Christian Temperance Union (WCTU) that it was men, not women, who poisoned the race, and even if they privately rejected such views, they rarely opposed them in public. One physician writing in the *Journal of the American Medical Association (JAMA)* in 1903 stated that "few publishers of schoolbooks could afford to risk the boycott of all their publications that might issue of a textbook on physiology which differed in its treatment of the effects of alcohol from the standards prescribed by the WCTU".[44]

The feminist view of men, alcohol, and racial degeneration associated with the WCTU was increasingly not wholly external to the medical profession, as American women obtained the right to train as physicians. A Dr Agnes Sparks, a physician at a private sanatorium for inebriates in Brooklyn, ingeniously articulated patriarchal inheritance customs with the biology of heredity by arguing that women are less likely to inherit and thus to transmit the alcoholic taint: "We know families in which the sons inherit the father's inebriety almost as naturally as they do his name or fortune, while the daughters show the strongest repugnance for the poison, especially if the mother be the inebriate."[45]

In Britain, however, it was women's drinking, not parental habits in general, that greatly preoccupied those worried about the decline of empire and race.[46] The British Society for the Scientific Study of Inebriety did not have proto-feminists to compare with Dr Agnes Sparks (probably because there were almost no women physicians in Britain); and the patriarchal-imperialist moral panic about mothering was tightly articulated with inebriety through the work of the Committee on Physical Deterioration, whose members were atypical of the medical profession in belonging (with one exception) to the Inebriety Society.[47]

As Lucia Zedner has pointed out in her study of the gender-specific enforcement of the Habitual Drunkards/Inebriates Acts, the British focus on the nefarious social and biological consequences of maternal drinking resulted in a situation where the vast majority of habitual drunkards put away under the Acts were women, and most of those were in turn mothers charged with child neglect through the surveillance work of the National Society for the Prevention of Cruelty to Children (NSPCC).[48] Dr Norman Kerr commented at the time that "the female parent is the more general transmitter of the hereditary alcoholic taint I have little doubt",[49] obviously expecting no disagreement.

British women doctors, who unlike their North American counterparts were unlikely to have been involved in feminist temperance
campaigns, did not show any sympathy for inebriate women, possibly
because of the belief that such women were found exclusively among
the urban poor. In an article entitled "Alcohol and the children of the
nation", Dr Mary Scharlieb painted a Hogarthian picture of "women of
the working classes" enjoying themselves in pubs while dosing their
babies with gin. Paternal drinking, she argued, was certainly an evil,
since it often led to physical violence, but maternal drinking was much
worse, both because it caused domestic chaos and because such
drinking was on the increase. (That working-class women's drinking was
on the rise was a 'fact' that everyone accepted; Dr Scharlieb gave as her
authority Charles Booth's middle-class informants' opinions.)[50] Fuelling
the flames lit by the 1904 Interdepartmental Committee on Physical
Deterioration, and coinciding with George Sims' highly successful 1907
journalistic campaign to remove children (and hence housewives) from
licenced premises, Dr Scharlieb grew passionate:

> Is it possible that from such homes as these we can bring forth the men
> and women who shall hold high our national name before the nations of
> the earth? It is in them that can be bred the men and women of the
> mother country to whom the younger nations of the Empire can look
> with admiration, and whose examples shall stimulate and nerve them to
> deeds of heroism, and to that noble self-respect that has hitherto made
> the name of England a talisman and a guard to her distant children?[51]

Whether one believed that drunken mothers were a national curse
because their behaviour was passed on to future generations or simply
because they were bad mothers, middle-class social observers could
agree that maternal drinking was a terrible thing. Either way, through
defective germ plasm or through vice, drunken mothers ended up with
dead infants and defective children. In her inaugural address as the first
woman president of the British Society for the Scientific Study of
Inebriety, Dr Scharlieb reiterated that

> the subject of Infant Mortality is very much before the public mind at the
> present time, and, in view of the falling birth-rate and of the imperative
> call from our colonies for a white population, we cannot but realize the
> importance of studying the relation of alcoholism to all these
> conditions.[52]

The doctrine, popularized from the 1880s onward, that women had a
particular responsibility to maximize the health not so much of their
particular babies but of 'the race'[53] often (although not always) relied
on Lamarckian views. The rejection of the view that conduct could be

The Inspector of Inebriates included photographs of inebriate women in his report designed to support his claim, made in the context of the moral panic about physical deterioration, that most such women were 'feeble-minded'. (British Parliamentary Papers, 1906, vol. xvi, pp. 97–98.)

inherited – the end of Lamarckianism – might therefore have signalled the end of the concern about maternal drinking. This possibility was raised by Karl Pearson, but quickly dismissed by virtually all other authorities. The strict Mendelian genetics championed by Karl Pearson and his collaborators at the National Eugenics Laboratory produced a study showing that maternal behaviour had no effect whatsoever on the quality of the germ plasm. Ridiculing the *British Journal of Inebriety* for publishing unscientific studies, Pearson dismissed both the popular Lamarckian view that drinking habits cause degeneration, and socio-logically oriented studies showing greater infant mortality and lower-weight newborns among drinking mothers.[54] For Pearson, it mattered little what pregnant women did or refrained from doing, for their destiny and that of their progeny was indelibly written in the unalter-able germ plasm, and their underlying problem was in any case low intelligence, not bad habits. As W.F. Bynum has noted, Pearson's study caused a great scandal, since, regardless of their views on the Lamarck vs. Weismann controversy, medical and social authorities in the United Kingdom were agreed that maternal drinking was more harmful than any other drinking.[55]

In contrast to Pearson's rigorous but unpopular work, some physi-cians who rejected Lamarck's theory about the inscription of vicious conduct into the physique of 'the race' did not want to conclude that working-class women's conduct was no longer of significance. Instead, they sought a new justification for the old programme of maternal governance by shifting the focus from the social environment to the fetal environment, in a number of articles disseminating scientific studies of fetal development.[56]

From 1903 to 1905, the readership of the *British Journal of Inebriety*, consisting largely of physicians, witnessed a heated debate on whether the alcoholic habits acquired by parents could be physically inherited, as Lamarckians believed, or not. The anti-Lamarckian physicians con-cluded that habits cannot be inherited, but that drinking by pregnant women could nevertheless physically affect the offspring. "Alcohol constitutes another form of injurious environment", causing damage to the individual baby but having no power to change the course of human evolution.[57] A well-known physician working in the prison service, Dr William Sullivan, carried out an extensive study of women inmates of the Liverpool prison, comparing their reproductive outcomes with those of their non-imprisoned and non-alcoholic relatives. This revealed that the infant mortality rate among drunken mothers was two and a half times greater than those of their sober relatives, and that, in all cases where it could be ascertained that conception occurred while the woman was drunk, *all* resulting children were stillborn or died soon after birth.[58] This study showed that choices and environments were more important than heredity, a conclusion indirectly supported by the sudden (and short-lived) scientific interest in documenting what we now call fetal alcohol syndrome.[59]

In other work, Dr Sullivan more directly critiqued degeneration theory, in particular its tendency to blame poor people for their own ills. In a book unusual for highlighting the sociology rather than the pathology of drinking, he went so far as to claim, as socialist and labour leaders did, that the notion of an alcoholic constitution or "inebriate diathesis" was "a figment", and that excessive drinking among the urban poor was caused by "industrial conditions".[60] But Dr Sullivan's well-meaning attempt to challenge the degeneration paradigm and its blame-the-victim approach to questions of poverty, while exonerating men, continued to target women/mothers, now under the banner of nurture rather than that of inheritance.

Dr Branthwaite, the Inspector of Inebriates, who shared neither Sullivan's sympathies for the working class nor his critique of degeneration, carried out his own study of fertility and infant mortality among inebriate women in 1909. He claims that he expected to find a strong correlation between prenatal drinking and infant mortality, but that this was simply not the case. Women who had been put away in inebriate asylums while pregnant gave birth to healthy babies in the same proportions as non-inebriate women; it was only inebriate women who had given birth and had nursed babies in their own homes who had higher rates of infant mortality.

> Maternal alcoholism during pregnancy is a possible cause of physical defect in offspring, but difficult of proof. It is reasonable to assume that the circulation of alcohol should have some injurious effect upon fetal development; but unfortunately for this assumption, the physical condition of the majority of children, born in the Reformatories, is good.[61]

Not surprisingly, given his job as inebriates inspector, Branthwaite's study showed that, contrary to Karl Pearson's fatalistic views, state intervention into the lives of poor pregnant women was not useless, but was, on the contrary, highly effective. In order to legitimize his policy and his work, he had to challenge the influential eugenic scientists on the question of alcohol and reproduction, although he was in general in sympathy with eugenics.

Fetal alcohol was thus of little or no interest to the degeneration experts who emphasized heredity rather than the conditions of pregnancies; and it was only of temporary and somewhat marginal interest to people like Dr Sullivan, who was more interested in the sociology of health than in medico-physiological issues. In the years 1900–14, in Britain, it seemed far more important to social and medical authorities to keep mothers and children physically away from pubs than to keep alcohol away from the fetus.[62] The moral hazards of the pub were intertwined with fears of imperial decline and maternal inadequacy that did not, in the end, rely very much on the notion of fetal alcohol, even though fetal alcohol syndrome had certainly been 'discovered'.

Toward the end of the Inebriate Acts' short life, the government named an assistant inspector, Dr Mary Gordon, whose special mandate was to manage the women detained under the Acts. Like a number of other early women physicians, Gordon was a fervent believer in eugenics.[63] She thus tended to subsume alcohol – or rather the narrower problem she was given to solve, namely female alcoholism – under the peril of 'feeble-mindedness', going so far as to advocate the "permanent detention" of inebriate women not under inebriate legislation but under the more powerful provisions of the Mental Deficiency Act of 1913.[64] This move to re-classify alcoholism not as chosen behaviour but as a symptom of mental deficiency/feeble-mindedness was not her own: Dr Branthwaite, her boss, had been paving the way for this since 1904. He had personally carried out scientific studies showing that two-thirds of the individuals put away under the Inebriate Acts were either "very defective (imbeciles, degenerates, epileptics)" or else "defective (eccentric, silly, dull, senile)".[65] This research was later cited by other experts to support the view (also held by Karl Pearson) that alcoholism was not a disease but rather an effect of feeble-mindedness. Since the vast majority of the inebriate asylum inmates were women, these studies had the effect of strengthening the discursive links between mental deficiency, the decline of the race, and female vice.[66] Significantly, the women's inebriate asylum run by the London County Council was, after 1913, turned into an institution for feeble-minded women, apparently with no change in the regime.[67]

The discursive slippage between 'female inebriates' and 'the feeble-minded' thus facilitated subsuming one large group of officially designated inebriates – working-class mothers – under the label of mental deficiency.[68] Fetal alcohol, having made a cameo appearance in the context of the debates between Lamarckians and anti-Lamarckians on heredity, habits, and environment, disappeared from view, not to be seen again in scientific alcohol studies until the 1970s. As shall be seen in chapter 7, contemporary campaigns against fetal alcohol, while differing markedly from the late Victorian strategies for regulating motherhood in many respects, also exhibit a marked lack of interest in maximizing the woman's own freedom or even utilizing her aspirations toward freedom to regulate her conduct.

The concerns about maternal drinking and fetal alcohol were a very important part of the more general turn-of-the-century campaign against the degeneration of the nation's population and of the Anglo-Saxon race, a campaign involving a number of interrelated projects. These projects have been extensively documented by social and legal historians, but no studies have thus far traced the connections between these population-based projects and the preoccupations of intellectuals (and of alcohol consumers) regarding the will, its freedom, and its compulsions. Let us return, then, to the main thread of this chapter – the issue of the will in science and medicine – first with a general overview of the debates about freedom and determinism in Victorian science, and then with an account of the treatments for diseased wills provided to individual private patients.

## THE WILL IN VICTORIAN SCIENCE

In Britain, the scientific attack on traditional religious and philosophical notions of the free will that underlay much of the discourse on the degeneration of 'the race' was most thoroughly carried out by the leading late Victorian psychiatrist Henry Maudsley.[69] Holding to a strict materialist, relentlessly anti-spiritual view, Maudsley argued that the existence of the will was a speculative theory based on no solid evidence, and that in our practical affairs we do not in fact behave as if we believed in the freedom of the will.[70] In addition to articulating a much more materialist view of evolution than most of his British colleagues, he also deployed the concept of the unconscious – or, as he called it, "infra-conscious" – in order to argue that even when we think we are acting freely, our actions are in fact unconsciously determined both by our heredity and by past habits that have petrified into a particular character. Ridiculing the traditional Victorian emphasis on conscious self-control and moral responsibility, Maudsley believed that, if we had more scientific insights into causality, even the most free of acts would be revealed as determined:

> What man is there who does not, in his manner of making love to his mistress, show some trait of character and behaviour which he never noticed in himself before, but which he might perhaps have noticed in his father had he been present at his father's wooing?

Continuing this thought and building a discursive link from Darwin to Freud, he wrote:

> To dissect any act of will accurately, and then to recompose it, would be to dissect and recompose humanity. Acts of will being acts and manifestations of self, outcomes of the person's essential nature, a thorough

self-knowledge is now, as it ever has been, an unattainable aim of
knowledge.

Rejecting the Christian view of the primacy of individual consciousness
in the same words used by Marx against idealism, Maudsley stated that
"it is not from consciousness but from life that obligation comes
primarily". The individual will is for Maudsley, then, but a derivative
crumb of Nature's purpose. Freedom is only a feeling we have, a feeling
rooted not in an individual soul but in the quiet workings of Nature
herself. "It may be that the sentiment of freedom that he [Man] has is
not really the sentiment of his own freedom, as he supposes, but the
sentiment of the freedom of nature working in him, he being a poor
channel of it; for as he by his nature as individual is part only of a whole,
he cannot in that relation be free."[71]

Maudsley's work was extremely influential in scientific circles not
only in Britain but internationally, helping to contribute to a certain
clinical fatalism in mental medicine/psychiatry.[72] In the medical circles
concerned with inebriety, his view that the will was the highest and
therefore most vulnerable product of human evolution – the theory
underpinning the concern that alcohol somehow dissolved the capacity
to will – was regarded as a well-known fact by medical authorities such as
the Edinburgh alienist Dr Clouston, as well as by popular writers on
alcohol's evil effects:

> The Will more than any other power of the mind determines the
> character and fate of the individual, as well as his influence upon society.
> Alcohol in attacking the 'temple' [i.e. body], strikes at the indwelling
> 'spirit'. Since will is the highest, most delicate and complex power of
> mind, the latest evolved, an injury to the integrity of the brain by such a
> poison necessarily produces its maximum harm to the will.[73]

Convinced that the will had a somatic basis somewhere in the nervous
system or the brain, a basis that had not yet been but would eventually
be discovered by science, Maudsley stated that alcohol and opium
intoxication could produce the same effects as inherited degeneration,
since alcohol enters the blood quickly and from there "the inmost
minute recesses of the brain".[74]

In France, Theodule Ribot, for years editor of the important organ of
materialist science *Revue de philosophie positive*, appropriated Maudsley's
materialist philosophy as a theoretical basis for his own work on the
pathologies of the will.[75] Ribot's much-read work *The diseases of the will*
classified inebriety as one of the conditions in which the will is unable to
control and inhibit the passions, much as Esquirol had done; but,
unlike Esquirol, Ribot linked this weak inhibitory power to degeneration. While conditions such as agoraphobia were classified as diseases of

a defective or absent "impulse" to act, the conditions formerly known as "monomanias" were attributed by Ribot to an "excess of impulse", conceived quasi-somatically as a force too great for the will to inhibit. In a statement building a rather shaky bridge from Esquirol to modern psychology via degeneration theory, Ribot tells his readers that "dipsomania, kleptomania, pyromania, erotomania, homicidal and suicidal mania are today no longer considered as distinct morbid forms, but as different manifestations of one single and the same cause: degeneracy, that is, psychological instability and lack of coordination".[76]

Maudsley's work was too relentlessly fatalistic to be consistently deployed even by his admirer Ribot, who was a secular republican but was nevertheless not nearly as enamoured of scientific determinism as Maudsley. In Ribot's work *Heredity*, the Maudsleyian view of the powerful effects of heredity is moderated by a concession to the mysteries of human freedom. Ribot concludes that, even though our actions are indeed shaped in ways only science can understand, nevertheless our actions are not completely determined; there is often room for personal freedom.[77] Strict determinism and its clinical corollary, fatalism, were also rejected by those clinicians who were working with inebriates, in Britain at least. Sir W.J. Collins, MD, used the title of Ribot's book, 'diseases of the will', not to somatize the will but, on the contrary, to cast doubt upon the physicality of inebriety:

> A disease it may be called, but a *disease of the will* (if one may couple terms derived from the opposite poles of the material and the volitional), and assuredly a disease in which the individual possessed has in many instances a most essential cooperative influence in his own worsement or betterment . . .
>
> I regret that I know of no royal road, no shortcut from vicious habit to the path of virtue . . . At a time when diagnosis by germ culture and treatment by the squirt have become familiar methods, and our advertising columns are full of serums good against anything from yellow fever to lockjaw . . . it seems, I confess, old-fashioned and unenterprising not to come forward with some new drug or serum good against habitual drunkenness.[78]

Collins' more consistently spiritual view was more typical of British physicians than Maudsley's strict materialism; but, on the whole, what is striking is the *lack of debate* between spiritualists and materialists. Most physicians seemed happy to write as if it did not matter very much whether diseases of the will were physical or spiritual, or, perhaps more accurately, to write as if the will were both at once.

A little book entitled *Inebriety: its source, prevention, and cure*, which sold very well in the United States, promoted this view of the will as an ontologically hybrid entity, with its corollary about inebriety as a hybrid condition.[79] The first chapter of the book gives a general overview of "the nervous-mental organization", explaining that heredity is often the cause of "the neuropsychopathic constitution", a general term including inebriety and neurasthenia. But spirituality is never far from the neurons. Chapter 4, for example, is entitled "The inebriate's continued progress in building up moral manhood". And at the end of the book, a fold-out diagram "of the moral manifestations resulting from the normal and abnormal conditions of the nervous-mental structure" popularizes Ribot's theory about excesses and defects of "impulse" in graphic form. Two lines, one pointing upward and one downward, are shown diverging from a straight line in the middle labelled "regularity of mental activity". The top line includes excessive conditions, such as avariciousness and maliciousness. The bottom line consists of those conditions related to a deficiency in mental and volitional powers, beginning with "lack of interest in life" and progressing to intemperance, melancholy, disease, and death.

Along the same lines, a Protestant minister who also had a PhD in psychology from Yale wrote a doctoral dissertation on alcoholism as if there were no conflict between his two affiliations. Moral and spiritual treatment was very important, he writes, but "the repair of will power comes through nutrition, while, conversely, loss of will is sure when the nervous force is lowered".[80] Elsewhere, an American physician describing the evil effects of alcohol on what he called "the moral nerves" explained:

> It is known that certain brain centers and brain fibres are the physical bases of the manifestations of the moral nature. When, therefore, alcohol disturbs and distracts the whole nervous system, its evil infuence is as certain to impress the moral as it is the intellectual or the motor capacities.[81]

## HYBRID TREATMENTS FOR A HYBRID CONDITION: BUILDING UP THE WILL THROUGH PASTORAL MEDICINE

The theory that inebriety was a hybrid condition, part physical and part moral, was implicit in many treatments used in private practice, and also in the numerous commercially produced home remedies obtainable without prescription. The back pages of the *British Journal of Inebriety* were covered with advertisements for Bovril, cocoa drinks, Ovaltine, and mineral water, suggesting to physicians that they build up their patients' nerve power with nourishing liquids. These adverts subsumed drunkards under the politer and broader category of 'convalescents' recovering from "neurasthenia, exhaustion, and brain fag".[82]

Probably not as common as beef teas, drugs were also used by many physicians. The *Journal of the American Medical Association (JAMA)*

# Did You Ever Know

## That Improper Food Often Causes the Liquor Habit?

It's a great proposition to get rid of a taste for liquor by changing food.

Improper food and stimulants like coffee and tea create unnatural appetites. The one who eats only proper food is normal in health and therefore normal in appetite.

By way of example take the case of a well-known business man of Lowry City, Mo., who says: "About three years ago my appetite failed me and my food disagreed with me. I got weak, nervous and dull and entirely unfit for business. Then like a fool I went to taking liquor to stimulate an appetite.

"For a time this worked well and I thought I had found a simple remedy, but I noticed I had to take more all the time and before long I found that I could not get along without the whiskey and I was in a pitiable condition.

"I tried to quit but it seemed impossible, as I needed nourishment and my stomach rejected food, and the more whiskey I drank the worse I got. I kept fighting this battle for more than two years and almost gave up all hope. Then I noticed an article about the food GRAPE-NUTS and concluded to give it a trial.

"I found I could eat GRAPE-NUTS with a relish and it was the first food that I found nourishing me in a long time. Soon my stomach trouble stopped, my appetite increased and then the craving thirst relaxed until all desire for drink was gone.

"I have used GRAPE-NUTS now for more than a year and I am now entirely strong and robust, entirely cured from drink and able to work hard every day. My gratitude for GRAPE-NUTS is unspeakable, as it has saved my life and reputation." Name given by Postum Co., Battle Creek, Mich.

A Free Sample of Delicious GRAPE-NUTS Food sent to any address upon request.

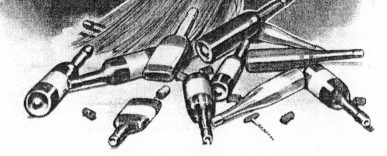

In the early twentieth century, drinking and eating habits were regarded as more closely intertwined than they are today. (*Everybody's Magazine*)

published many notes from subscribing physicians, listing their favourite drug cures for alcoholism: strychnine, nux vomica, chloride of gold,
and sedatives such as opiates and valerian.[83] None of these drug cures
ever gained general acceptance, however. Most American and virtually
all British therapeutic discussions tended to confine the therapeutic
effect of drugs to helping people in the withdrawal stage: no drug *cure*
for alcoholism was ever claimed by physicians (then or now). Drugs
were often used to "build up the nerves" or to sedate patients in
withdrawal; but it was generally emphasized that the moral process by
which patients formed a resolution and mustered their emotional
resources to maintain it was the real key to cure.[84] In fact, physicians
sometimes rejected claims about magic bullets as quack remedies of no
scientific value.

If drugs were considered inadequate, so was hypnosis. Two isolated
reports in *JAMA*, both originating from the same physician, stressed that
hypnosis or suggestion could be effective, but "the patient must be
willing to be cured". One of these two treatment notes ends by
emphasizing that "the object of the treatment is not only to cure the
craze, but to strengthen the will".[85]

A typical compromise between moral and medical treatment is found
in the advice of a physician running a private sanatorium in England,
who, after describing strychnine injections, purgatives, and other
medications, concludes that drug treatment operates chiefly to restore a
weak nervous system, but that a separate effort needs to be made by
both physician and patient to morally build up "a relatively inadequate
will-power".[86]

What is most striking for us today in the medical advice about
alcoholism of the turn of the century is the way in which the therapeutic
discourse placed physical remedies such as strychnine injections very
much on the same level as moral support for the inebriate's resolve to
stop drinking. The advertorials published in the *British Journal of
Inebriety*, which gave explicit medical endorsements to commercially
produced non-alcoholic drinks advertised in the journal, were written
as if by drinking Cadbury's cocoa one directly imbibed moral resolve
along with nutritious matter, thus showing that the mixed moral–
physical language of the inebriety texts cited above was used in commercial venues as well as in texts on science and health.

If the will had been successfully defined in somatic terms, then drugs
or other physiological treatments or prevention measures would
probably have become dominant. And if the will had been successfully
monopolized by religion, then evangelistic discourse would have been
everywhere prescribed. The former approach would have emphasized
necessity and determination, and the latter, spiritual freedom. But it so

happened that most people regarded diseases of the will as hybrid conditions, and this is clearly seen in then-current recommendations for inebriety treatment. Dr Norman Kerr presented a theoretical framework in keeping with the somatic theories of nervous diseases current in the 1880s and 1890s, and strongly influenced by degeneration theory. But, despite his quasi-somatic claim that inebriety is defined as "the will being paralyzed", he has little doubt that the volitional paralytics' efforts to get up and walk constitute a glorious chapter in the history of human/British freedom. Recovering inebriates, Kerr states, are "inspired with the determination to strike a blow for freedom, and casting off forever the yoke of their oppressor".

> The continuous and victorious struggle of such heroic souls with their hereditary enemy – an enemy the more powerful because ever leading its treacherous life within their breasts, presents to my mind such a glorious conflict, such an august spectacle, as should evoke the highest efforts of the painter and the sculptor. Before so protracted and lofty a combat, the immortal group of Lacoon contending with the serpents, grand though that great work of art is, must pale its ineffectual fires.[87]

The *British Journal of Inebriety* went so far as to grant an anonymous "ex-patient" space to discuss his own views on treatment methods and to make a rousing argument for the need to treat alcoholics (or, more narrowly, inebriate gentlemen like himself) as free and moral beings, not as helpless degenerates. The ex-patient emphasizes "the mental and moral sufferings of the inebriate, the remorse, the regrets . . ." and, anticipating AA, calls on the public to appreciate "the moral courage of inebriety".[88]

The therapeutic regimes used for inebriate gentlemen were pastoral in Foucault's sense: the regimes were individualized and involved personal, face-to-face discussion as well as spiritual direction. In contrast to the scientific studies carried out on the population of inebriate asylums, physicians treating inebriate gentlemen did not do surveys or keep statistics. Instead, they reported on individual cases at some length and with much sympathy for the patient's struggles.[89] One doctor even provided a lengthy report of how he, along with his patient, went through a series of experiments designed to find a suitable alternative to alcohol:

> He started on milk; I began on milk-and-water. We both shelved that diet. He diluted his milk down with water, Vichy, soda water, barley water . . . Then we went to weak veal broth and barley water, and that did pretty well for a longish winter time. But the summer came, and we both shied at animal broths, however well-prepared, and went to barley water and lemon . . . Then we started again. This time it was ginger-ale.[90]

Contrary to the view that pastoralism is a pre-modern form of power displaced by the technologies of discipline and normalization, my research shows that pastoral methods were by no means dead at the dawn of the twentieth century, even among educated physicians.[91] Clinical fatalism and materialist determinism may have dominated the major scientific works produced by asylum physicians, but they did not necessarily shape the everyday work of physicians. This was particularly true of physicians dealing with patients with whom they could identify, both through their shared class and sex and through the fact that heavy drinking was never stigmatized in the same way as lunacy or homosexuality. The Salvation Army's work with lumpen alcoholics, begun in the 1880s, constituted a very important form of pastoralism, and one that is still practiced today. But even scientifically minded physicians participated in pastoral–clinical practices quite out of keeping with the standard image we have of turn-of-the-century medicine. Certainly, the camaraderie shown by the physician who collaborated with his patient in devising palatable alternatives to alcohol, as if they were AA members *avant la lettre*, shows starkly how the problem of inebriety could unsettle the authority of physicians as well as the legitimacy of science. The mutual support of the two men trying out various homey techniques for avoiding a relapse into inebriety is a curious page in the history of medicine.

It must be underlined, however, that the odes to the moral courage of the recovering inebriate found in medical literature were sung almost exclusively in honour of gentlemen inebriates. In Kerr's massive book on inebriety, there are numerous case studies of "ladies" suffering from either alcoholism or "the morphia habit": all of these stories focus on their helplessness in the face of both heredity and the specificities of female physiology, saying little or nothing about the strength of their willpower.[92] And as for the largely female and universally poor individuals put in inebriate reformatories, we have already seen how their alcoholism was subsumed under the banner of feeble-mindedness, a label which excluded them completely from the purview of moral freedom.

The treatments for alcoholism explored by turn-of-the-century physicians with privately paying male patients constituted a distinctly empowering version of moral treatment. The older moral treatment depended largely on the willpower of the physician.[93] The phrase used by Morel to describe moral treatment for temporary insanity – "the transfusion of the will of the physician into that of the patient"[94] – suggests just such a one-way relationship of doctor to patient, akin to mesmerism or hypnotism. Speaking of Pinel's treatment, Robert Castel has emphasized the despotic features of such psychiatric techniques:

"The return to reason can only be effected by the insane person's interiorization of a will to rationality that is at first foreign to him ... When the alien will enters into him, gradually narrowing the area of agitation and delirium until it subjugates them completely, then the cure occurs."[95] And yet, if we attend to the pastoral as well as to the despotic elements of psychiatric practice, we can see that the patient/disciple is simultaneously free and unfree: insofar as the therapeutic or spiritual relationship is willingly assumed by the subject, the transfusion metaphor is not wholly adequate.[96]

The history of alcoholism treatment, therefore, offers a different view of the evolution of the physician–patient relationship than that provided by existing critical histories of psychiatry. In studying alcohol and addiction issues, it becomes clear that pastoralism is not purely medieval, and that the clinical gaze is not universally disciplinary and/or despotic. Even at the height of the deterministic discourse of degeneration, some deviants at least were treated not despotically but through their very freedom.

Since governing individuals through their very freedom became in the mid-twentieth century absolutely commonplace,[97] the study of the 'empowerment' of inebriates has a significance for all of us today, whether or not we are interested in the history of medicine. The genealogy of alcoholism, it turns out, takes us far beyond the sphere of medical history: it begins to offer elements toward what we might call the genealogy of the free will.

To look more closely at the institutional basis for the liberal transformation of moral treatment and the practical implementation of projects to repair the will, however, we need to turn to a closer study of both the empowering institutions for inebriate gentlemen and their coercive counterparts for inebriates imprisoned under the British Habitual Inebriates Acts, in a historical analysis of what we will call the social stratification of the free will.

CHAPTER 3

# THE FRAGMENTATION OF INEBRIETY

The attempt to manage harmful or disorderly habits of consumption through the category of inebriety had many components, from expert discourses to clinical regimes and experiments. In this chapter we will turn away from both medical texts and clinical practices in order to analyze the political efforts of organized inebriety specialists, with the British Habitual Inebriates Acts as the prime instance of such governmental activity. We will show that the medico-legal category of 'inebriate', the keystone of the policies and the institutional practices described in this chapter, contained the seed of its own destruction. The inebriate was never a stable identity even in the few instances where public funding was made available for collecting, managing, and treating people under the banner of inebriety; and with the onset of World War I, this unstable and already fragmented identity quickly descended into near-oblivion.

The case study of inebriety challenges the conventional Foucaultian wisdom on the transition from the act-based governance of the criminal law and other forms of sovereign power to the more modern identity-based governance typical of disciplinarity. Much contemporary governance does rely on the construction of distinct identities through various knowledges: for instance, sexuality is today largely regulated through dividing it into two identities, homosexuality and heterosexuality. But not everything is governed through the construction of such identities as homosexuals, battered women, or addicts; and not every identity is constructed through the professionally certified knowledge of such experts as psychiatrists and physicians. As may be clear by now, one of the aims of this book is to encourage others to pursue Foucaultian and feminist critical studies of social governance mapping

68

THE FRAGMENTATION OF INEBRIETY

the transmutations and ambiguities that are often left out even in accounts that claim to be genealogical.

As well as emphasizing the complex dynamics of the process of identity construction, deconstruction, and reformation, this chapter also develops a parallel argument not only about complexities of identity governance but also about its limits. We are indeed governed through identity categories, and we sometimes even govern ourselves and our loved ones through disciplinary mechanisms. But both theorists and historians have generally neglected to study a process that has always existed alongside both sovereignty and discipline, a way of governing that lies in the borderland between act and identity: habit. The ways in which habit can be creatively used to undermine the binary opposition of freedom vs. necessity that runs right through Western culture are documented elsewhere in this book; in this chapter we will focus on the relation of habit to the Foucaultian narrative of the rise of disciplinary governance driven by expert knowledges of medico-social identities. That a British official inquiry into the operation of the Inebriates Acts – an inquiry populated by the archetypal medical experts – would be led to conclude, in 1908, that excessive drinking was, in the final analysis, neither a vice nor a disease but more simply a "habit", is a point of some theoretical as well as historical significance.

Governing out of habit, it will be argued, does not correspond to any historical epoch – it is not as if phenomena are first governed as acts and then as habits and then as identities. The governance of conduct through the well-worn, usually unnoticed mechanisms of habit formation and habit reform existed since well before modernity, and continues to exist today alongside multiple other forms of governance.

THE MEDICALIZATION CRUSADE IN NORTH AMERICA

The British temperance doctors who launched the Society for the Scientific Study of Inebriety in 1883 had the impression that, in the United States, there were already numerous state-supported inebriate asylums dedicated to the exclusively medical treatment of excessive drinking, and they derived much hope for their political project from this supposed fact. Speaking at the 1884 meeting of the society, a former mayor of New York City explained that thirty-seven American states had provision for the compulsory detention of habitual drunkards, and he made the grand claim that "American legislators" had agreed that "the dipsomaniac" was to take "his legal place beside the Monomaniac, or the Homicidal maniac, or the Delusionist". The only indication his audience might have got that American legislators were not as universally enlightened as the speaker suggested was a brief statement at the end of the speech admitting that fully public institutions were not always available, and that "in some states subsidies are given (of public moneys raised by taxation, or out of the proceeds of licence fees for the sale of liquors) to private retreats for the treatment of inebriety as a disease".[1]

This speech was misleading in a number of ways. First of all, there were very few inebriate homes of any kind in the United States. Secondly, a good proportion of them (the vast majority, in the nineteenth century) were for voluntary admissions only and were run by self-help temperance groups, such as the Washingtonians or the Sons of Temperance, on strictly non-medical lines.[2] The American Society for the Study and Cure of Inebriety, founded in 1870, although initially including the superintendents of a couple of "Washingtonian" temperance homes as well as physicians, soon attempted to eliminate the temperance movement from the management of excessive drinking and to create a medical monopoly. Its members suggested in often shrill tones that inebriates were monomaniacs or close to it, and thus needed strict medical supervision.[3] But this society had small numbers and little influence. It quickly provoked much opposition from the much more numerous temperance activists, and (by contrast with the British Society for the Scientific Study of Inebriety) it became not a scientific society but rather a very small group of administrators of struggling institutions desperately seeking political support for their establishments. By the early twentieth century it appears to have become a one-man operation, and it died soon after the death of its leader, Dr T.D. Crothers.[4] Even Dr Crothers, although fanatically devoted to the cause of medicalizing drunkards, admitted that the prospects for medicalizing drinking through an analogy with lunacy were not good, given the state of public opinion. He was not being overly pessimistic, since even in France, where the power of psychiatry to define conduct was probably greatest, turn-of-the-century alienists rarely claimed that alcoholics who committed crimes were exempt from legal and moral responsibility.[5]

The first medicalized asylum for inebriates in the United States, set up by a Dr Edward Turner in Binghamton, New York, in 1864, confined patients for a minimum of one year, locked them up at night, and used the strictest of treatments. Dr D.G. Dodge, its superintendent in 1870, declared that "certain *restraints* are absolutely necessary" for inebriates as for lunatics, and ominously added that "to be effectual, the restraint must be rigid".[6] Dr Crothers later opined that these methods "were far in advance of that time", and that the patients and their families were too unenlightened to see that deprivation of liberty was an essential part of the cure:

> The patients themselves, after the immediate recovery from the effect of spirits, protested against the confinement and doctrine of disease, and

> sought in every way through their friends to break up the methods of treatment . . . The patients and their friends insisted that, while the case might be diseased, his recovery depended largely upon his liberty and promise to get well; that restraint was irritation and injury; and that appeals to his honour and manhood were the real agents of final cure.[7]

The board of the asylum ended up siding with the patients and their relatives and against the physicians, and eventually the state legislature ended the experiment and turned the inebriate asylum into a regular lunatic asylum. Crothers' language of "honour and manhood" suggests that the patients were supported in their anti-psychiatry campaign by the temperance movement, and indeed he notes that temperance activists opposed the medicalization project because they believed it tended to "diminish human responsibility".[8]

A few years later, Dr Crothers, in the course of delivering the Norman Kerr Memorial Lecture in London, recognized that most of the thirty-seven US state laws permitting state inebriate asylums were dead letters.[9] (Some had even been declared unconstitutional by the courts, although Crothers did not mention that.)[10] He also admitted that the attempt by physicians to circumvent the state by setting up private retreats was not meeting with great success, for practical reasons:

> In America several states have organized institutions, but they are still under the influence of politics, and lack legal power and concentration of effort . . .
>
> Nearly all the institutions in the early days were the work of private enterprise, managed with limited knowledge and experience, and as a natural result they were unable to sustain themselves in face of this opposition . . .

And in a comment that revealed more about his own stance toward patients than perhaps he intended, Crothers complained that "in America the bitterest critics and most unrelenting opponents of asylums have been the inmates of such institutions and their friends. For years they have influenced public sentiment . . ."[11]

Despite Crothers' belief that patients and their temperance allies conspired against the asylum project, the failure of medicalized institutions is not directly attributable to the success of voluntary temperance homes. As Jim Baumohl has shown, temperance homes were plagued by problems of their own, mainly lack of funding and instability in the semi-evangelical organizations sponsoring them. By the early twentieth century, few such homes existed. The decline of self-help homes for recovering drunkards was rooted in a marked shift in the aims and techniques of the North American temperance move-ment: the reformed drunkards giving slang-filled speeches at mid-nineteenth century revival meetings had been largely replaced, by the 1910s, by sober middle-class women and men much more interested in keeping their own respectability than in saving the fallen.[12]

A potentially more serious threat to Dr Crothers' project to treat inebriates as lunatics[13] was that posed by the 'quacks' who ran homes for privately paying patients, such as the chain of Keeley homes specializing in a proprietary gold chloride cure for habitual drunkenness.[14] Whether or not they were physicians, the administrators of these homes certainly agreed that inebriety was a disease. However, they saw it not as a form of lunacy but rather as a mixed physical and moral condition similar to neurasthenia, and hence not justifying legal measures of commitment and confinement. Privately run homes for nerve diseases, widely advertised in medical and other journals and used with reasonable frequency by the middle and upper classes, tended to regard inebriety as a minor variation within the array of nerve illnesses that were never sharply differentiated from each other and that were all treated with rest cures, fresh country air, protein-rich diets, and beef teas.

Support for discursively recognizing inebriety while in practice merging it with hysteria, neurasthenia, and non-specific debility was given by the American physician who made his fame and fortune through the ill-defined diagnosis of neurasthenia, Dr George Beard. In a move undermining the project of specific inebriate institutions, Beard stated, to a meeting of the American society of inebriety-home physicians, that there was no clinical distinction between the symptoms of alcoholics and those of hysterics and neurasthenics.[15] But whatever their theory of inebriety, the administrators of privately run homes were in any case unlikely to use the authoritarian techniques popular in lunatic asylums, since their patients were also their paying customers.

That the real threat to the medical claims in regard to inebriety and drinking lay in the commercial sector rather than in the temperance movement is suggested by the usually veiled fears and threats voiced in the medical journals. A physician writing in the *New York Medical Journal*

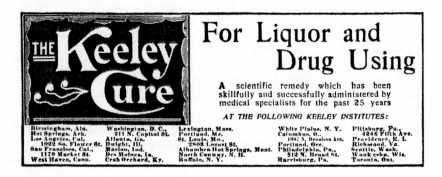

Around 1900, a great deal of the business of alcoholism recovery was in the hands of commercial rather than medical establishments. (Left: *Harpers*, May 1905; above: *Harpers*, April 1906.)

to support the compulsory state committal of inebriates typically complained that the partial success of some proprietary inebriety cures was being used to undermine medicine itself:

> Any mode of treatment, secret, patent, proprietary, natural, supernatural, or scientific, will cure some cases of inebriety . . . But they have been, are, and will continue to be, wholly impotent to make any impression upon inebriety as a scourge to the peoples of the world or to thwart its disease-producing capacity.[16]

Another physician used similarly defensive language to draw a sharp distinction between properly medical institutions, such as the Binghamton asylum, and the 'quack' homes dispensing proprietary remedies:

> The many private sanatoria for the treatment of alcoholism now found throughout the country testify that the seed sown by Dr Turner has taken root and is now bearing a beneficent harvest. I, of course, do not here refer to those widely advertised institutions where secret nostrums are used in a routine way . . .[17]

Little evidence was ever provided that the 'quack' institutions that generally avoided stigmatizing their patients as inebriates were substantially different from the ones run by physicians: as we saw in the last chapter, some respectable physicians used chloride of gold (Keeley's secret ingredient) and other drugs along with moral support, and this therapeutic combination did not differ significantly from those provided through non-medical commercial channels. The attempt to discursively demarcate a *disease of inebriety* that predisposed people to heavy drinking, thus constituting a new distinct identity somewhat independent of the person's behaviour, did not in the end do much to further the physicians' monopolistic ambitions. Official medicine was never able to offer an agreed-upon therapy for inebriety, whether physical or psychological, other than the general hygienic regimes used for all nerve diseases. Just as twentieth century physicians have been in the difficult position of having to admit that AA is not very scientific but that it often works, so too the inebriate doctors were in the uneasy position of having to defend medicine against its rivals in a terrain in which medicine had little to offer by way of therapy.

In Australia, the campaign to institutionalize inebriates under a more or less medical rationale was, at the legal level, more successful than in Britain: the state of Victoria passed an inebriates law in 1871, eight years earlier than Britain, and by about 1900 most states had passed relatively draconian measures allowing for compulsory committals. Nevertheless, the rigours of the law were brought to bear on very few inebriates, since little public funding was made available for asylums.[18]

In Canada, although the complete story of inebriate institutions has never been researched, a similar failure of medicalization seems to have taken place.[19] Several provinces followed the American example of passing laws allowing for the committal of inebriates, but these also remained, with some short-lived exceptions, dead letters. In Ontario, which generally led the rest of Canada in terms of social policy and the building of public institutions, an 1872 law did result in some committals of public patients to private facilities, but there was never sufficient support to fund a separate, wholly public inebriate institution. In 1889 the (male) citizens of Toronto voted against the plan to devote $30,000 to the building of an inebriate asylum, a vote which is not so remarkable in its result as in the fact that the question was put to a plebiscite in the first place, since the much more expensive lunatic asylums were never the subject of direct democracy.[20] Faced with a question essentially asking the public whether inebriety/ alcoholism is a disease deserving of public funding, the citizens voted no.

This 'no' to the theory of inebriety as a fully medicalized disease entity was not a one-off instance of popular resistance to medicine. It is significant that in 1953, at a time when the notion of alcoholism as an identity was as popular as it ever has been (thanks to AA and to both popular and medical discourses on the alcoholic personality), the citizens of Canada were once again asked to express their views on the nature of alcoholism, through the emerging technology of the public opinion survey. This poll found that a quarter of Canadians believed alcoholism to be a disease, 45 per cent thought it was "lack of self-control", and, perhaps most significantly, 26 per cent thought that it was both a disease and a vice.[21]

In keeping with this mixed popular opinion, public funding for alcoholism treatment has been provided in fits and starts in North America for the past forty or fifty years. Even in Canada, which unlike the United States has universal public medical insurance, public treatment facilities are few and far between. The number of people treated in such facilities is far smaller than the number of people who seek out AA groups. In the United States, public hospitals, while treating alcoholics for various physical consequences of heavy drinking, have tended to do so reluctantly and with little faith that medicine could ever cure alcoholism itself.[22] Privately run treatment facilities do offer recovery programmes and are often reimbursed by their patients' health insurance plans (under the DSM-IV category of alcohol dependence), but many of these addiction-recovery programmes, while funded as if they were medical, borrow heavily from the non-medical, explicitly spiritual techniques of Alcoholics Anonymous.

## THE BRITISH EXPERIMENT WITH 'HABITUAL DRUNKARD' LEGISLATION

That the British Habitual Inebriates Acts of 1879 and 1898 cannot be categorized as an instance of the relentless medicalization of deviance is clear from the fact – not noticed by historians of the Acts[23] – that medical testimony was never deemed necessary in order to have people committed under the Acts. The Acts did come into being through medical pressure, and did provide official recognition (and additional clients) to a number of inebriety treatment homes run by physicians. But the Acts did not even attempt to construct a homogeneous population of medicalized inebriates. Rather, they sought to govern three distinct groups in different ways. The first group consisted of middle- and upper-class inebriates who entered privately run but publicly inspected and recognized treatment homes known as "retreats". These patients were not committed by the state, although as the Inspector and other commentators noted, financial and moral pressure from their families was usually instrumental in obtaining their consent to be institutionalized for periods ranging from a few months to two years. This first group was the only one to which the 1879 Act applied.

The 1898 Act had a very different, much more criminological character. It addressed two pre-existing groups of particularly problematic offenders. One consisted of the police-court recidivists, many of them charged with drunkenness offenses, who populated the lower courts, in the United Kingdom as in other countries. Such offenders were by the 1890s increasingly considered as the new barbarians, a social menace not deserving of due process. This group of recidivist offenders was targeted by section 2 of the 1898 Act, which allowed courts to commit those charged with drunkenness offenses four times in one year to three years in an inebriate reformatory, rather than the usual, very short jail term. (This laid the groundwork for the later enactment of habitual offender legislation.)

The third group of habitual inebriates was brought into being by section 1 of the 1898 Act. This allowed for those convicted of indictable offenses to be committed to an inebriate reformatory in addition to or instead of the usual sentence. This commitment was not dependent on medical testimony: the prosecution simply needed to "state that the offender is a habitual drunkard" and to convince the jury.[24] In theory, this clause could have been used against men convicted of drunken assaults in pub brawls or in domestic settings; but such committals were virtually non-existent. In practice, section 1 inebriates were made up almost exclusively of mothers charged with child neglect by the National Society for the Prevention of Cruelty to Children (NSPCC). At the peak of the Acts' enforcement (1906), 80 per cent of the 364 people who had, since 1898, been committed under section 1 were mothers charged with child neglect. (Most of the other section 1 cases, incidentally, were attempted suicides; there was only one person convicted of manslaughter who was additionally labelled as an inebriate.)[25]

The original 1879 Habitual Drunkards Act was largely the offspring of Dr Darlymple, an MP who also operated the largest private treatment home for gentlemen inebriates. Darlymple wanted the government to regulate the inebriate home business – possibly because of competition from 'quacks' – but in addition, he, like his American counterparts, wanted the state to compulsorily commit certain individuals to these homes. In this he drew much support from the small group of physicians in the American Society for the Study and Cure of Inebriety, who eagerly travelled to London and participated in parliamentary inquiries. His proposed bill was watered down to the point of ineffectiveness, however. Establishing a peculiar dialectic of freedom and coercion, the Act permitted privately paying clients/patients to voluntarily sign away their freedom by declaring in front of two JPs or magistrates that they were indeed habitual drunkards and thus requested/required institutionalization in retreats. "No wonder that few have been found willing to make a voluntary surrender of liberty on such terms", exclaimed Dr Alexander Peddie some years later.[26]

The definition of habitual drunkard set out in the 1879 Act, and retained throughout the life of the Acts, was as follows:

> . . . a person who, not being amenable to any jurisdiction in lunacy, is notwithstanding, by reason of habitual intemperate drinking of intoxicating liquors, at times dangerous to himself or herself or to others, or incapable of managing himself or herself and his or her affairs.[27]

The text of this definition is clearly rooted in the Victorian alienists' project to construct a medical mechanism for governing the zone between lunacy and reason. But, as noted above, there was no process for using medical expert witness testimony to diagnose inebriates; and what is more significant, the records of the British Society for the Scientific Study of Inebriety show no concern about the absence of that technology. The physicians agreed that inebriety was a disease, but one diagnosable by every JP in the land. This may have been not so much an admission of the limits of psychiatry's explanatory powers but simply a pragmatic move acknowledging that, if British judges and juries were not too likely to defer to psychiatrists in murder trials, they would be even less likely to defer to expert testimony in the case of the common situation of drunkenness.

The initial 1879 legislation contained a provision that stood in particularly stark contrast to medico-legal practices around lunacy and insanity: although inebriates were defined as incapable of managing themselves, they could *never* be committed against their will. This provision for self-committal, which completely undermined the 1879 Act, was vigorously opposed by the physicians, and it was eventually supplemented by coercive measures in the 1898 Act. And yet the mechanism for voluntarily signing away one's freedom remained. Although it was used by a small number of inebriates, it has some significance as a crystallization of the commonsense wisdom that alcoholics can only be cured if they want to be cured.

Despite providing a single definition of "habitual drunkard" (or, after 1898, "habitual inebriate"), the Acts sharply distinguished between the inhabitants of privately run retreats and the criminalized population committed to the inebriate reformatories. The distinction between the two institutions was circularly justified by reference to the alleged differences between upper-class and working-class inebriety. In the words of the Inspector:

> On leaving the former [retreats] we completely turn our backs on the principle of voluntary admission, and with it what may justly be called the 'drawing room' aspect of all efforts toward inebriate reform.[28]

We will thus discuss the retreats and their 'drawing room' addiction-recovery methods first, and then turn to the reformatories.

"THE DRAWING ROOM ASPECT OF INEBRIATE REFORM":
THE RETREATS

It is impossible to determine how many retreats existed at any one time, since there was considerable turnover in the institutions listed in the official reports. The Inspector surmised that about twenty such homes were officially recognized in an average year. From 1879 to 1912 just over 10,000 persons were admitted to these homes,[29] although the majority of them were private voluntary patients, patients who had not committed themselves or been committed by others under the Acts.[30]

The retreats were in turn divided by sex. The ladies' retreats fell into two categories: some were religious institutions operated by temperance organizations, while the rest were more or less medical homes catering to ladies suffering from nerve diseases, including inebriety. One of the medical/commercial homes, in Lanarkshire, described its regime as follows:

> The Retreat has been opened for the treatment of lady patients only; it has been licensed under the Inebriates Acts, and ladies can be received either as statutory or as voluntary patients. The Acts provide for the

compulsory treatment of patients for such period, not exceeding two years, as may be agreed to by the patient before admission . . . Voluntary patients, though not subject to the regulations imposed by the Inebriates Acts, must conform to the rules of the establishment, which confer upon the Superintendents such powers as past experience has proved to be beneficial in the treatment of inebriety.

The Retreat is also adapted for such as suffer from other perversions, neurasthenia, hysteria, and other such disorders. No patient under certificate of insanity can be admitted.[31]

From the evidence contained in the retreats' reports to the Inspector and in their published advertisements, it appears that the medically run ladies' retreats used the mix of isolation, moral treatment, and hygienic therapy that was thought appropriate for neurasthenia, hysteria, and nerve diseases generally. Indeed, the retreats may not have differentiated their inebriate patients from their hysterics except for the purposes of being inspected; no mention is made in any of the available reports of any therapies specifically aimed at inebriety.

But the medically run establishments for nervous ladies that advertised heavily in medical journals did not have a monopoly over inebriate ladies. Temperance organizations also ran retreats, especially those for women. It is a tribute to the zeal and ingenuity of middle-class British female philanthropists that some of these homes explicitly challenged the strict duality of freedom–coercion set out in the Acts, and the class divide that underpinned it. Instead of separating the ladies under voluntary admission from the criminalized neglectful mothers, some establishments developed a gender-specific and class-inclusive Christian pastoral maternalism.

The largest religious retreat in the early days of the Inebriates Acts was The Grove Retreat for Inebriate Women, in Fallowfield, which opened in 1890. It was operated by the Manchester Women's Christian Temperance Association and run by a hired matron (not a physician). It admitted both women who could pay small amounts and those who could not pay at all, the latter being employed in the usual rescue-home labours of laundry and domestic work. The women attended religious services twice a day and listened to local clergymen read from the Bible, and were assiduously visited by a committee of temperance ladies from Manchester and Salford.[32]

Some years later, Lady Somerset's Duxhurst Home provided similar gender-specific religious treatment. This institution, the largest of the retreats, attempted to integrate the paying lady patients with poor women who worked for their keep in the farm on the premises.[33] Lady Henry Somerset, leader of the women's temperance movement in the United Kingdom and at one point leader of the world Women's

Christian Temperance Union (WCTU), went so far as to tell the physicians of the British Inebriety Society that, in her view, only "THE DIVINE PHYSICIAN" could cure female inebriates.[34]

The divine physician, however, did not succeed in effecting the ambitious project of treating all women in a single institution regardless of class and of the closely related variable of legal status. Even though the ladies were housed in a "Manor House" somewhat removed from the farm colony for the poorer women, mixing the freedom of the "drawing room" with the coercion of state reformatories in a single institution did not work. Duxhurst eventually got rid of its reformatory cases and became a purely voluntary retreat, as had already been done by some American temperance homes for men, which had rejected people committed to them by the courts.

The Salvation Army also ran several licenced retreats. If the physicians in the British Inebriety Society objected to such organizations running inebriate homes, they never said so in public. In marked contrast to their counterparts in the United States, they listened politely to speeches by Salvation Army leader Catherine Booth on several occasions.

The temperance organizations appeared, therefore, to have been given medical permission to run women's homes and to specialize in "female inebriety"; but they were not so prominent in the business of gentlemen's homes. The Church of England Temperance Society did run a men's home, but most gentlemen inebriates seem to have sought help in small, exclusive homes run directly by physicians charging very high fees. The most important of these was the Darlymple Home, run first by Dr Darlymple and then by Dr Branthwaite (who in 1898 became inspector of inebriate reformatories). This retreat – the only male one licenced at the beginning of the Acts, in 1879 – was also the only one providing a detailed breakdown of its patients' occupations. The largest categories were "merchants" (probably including publicans) and "gentlemen of no occupation", followed by clerks, manufacturers, physicians, and army and navy officers.[35] Although this retreat was designed specifically as a medical pilot project, it borrowed recovery techniques from the temperance movement. As its medical superintendent stated in 1911:

> With regard to the treatment of alcoholic cases, my aim is to restore a patient to physical and mental health, to make him realize that his cure is in his own hands, and that total abstinence from alcohol for the remainder of his life is an absolute necessity, and to help him build up his self-control, and to cultivate his power of resistance.[36]

Other gentlemen's retreats, run on more commercial lines, appear to have relied on a regime of alcohol deprivation softened by plenty of manly sports, such as billiards, hunting, and fishing. One retreat, located near Fife, in Scotland, advertised in the following terms:

> For the treatment of Gentlemen suffering from the alcoholic and morphine habits, and narcomania from such drugs as cocaine and chloral. The retreat possesses many unique advantages. It is in an isolated part of the country where there is freedom from temptation. The grounds are very extensive, there being 130 acres for recreation and 800 acres of low-ground shooting; a stream flows through, and a lake is situated in the grounds, in which there is trout-fishing ... Sports: shooting, fishing, golf course, tennis, badminton, cricket, photographic darkroom, billiards, skating, etc.[37]

A similar home in rural Wales, also licenced under the Acts, advertised itself as "devoted to the care of Gentlemen of the Upper Classes only, suffering from Inebriety, Neuritis, Debility, Neurasthenia, and the abuse of drugs ... Well-preserved shooting over 22,000 acres, containing large grouse moors, pheasant coverts, and enclosed rabbit warren. Four game-keepers kept ... Private golf links, lawn tennis, croquet, bowls, etc."[38] Institutions not licenced under the Acts also advertised their provision of gentlemanly pastimes more than their medical facilities, and often stressed that, unlike the licenced retreats, they allowed patients to stay for a few weeks only. In treating their patients as valuable customers, they operated more as health retreats than like asylums.

At the same time, then, that there was an effort to differentiate inebriety as a specific disease, the treatment facilities provided had two distinct but related effects that made inebriety disappear. First, the very different regimes provided for different classes of patients had the effect of disaggregating inebriates; and, secondly, since none of the treatments was specific to alcohol abuse, inebriety itself disappeared under broader or more fundamental categories. The religiously run homes for the middling classes dealt with alcoholism as a form or an effect of vice, treating it with doses of Christian speech in exactly the same way as other vices. The more luxurious, less religious institutions for the upper classes, on their part, made no therapeutic distinction between inebriety and nerve diseases such as neurasthenia, narco-mania, or simple "debility", treating alcoholism through rest, sport, and luxury (with considerably more sport and more luxury available for gentlemen than for ladies).

Inebriety among the upper classes, then, was never a distinct object of governance, despite the creation of supposedly specific retreats. The retreats run by physicians did not provide any specific treatment for inebriety, and indeed seem to have considered it as a minor variation on neurasthenia. Those run by religious groups, in turn, merged drinking into the capacious categories of sin and vice.

Unlike the prison-like reformatories for compulsorily committed 'habitual inebriates', private establishments offering residential treatment were often as luxurious as today's health spas. (Recurring advertisements from *British Journal of Inebriety*, c. 1910–14.)

*THE BROKEN-HEARTED !*

ADDICTED TO INEBRIETY.

**SPRINGFIELD LODGE,**

Grove Hill Road,

Denmark Hill, LONDON, S.E.

*(Under the direction of Mrs. BRAMWELL BOOTH.)*

THIS HOUSE and LARGE GARDEN are especially set apart for LADIES who are the Victims of Alcohol or Drugs. Considerable success has been achieved with Patients from various ranks of Society. Denmark Hill is a very pleasant Suburb of London— air good, view extensive.

OR **APPLY NOW FOR TERMS!** To Secretary, 259 Mare St., HACKNEY, LONDON, N.E.

## "THEY DO NOT WISH FOR TREATMENT AT THE EXPENSE OF THEIR FREEDOM": THE INEBRIATE REFORMATORIES

Meanwhile, inebriety among the poorer classes also fragmented and disappeared even as it was being institutionalized. The 500 or so neglectful mothers put away for three years under section 1 of the Acts were mothers of the nation/empire first and alcoholics second, as is clear from the fact that it did not occur to the NSPCC to use the Inebriate Acts to prosecute abusive drunken fathers.[39] On their part, the 3,000 women and 700 men put away in "certified inebriate reformatories" under section 2 constituted a different sort of national menace. As David Garland has documented for the United Kingdom, and Robert Nye and Ruth Harris for France, the 1880s and 1890s witnessed the rise of a great fear about habitual offenders and other criminals who, although not necessarily guilty of major crimes, were thought to pose such a danger to the social order as to justify measures contravening the niceties of due process and proportional punishment.[40] Section 2 of the Inebriates Acts, allowing for the designation of those repeatedly convicted of drunkenness offences as inebriates, seems to have been used against just this type of fin de siècle social menace, with the specific twist that it was

83

largely female public-order offenders, not young male delinquents or vagrant men, who were targetted by police (especially in London) and by the courts. The habitual offender was, both in popular discourse and in criminal justice practice, male: but the habitual inebriate was (in Britain only) female.

The certified inebriate reformatories were not a glowing success in anyone's opinion, particularly insofar as the more numerous police-court recidivists were concerned. (Many of the neglectful mothers were apparently reformed, by contrast.) The recidivist inmates were not slow to complain that a "simple drunk" ought not to result in being imprisoned for three years; and, in general, they did not seem inclined to regard their drinking habits as requiring reform. Women of Irish origin were described as particularly stubborn. A prison doctor expressed surprise to find that such women "have a strong sense of the importance of their liberty and a corresponding idea of the proper penalty that should attach to a 'simple drunk' . . . They do not wish for treatment at the expense of their liberty."[41]

The difficulties of managing the certified inebriate population led to the provision of three frankly penal "state" reformatories whose purpose was simply to siphon off the unreformables in order to allow the other reformatories to get on with their work without the constant disturbances caused by the most rebellious inmates. This separation, however, was not sufficient to ensure that the certified inebriate reformatories met with anything remotely resembling success. In his 1909 report, Inspector Branthwaite allowed himself to vent his frustrations. He repeated the claim made in his earlier surveys of reformatory inmates to the effect that two-thirds of female inebriates were feeble-minded, and that their drinking habits were neither willed acts nor the result of a specific disease of inebriety, but rather a symptom of mental deficiency. Under the heading of "mental defect", he then proceeds to unwittingly give evidence of these women's intellectual powers:

> In their view lawmakers are tyrants, and the servants of the law instruments of organized persecution . . . Drunkenness is justifiable, prostitution is justifiable, everything they do is justifiable, so long as they can show (to their own satisfaction) some so-called 'reason' for their conduct . . . They do not care in the least for the opinion of others in matters relating to conduct.[42]

The reference to prostitution is not casual. The same report states that over 50 per cent of these section 2 habitual female offenders had prior prostitution convictions. This figure indicates that the police (in London, at least, where this section was used much more than in any other place) were using section 2 of the Inebriate Acts against the old

Victorian fallen woman – a woman who drank in public and who was likely to be convicted of prostitution offenses. In other words, they were using the modern legal machinery of the Inebriates Acts not to create a modern medicalized identity but to continue targetting urban working-class females who misbehaved in public. The Acts allowed the London police to increase their power over such fallen women, although this power was undermined by the ongoing fight between the London County Council (LCC) and the central government about the financial responsibility for the largely female population of inebriates.

Overall, the 1898 Acts never worked very well, primarily because they were permissive only, and local governments showed much reluctance in identifying their inebriates and even more reluctance in paying for three years' confinement for each of them. In addition, there was a lingering confusion in the public mind about the distinction between retreats and reformatories. The awkward marriage of the soft medica-lization approach of the 1879 Act with the harsh penal provisions of the 1898 Act was never a success, despite the strenuous efforts of the Inspector to explain the rationale of the system and to make it work.

One technique used by the enterprising Inspector Branthwaite to maintain coherence in the system was to distribute individuals among institutions according to their socioeconomic status, even in cases where such distribution went against the letter of the law. In 1903 he stated that he had ordered that three upper-class inebriates who had fallen afoul of the Act be transferred from reformatories to retreats. In 1907 he reported that "in a few instances some well-educated, better class persons have been committed under the Act", adding that these individuals were quickly taken out of reformatories and put in retreats "in order to give them the advantage of association with persons of their own condition".[43] This legally questionable move starkly revealed the administrative weaknesses caused by the circularity of the committal process: socioeconomic difference was translated into a differential relation to freedom, with this alleged ontological distinction between the 'drawing room' and the criminal populations then being used to justify the existence of a dual system of institutions. Once in place, the dual system of institutions in turn had the effect of producing different populations of inebriates. The two-track system, far from giving coher-ence to the overall category of inebriate, in fact fragmented it.

The administrative difficulties of enforcing the supposedly rigid distinction between free patients of retreats and coerced criminals were multiplied by the fact that the majority of the inebriate reformatories as well as the retreats were operated by philanthropic or otherwise private bodies. This meant that beyond the minimal requirements set out in the Inspector's brief, there was little opportunity to standardize, much less to study or evaluate, any treatment offered – in sharp contrast to the research opportunities afforded to psychiatry by the network of lunatic asylums. No doubt realizing that research on inebriates was a necessary component of the project to govern through inebriety, the Inspector valiantly attempted to personally carry out research studies, on such topics as infant mortality and feeble-mindedness, upon the population of inebriate reformatories, as documented in the previous chapter. (It did not occur to him to undertake any scientific study of the 'drawing room' methods of the retreats.)

These administrative troubles were further compounded by the serious financial difficulties caused by the refusal of the central government to fund anything except the few small reformatories for the most 'hardened' inebriate offenders, two for women (one for England and one for Scotland), and one for men. The LCC, which had set up a special committee on the Inebriates Acts chaired by inebriety physician Sir William Collins, fought a long battle with the central government about financial responsibility for inebriates. Eventually, the LCC stopped paying for committals, and this was the kiss of death for the Acts. In 1914 they ceased to be enforced in England and Wales, and soon after that in Scotland and Ireland as well.

Tellingly, Inspector Branthwaite moved on to a more rewarding position with the new liquor control board, set up (as part of the war effort) to govern pub licences, to lower the legal limit for alcohol content in beer, and to manage other alcohol-related questions.[44] Inebriates and inebriety simply disappeared from the scene, leaving so few traces that nobody remembered to repeal the Inebriates Acts until 1976.[45]

In the years after 1914, gentlemen and lady inebriates undoubtedly continued to be pressured by relatives into temporarily residing in either temperance-run or medical/commercial retreats. As for the inmates of inebriate reformatories, the police-court recidivists (many of whom, as we have seen, had prior convictions for prostitution as well as drunkenness) likely came to be managed under non-alcohol-related provisions regarding persistent offenders and mentally deficient indi-viduals. Although the failure of the Acts was due to a series of contingent factors and cannot be explained in a functionalist manner, the absence of a protest campaign to bring them back can certainly be attributed to the fact that the various populations making up the habitual inebriate were now manageable through other means. As David Garland has observed, the Inebriates Acts, whatever their practical problems, "operated as a kind of precedent or model for similar measures in regard to the feeble-minded, vagrants, habitual criminals and even 'normal' offenders"[46] – although Garland fails to note that it may well have been the gendering of inebriates as largely female that allowed the Inebriates Acts to serve as the vanguard of legislative moves to undermine classical legal ideas about crime, the criminal, and punishment.

While upper-class inebriates melted into the diffuse shadow zone between madness and reason signified by the capacious term "nerve diseases", working-class drinking problems – which had in turn put a disproportionate focus on women/mothers – disappeared into the other shadowland of Reason, that created by the term 'feeble-mindedness'. Much like inebriates, the feeble-minded were defined as falling neither within the narrow scope of nineteenth century "idiocy" nor within legal lunacy, but still as unable to manage their own affairs.

The Mental Deficiency Act of 1913 had two sections under which women formerly designated as inebriates could be re-classified and, more successfully, re-institutionalized by the state. Section 2b (iv) provided for the committal of anyone, whether or not they committed a crime, who qualified as a "defective" and also as "an habitual drunkard within the meaning of the Inebriates Acts". Also relevant to the largely female population of inebriate asylums was section 2b (vi) of the 1913 Act, providing for the institutionalization of "defectives" who gave birth to an illegitimate child while on poor relief. In addition, the Children Act of 1908 empowered authorities to remove children from the custody of inebriate parents, thus making the NSPCC prosecution of neglectful mothers under the Inebriates Acts unnecessary.[47]

In contrast to the scientific success in defining and managing intelligence through the campaign against the feeble-minded, the will was not – and indeed, has never been – fully captured by what Foucaultian scholars call the psy sciences. If the will had become as much of an object of scientific expertise as intelligence, inebriety would probably have prospered, evolving smoothly into alcoholism the way that feeble-mindedness evolved into mental retardation. But with twentieth century scientific psychology losing the Victorian interest in discovering the mechanisms of free will,[48] the question of whether people who drank too much could stop drinking was never monopolized by science.

The Inebriates Acts governed many things, therefore, but they did not govern inebriety as such, and did little to govern alcohol consumption. The urban issues of street disorder and street prostitution; the national and imperial problem of working-class mothers neglecting their maternal duties; the emerging question of the danger posed by the weak-minded to society; the criminological problem of the habitual offender and the frustrations of revolving-door lower court justice; the rather different, more delicate problems of well-bred people who abused alcohol or drugs due to a nervous constitution . . . these were the major fault lines on top of which the shaky edifice of the Inebriates Acts was built. The edifice was no longer needed after 1914, for there were other programmes in place for governing maternal duties, urban crime/order, and, for that matter, the anxieties and habits of the rich. Governing through inebriety, then, was a temporary strategy, and one that had little to do with governing alcohol.

## PASTORALISM FOR THE POOR: THE SALVATION ARMY'S WORK WITH DRUNKARDS

Robert Castel's classic work on insanity and asylums in France argues that paying patients have been able to escape the notoriously authoritarian methods of asylums, as physicians developed psychotherapeutic techniques for their bourgeois clients that worked through, rather than against, the patient's freedom: "personalized care for those who pay for it, mass regimentation for the poor".[49] This applies to inebriety treatments to a large extent: as we have just seen, personalized clinical and/or pastoral care for inebriety was found in retreats but not in reformatories.

But there are exceptions to this general rule about the class specificity of care. Clinical medicine may have reserved its liberal methods of working through the patient's freedom and respecting the patient's individual features for those patients who could pay, not only because they paid but also because they shared the physician's own cultural capital. But clinical medicine is not the only system for providing individualized care. Spiritually oriented organizations have for centuries been involved in providing care that, while not liberal in the Foucaultian sense,[50] acknowledges and values individual variation and avoids the perils of normalization. In particular, a number of religious organizations have attempted to provide personalized care for the poor alcoholic. Roman Catholic orders, especially of nuns, have received little attention from historians of madness and crime, but they have played important roles in consoling the poor and fallen with techniques that have ancient roots but are still in effect today. But perhaps most significant in the English-speaking world is the Christian organization that down to the present day specializes in the urban degenerate: the Salvation Army.

In the late 1880s, the Salvation Army's officers turned their attention away from purely evangelical pursuits and began to emphasize charity and social work with the urban poor, in the United Kingdom but also in the United States, Canada, New Zealand, and elsewhere in the British Empire. Unlike more respectable groups of urban missionaries, such as the Methodists, the Salvation Army embraced those considered by others as unreformable, including prostitutes and drunkards.[51] The Army avoided using the medicalized language of dipsomania and inebriety, preferring the old language of 'the sin of drunkenness'. Even when the modern terms appear, the medical model is quickly undermined. A typically melodramatic autobiographical article in the Army's *Social Gazette*, entitled "The experiences of a dipsomaniac", prefers to use the word "drunkard" in the body of the text, and the anonymous author calls himself "a converted boozer".[52] And the homes opened up for alcoholics by the Army in various English-speaking cities around the world were always called "Homes for Drunkards", not homes for inebriates or alcoholics. The Army did give in to the classificatory mania of the turn of the century to some extent, possibly out of fundraising considerations, but most of its institutions did not in fact serve or produce distinct populations. Rescue homes for women, for instance, were described in fundraising appeals as rescuing women specifically from prostitution, but in practice many other poor and homeless women were admitted to them. From descriptions provided in the Army's social-work reports,[53] it appears that a very large number of down-and-out alcoholics received some care, and most of these avoided being labelled as inebriates.

The evangelical Protestant theory of grace and salvation is sufficiently well known that it need not detain us here. Worth analyzing, however, are the practical techniques used by the zealous officers of the Salvation Army's early days to reach precisely that group considered as hopeless by all other authorities – that ill-defined group known as the residuum, "outcast London", the submerged tenth, or the lumpenproletariat.

The Army's work with inebriates at the turn of the century, especially that led and influenced by Catherine Booth in London, did not regard heavy drinking as rooted in a constitutional weakness or nervous diathesis. It regarded it as a normal part of life in the slums. Countless narratives published in Salvation Army sources, many of them autobiographical, of ordinary poor people driven to drink by poverty, by domestic violence, by seduction and abandonment, or by other everyday traumas of the urban poor, suggest that there is nothing pathological about drinking. Drinking heavily is simply an aspect of life in a fallen world.

A remarkable feature of such autobiographical accounts, many written with melodramatic flair, is that, although their primary aim is to promote the life of the saved, they often devote pages and pages to recounting the escapist pleasures of alcohol in vivid detail. The tales of life in the underworld always involve a slippery slope downward and an in-the-nick-of-time intervention by a Salvation Army officer or by God himself; but, nevertheless, a great deal of time and creative effort is devoted to documenting the everyday life, the pleasures, and the troubles of the 'perishing classes'. Although later in the twentieth century the Army's work became more infused with the objectifying methods of social case work, their early social work is notable for its sympathy with the fallen. A typical example is a 1897 story about a respectable Scottish woman who emigrated to Canada and was in

> ... an unfortunate marriage to a man who proved a slave to drink, which brought all the wretchedness and misery so common in the home of the drunkard, until the idea of a home had to be abandoned and the children placed in institutions, while the wife and mother sought employment by which to obtain the funds needed to maintain them there. But, sad to relate, before this took place she had many a time sought temporary relief from her trouble in the accursed cup, and was fast becoming as great a slave to it as her husband. After she went to a situation he spent all his own earnings in drink, and then when he knew her wages were due would hang around the place and often manage to get her out to spend her hard earnings with him, and frequently finished up by beating her because she had no more to give him.[54]

The sympathy shown here for a mother who drinks and abandons her children stands in sharp contrast to the judgements made by the British Inebriates Inspector and by the inebriety physicians, including Dr Mary Gordon and Dr Mary Scharlieb, about inebriate women. Indeed, despite the fact that Catherine Booth attended some meetings of the British Inebriety Society and was admired by many of the physicians for taking on the hopeless cases, she made no bones about her critical views of the medical profession, especially those physicians who called for coercive measures against the feeble-minded:

> One of the things the Salvation Army can do to-day is to protect such sufferers from the doctors; for it seems as if we are coming under a kind of tyranny on the part of these professional people! ... [The feeble-minded] will need to be delivered from the tyranny of the medical profession! You must take this as my personal opinion.[55]

Unlike more middle-class sectors of the temperance movement, the Army realized that preaching temperance would be useless if no alternative places of leisure-time recreation were provided: hence their brass-band music, which stood in sharp contrast to the well-bred choirs and organs of traditional churches. Unlike most middle-class temperance organizations, the Army usually attempted to provide alternatives to the evils of pubs and saloons, not just to close them down, going so far as to make Army meeting halls look and feel like pubs rather than like churches. As Catherine Booth said:

> We think that the same enterprise which actuates business men with respect to their buildings should be incorporated into religion. What care and sagacity are exercised as to the situation and suitability of business premises . . . opening the theatres, dancing halls, and gin palaces every day, and making them attractive every night by flaring gas, music and other attractions . . .[56]

Although the Army's special vocation was caring for and converting the lumpenproletariat, they also operated inebriety homes for paying patients, partly for reasons of financial gain and partly because, as evangelical Christians, they believed sin was found in every class of society. In these homes, religious pastoralism was the main therapy, but hygienic measures were not neglected; a vegetarian diet was used in the English homes, for instance.[57]

In many ways, then, these Salvation Army homes – not the medicalized asylums – were the rightful heirs of the early nineteenth century moral treatment movement pioneered by the Quakers at the York Retreat. At the turn of the twentieth century, at a time when medicalized institutions tended to fatalistically write off degenerates, Catherine Booth and her optimistic troops continued to believe that anyone, no matter how fallen, could be healed and transformed. The care provided by the Army was, at one level, always the same but, at another level, always individualized. The melodramatic narratives of sin and salvation all have identical endings, but each sinner's long road to the freedom of salvation is portrayed as highly individual, and much effort was spent documenting these struggles in all their colourful variety. Just as psychiatrists from Esquirol to Freud revelled in the peculiarities of the case study even as they purported to uncover the fundamental unchanging laws of the psyche, so too the discourse of evangelism reconciled the endless variety of actually existing sins and vices with the ideal of a single redemptive truth.

The religious version of moral treatment practiced by the Salvation Army, although ridiculed by most twentieth century physicians, was successfully taken up by Alcoholics Anonymous and re-deployed through the new technology of the small, semi-private, anonymous self-help group – a technology more suited to mid-twentieth century urban life than the Army technique of open-air brass-band meetings. In tracing the history of alcoholism treatments, it is possible to discern a certain genealogy of moral treatment neglected by existing historical studies of the psy sciences, a line that goes from Willis, Tuke and Pinel, through evangelical 'rescue' work, to today's AA.

THE RETURN OF HABIT

As a network of new laws and institutions was being developed in such a way that inebriate institutions would become redundant, the inebriety experts were busy unwittingly undermining the very notion of inebriety as a single disease. The departmental committee on the operation of the Acts, consisting of some MPs and a number of prison doctors and inebriety experts, wrote a learned and highly detailed report in 1908 calling for harsher committal powers; but, in a classic deconstructive move, the committee undermined its own recommendations by providing a theoretical justification that challenged the very idea of inebriety as a disease. In one part of their report, the committee constructed a unified and medicalized inebriate identity by contrasting the true (diseased) inebriate with the "bank-holiday drunkard".[58] But, on the next page, they divide up inebriety into three distinct conditions.

The first type of inebriate consists of "persons born with an excessive degree of the common capacity for deriving pleasure from the use of alcohol"; these are often "superior", well-educated persons, who have plenty of willpower but simply possess too much desire, too much virility. These individuals (clearly gentlemen) have stronger desires than working-class men, but typically they also have stronger wills. The second type of inebriate consists of "persons deficient in self-control", who are often violent and of low intelligence. Their desires may not amount to more than whims, but they lack even the small amount of willpower necessary to resist them. The third type, consisting primarily of "women" (read 'ladies'), is made up of inebriates "by artificial culture rather than nature". (The reference here is to the belief that most ladies became addicted to alcohol or drugs through overprescription.) The ladies, though not possessed of any great desires, could therefore also become inebriates in a peculiarly passive way. They then attempt to combine this fragmented etiology with a unified therapy by suggesting that, for all three types of inebriate, the aim of treatment is to "alter the ratio between self-control and desire".

The committee's formula for inebriety (a ratio of quantity of willpower or self-control to strength of desire) is one of the more interesting theorizations of alcoholism that has ever been produced. It cleverly combines the ideal of a unified disease entity with the existence of divergent treatment programmes for distinct populations in a formula that, because it is a ratio, avoids the problem of defining what is or is not excess consumption in absolute terms. The formula, however, together with the threefold classification of types of inebriety that mirrors the stratified reality of treatment programmes, explains far too much. Like those feminist overdeterministic explanations that make one wonder how any woman can even open her mouth, the committee members' ontology of inebriety made it into a normal condition for each social group: for what lady did not suffer from passive submission to medical advice, and what gentleman who served his nation and his empire did not at least occasionally suffer from too much virility? That gentlemen had both stronger desires and stronger inhibitions than ladies, and that the urban working class lacked the ability to restrain the whim of the moment, were conventional views about the differentiation of human capacities by gender and by class. But this theory of the social stratification of the soul – like the parallel views about the inability of "native" races to control their drinking – had little to do with alcohol, and did not begin to explain why, within the same group, some people were able to control their drinking and others were not. The theory of the social stratification of both willpower and desire, then, generated three different types of inebriety corresponding to pre-existing types of soul. It did not construct a distinct disease of inebriety.

The committee might have stopped with those comments, which fragmented inebriety into three distinct conditions with their own etiologies and therapies but did not directly challenge the medicalization of drinking or other practices of consumption. But they did not. More sensitive to popular skepticism about the medicalization of drinking than one would expect from an official body, the committee mused that inebriety, whether fragmented or unified, was in any case not a real disease, not like influenza: it is rather a "constitutional peculiarity", perhaps even just a "habit".[59]

By labelling it a habit, they were by no means saying that it was trivial: Victorian and Edwardian discourses on topics such as health, hygiene, sex education, intellectual training, and ethics were absolutely full of information on how to monitor and re-shape one's habits, for habits were regarded as the bricks and mortar making up the edifice of character, and character was in turn the basis of both individual moral worth and national prosperity. But while in 1908 people paid more conscious attention to their own habits and those of their loved ones than we do today, habits have never been the province of either psy experts or the law.[60] The law treats human conduct as a series of discrete acts, with notions such as habit and character playing a secondary role, often only at the level of sentencing. The psy sciences, on their part, tend to regard habits as mere symptoms or indicators of the more fundamental reality designated by terms such as 'personality'. By declaring drunkenness/inebriety to be a habit, the committee members were putting it on the same level as exercise, drinking coffee, or eating sweets: something to be regulated, but regulated through our own knowledges and our own idiosyncratic mechanisms, not through either clinical medicine or law.

## THE END OF LEGAL INEBRIETY

Not coincidentally, the British Society for the Scientific Study of Inebriety took a sharp turn in 1914. Maternal drinking was still a concern, as were the drinking habits of working-class men. But much hope was placed on the new wartime restrictions on pub hours and pub location. Rather than target a small group of vicious/criminal inebriates for direct control through a stigmatized identity (inebriate/alcoholic), the emphasis was now on re-shaping the habits of the urban working class as a whole. In the United Kingdom, as in North America after Prohibition, drinking came increasingly to be governed through environmental rather than disciplinary measures, through liquor control and the micromanagement of pub hours and drinking conditions, rather than through pathologization. After 1914, the British working classes could no longer get a drink first thing in the morning, and they could no longer while away the whole afternoon at the pub. This risk-management strategy, the doctors of the Inebriety Society believed, would be a much more effective measure against alcoholism than the Inebriates Acts. Not incidentally, the new risk-based strategies of controlling the sale of beer in pubs did not affect the upper-class inebriates, who had distinct, more privatized consumption patterns that were little affected by the endless debates on pub licencing.

Environmental measures aimed at changing the drinking habits of the working class as a whole were not the only programme for governing alcohol. The drawing room methods of addiction recovery used by physicians and other personnel treating 'morphinomania', neurasthenia, and drinking problems continued to develop and change over the years after World War I. The development of treatment regimes for alcoholics and addicts, however, would take place largely outside of the gaze of government inspectors. With the exception of some hospital programmes, alcoholism among the middle and upper classes became, after World War I, a private problem for which individuals and families sought medical and, increasingly, psychological advice with little or no interference from the legal system. This advice would come to be cast neither in the deterministic terms provided by the degeneration paradigm nor in the chipper tones of temperance tracts, but rather in the new scientific terms provided by the resources of psychological clinics and private psychiatry. In mid-twentieth century psy practice, the issues formerly gathered under the sign of inebriety would come to be reorganized as problems of neurotic personality development. Once more, then, alcohol would recede into the background, as the psy sciences explored in detail the underlying problems of which drinking was, for them, but a rather insignificant symptom.

The alcoholic personality, as we shall see in the next two chapters, was, in sharp contrast to inebriety, a successful programme for governing. Although no strictly medical treatment ever became generally accepted, people in English-speaking countries came to believe that a minority of drinkers were indeed alcoholics, a different kind of person, a type of human being with distinct features. But, perhaps because of the lack of a generally agreed-upon course of treatment, the alcoholic identity began to unravel in the 1970s. In Britain, the Royal College of Psychiatrists decided that alcoholism was no longer the object to be governed: rather, drinking in general, aggregate amounts of drinking across the nation as a whole, were now to be governed. And how were overall amounts of alcohol consumed to be governed? By changing the habits of the population. The chapter on treatment in the widely sold paperback *Alcohol and other drugs*, issued by the Royal College in 1986, contains a section entitled "The process of changing habits". This contains homey advice to drinkers who want to drink less: try to change your transportation habits so you no longer stop off at the pub on the way home, they tell us; make sure you always have non-alcoholic drinks in the house; and so forth. The advice is sensible enough, but it is strikingly non-psychiatric. We are now told, even by psychiatrists, that we can change our drinking patterns without any need for deep explanation, but simply by deploying the same tricks we use to not forget our keys. We tell ourselves: go here, don't go there, try substituting mineral water for beer, and so forth, just as people have done ever since the Greeks came up with the notion of regulating drinking and eating as a question of care of self.[61]

Many organizations and individuals – from nineteenth century clinical-pastoral medicine, through AA, to contemporary social workers dispensing commonsense advice and support to alcoholics and their families – have developed a rich array of practical measures that have indeed helped a good number of people who feel that they have lost control over drinking. But this practice-based wisdom has seldom been used as the basis of scientific knowledge. The American social scientists who, around 1940, began to build up a network of research and treatment projects focussing on alcoholism began their work – in what is perhaps a typically American fashion – as if alcoholism had no history, as if neither the inebriety physicians nor the Salvation Army had existed. Starting from scratch with little knowledge and less interest in their own antecedents, it is perhaps not surprising that they proceeded to fall into many of the same dilemmas of the free will as their nineteenth century predecessors.

# CHAPTER 4

# 'ENLIGHTENED HEDONISM': THE EMERGENCE OF ALCOHOL SCIENCE IN THE UNITED STATES

During World War I, the United States and Canada implemented prohibition, while, in the United Kingdom, the availability of alcohol was severely curtailed. Existing concerns about excessive drinking were articulated to the sudden transformations of a wartime society through the diagram of the free will discussed in the previous two chapters. The late Victorian/Edwardian argument, it will be recalled, ran roughly as follows: the will's ability to control and even suppress the desire to drink is crucial for individual moral and physical health as well as for national success; alcohol damages the will, and pre-existing deficiencies in the will are revealed and aggravated by drinking. Therefore, curtailing drinking opportunities ensures that individual and collective energies can be concentrated on building up both individual and national willpower.

During World War II, by contrast, alcohol sales – even to uniformed soldiers – were rarely restricted. Although cigarettes were perhaps the soldier's most important vice during this war, alcohol, while not as easy to carry as cigarettes, was made generally available to both civilians and soldiers. The sight of very drunk soldiers and sailors returning to base after a furlough was a common one, with officers regarding this as a problem only if the men got belligerent.[1] The striking contrast between World War I and World War II on this issue is, I will argue in this chapter, indicative of a major shift in the ethics of drinking – a major shift in the relations linking volition, desire, and consumption.

By the time that World War II broke out, the temperance ethos that had given rise both to prohibition and to medical theories of inebriety as a disease of the will was regarded as old-fashioned. The belief that morality consisted in purification, in suppressing desire, had come to be ridiculed, at least among the intellectual elite. A Boston psychiatrist writing in the very first volume of the *Quarterly Journal of Studies on Alcohol* drew on Freud's views on the pleasure principle to argue that pleasure seeking is normal and natural, and that it is asceticism, not hedonism, which is culturally peculiar. While refraining from directly stating that it is the neuroses of puritans, not those of alcoholics, that ought to be investigated, Dr Abraham Myerson argued, in a passage expressing the general tenor of the journal, that the policy goal of the new science of alcohol ought to be a "healthy" attitude promoting "moderate" drinking. "Enlightened hedonism" does not mean lack of regulation: neither Myerson nor his colleagues ever proposed putting an end to the problematization of alcohol as a particularly dangerous substance. "This does not mean a lessening of social control in the use of alcohol. It means taking account of human pleasure and human needs. It means we must not minimize the pleasure principle."[2]

Thus, although alcohol remained more problematic than other liquids – for reasons considered too obvious to merit mentioning – the mode of problematization changed. In the new, consumer-society for-mulation, the fact that alcohol is associated with relaxation, intimacy, and disinhibition, and that it is consumed for pleasure and not for nutrition, did not arouse automatic suspicion, as had been the case before World War I. The pleasure of consuming alcoholic drinks had now become a potentially positive, socially functional force to be channelled into healthy consumption. Just as in the sexual arena the generalized suspicion of female sexuality typical of the turn of the century quickly gave way, first in the interwar period but more markedly in the 1940s, to an emphasis on the legally sanctioned enjoyment of normal sexual desires – in a shift through which frigidity, a concept not available to Victorians, suddenly became a problem – so, too, in the field of drinking, total abstinence began to appear as less socially productive than moderate, legal, orderly drinking.

The quest for techniques to promote moderate drinking, and more generally a socially functional hedonism, was the driving force of the alcohol studies movement pioneered by sociologists and physiologists at Yale University in the 1940s. How could a civil society and a government that had been torn asunder in the prohibition battles now transcend the legacy of prohibition? Alcohol science answered that a scientific approach would help to promote an attitude toward drinking that fostered enjoyment and acknowledged pleasure while maintaining a watchful eye for anarchies and dysfunctions.

Since alcohol science wanted to be based on facts, not utopias, a number of potential models of moderate drinking marrying pleasure to social regulation were canvassed. One strategy placed regular, social drinking in the patriotically drawn context of the days of the early American republic, the time before the temperance movement. This move, constructing the heavy drinking of the late eighteenth century as more authentically American than nineteenth century temperance, was rarely repeated – perhaps because the amounts of alcohol consumed in late eighteenth century America were shown to be the highest in history and a dubious model for moderation.[3] But the alcohologists found it easy to replace inconvenient facts with more convenient ones. As the last section of this chapter will outline, most of the empirical studies undertaken with the hope of inspiring America on the road to enlightened hedonism looked to ethnic and cultural diversity, not to history, for information and inspiration.

Enlightened hedonism was also a theme in the transformation of British approaches to addiction in the 1940s and 1950s. But British alcohol science remained dominated by medical doctors, and social and cultural issues tended to remain in the background. The annual meetings of the British Society for the Scientific Study of Inebriety ('Addiction' after 1946) consisted of ritual battles between the advocates of somatic theories of alcoholism and those defending newer psychiatric theories of repression and personality. The physicians who dominated expert discourses on addiction in the United Kingdom remained mired in discussions of disease entities and diseased individuals, showing little interest in using sociological and/or marketing techniques to lead the general population toward relaxed, well-adjusted patterns of consumption.[4] The psychological research on consumption developed in the London Tavistock clinic was employed to market beer,[5] but although it could just as well have been employed to develop programmes for moderate drinking, it was not used in this way, at least in the postwar period.

The hegemony of British psychiatry over the question of alcoholism seems to have functioned to retard the progress of alcohol science in Britain, isolating it from what would become the major international trends in alcohol studies from the 1940s onward. At the Yale Center for Alcohol Studies (which relocated to Rutgers University in 1960),[6] and soon after in alcoholism research institutes in Toronto and in Helsinki, the assumption was made that alcoholism was not strictly a medical concern, whether psychic or somatic, but was rather an inherently *interdisciplinary* problem. Building up well-funded research institutes around interdisciplinary social problems was not a strategy unique to alcohol: the similar field of criminology comes to mind. But criminology had maintained a close connection to the social sciences since its inception in the 1880s, with crime being generally defined as a problem with a heavier social than medical involvement. The deployment of the strategy of interdisciplinary studies of the social within a field that had historically been claimed by medicine – alcohol/ism – involved, in contrast to criminology, a serious challenge to the authority of medicine. This challenge would undoubtedly have resulted in the marginalization of alcohology, but for the fortunate (for the social scientists) fact that, as the previous two chapters document, medicine had continually tried but failed to produce a successful inebriety/alcoholism diagnosis and a generally accepted treatment.

As inebriety was slowly replaced by alcoholism in everyday and medical speech in the 1920s and 1930s, the term 'alcoholism' was as likely to be used and defined by temperance activists and, after the mid-1930s, by members of AA, as by physicians.[7] Even in 1956, when the American Medical Association, under pressure from the alcoholism lobbies, issued a statement urging physicians to provide care and treatment for alcoholics, the profession's ambivalent view about the status of alcoholism as a disease was revealed in the unusual statement declaring that medical provision "must be made *for such patients who cooperate and who wish such care*".[8]

Physicians felt that most alcoholics were uncooperative and that they would undermine any medical regime. They also knew that no strictly medical treatment existed – other than the drug Antabuse, which did not treat alcoholism as such but simply supplemented the patient's will to stop drinking by providing an automatic physical punishment for drinking.[9] The reluctance of physicians to assume responsibility for alcoholism and alcoholics meant that a space existed within which the Yale social scientists were able to create a new scientific field that overlapped with medicine's jurisdiction but was largely autonomous from it.

This scientific field, which I am calling 'alcohology', by analogy with criminology, was first defined as alcohol*ism* studies. Distancing itself from the traditional religious and sociological interest in such topics as 'poverty and drink', the group that was the germ of the Yale Center, the Research Council on Problems of Alcohol, decided in 1939 to devote all of its energies to *alcoholism*. This move was not unrelated to the fact that they initially obtained their funding from the liquor industry.[10] Liquor interests were, in the aftermath of prohibition repeal, very keen to show that alcohol was not itself a problem, and that the problems of drinking were really caused by a small minority of people who had pathological patterns of consumption. Funding from the liquor industry, however, was unlikely to have totally determined the university-based work of the Yale academics. The focus on alcoholism would not have been chosen, regardless of funds, if it had not been an excellent choice for other reasons. First of all, focussing on *alcoholism* satisfied the Alcoholics Anonymous constituency (which as early as the mid-1940s was influential among American experts), since AA's premise is that only that minority of individuals who are already alcoholics before they begin to drink are likely to drink uncontrollably. Secondly, and most importantly, the focus on alcoholism also helped to circumvent the battles between wets and drys that had plagued American inebriety circles and retarded the development of alcohol science in the United States from the 1880s right up until prohibition. If wets and drys disagreed on the nature of alcohol, they could nevertheless agree that some people, at least, engaged in antisocial and unhealthy patterns of consumption.[11]

Alcoholism remained the focus of the Yale Center's work for some time, and it was the most discussed issue in the *Quarterly Journal of Studies on Alcohol* from its founding in 1940 until well into the 1960s. But without abandoning the focus on alcoholism and alcoholics, the scope of alcohology was fairly quickly extended to include the study of diverse alcohol "problems", from traffic accidents to licencing strategies.[12] This was perhaps not surprising, since the discipline that was best represented in American alcohology was sociology. But with the shift from alcoholism to alcohol problems, the political and moral battles around alcohol that had been officially expelled by the Research Council in 1939 found themselves brought back in. The main difference was that these social–moral concerns were no longer located under the banner of Progressivism, the social gospel, or temperance, but rather under the more politically neutral and scientific name of university-based social science.

The marginalization of psychiatry and of psychiatry's focus on individual deviance was accomplished quietly and without fanfare. The Yale Center started out in the university's physiology lab, run by Dr Howard Haggard. When Haggard retired, he was replaced first by the eclectic statistician E.M. Jellinek and then by the sociologist Selden Bacon. Bacon and his graduate students seem to have dominated the centre's work, particularly after Jellinek left Yale for the World Health Organization. Mark Keller, for many years the editor of the *Quarterly Journal of Studies on Alcohol*, describes the formation of the Yale non-medical interdisciplinary research team as if the issue of medical jurisdiction over inebriety/alcoholism did not even exist:

> The universities were not interested. I think it had to do with the stigma on alcohol. The academic world shied away from it. So that we were, in the 1940s, really alone in trying to do something in this line at Yale. We started with a small staff, but we kept acquiring more people. We acquired a sociologist – Selden Bacon. He came around the laboratory one day because he had a project in the jails . . . and had discovered that most of the people were in jail because they had been drunk. We acquired a legal scholar . . . an educationist . . . another sociologist . . . an experimental

> psychologist . . . a librarian, an industry specialist . . . and for brief periods
> an anthropologist, an economist, and others.[13]

In his introductory address to the influential summer school on alcohol issues held at Yale in the 1940s and attended by a mix of academics and practitioners, the school's organizer, E.M. Jellinek, paid due homage to the importance of psychiatry in alcohol studies. But, significantly, none of the three lectures on treatment was given by a psychiatrist: one was by a member of AA and the other two by religious people.[14] Overall, the Yale summer school curriculum suggested that sociologists were the chief scientists of alcohol, with assorted others being expected to put the findings of sociological and social psychological research to good use in policy measures and treatment facilities.

The ascendancy of sociology and social psychology in alcohology was made possible by an intellectual vacuum that appeared after the somaticist degeneration paradigm discussed in the previous chapter went out of fashion. By the 1940s, the degeneration paradigm had been discredited for a number of reasons, not least its close link to Nazi eugenics. Liberal-minded social scientists – many of whom were Jewish and/or anti-fascist – were engaged in pursuing approaches to sociology, anthropology, and psychology that rejected not only the degeneration paradigm but, more generally, any attempt to use body types, inheritance, and physiological factors of any kind to explain such problems as alcoholism, sexual variation, and crime. Jellinek (who was himself Jewish) emphasized that alcoholism was not "a problem in eugenics",[15] and most alcohologists of this period went so far down the anti-physiological route as to roundly deny that pregnant women's drinking had any ill effects on the fetus.[16]

American alcohology acknowledged that alcoholism ran in families, sometimes adding that inheritance played a role in at least some cases. Nevertheless, their research projects did not include attempts to link bodily features to alcoholism. They did not ask about somatic types, but rather about personality types, debating amongst themselves whether there was an alcoholic *personality*, not an alcoholic body. The disappearance of the body that can be observed across a number of fields of study in the period from the 1930s to the 1950s[17] opened the door for two quite different and often conflicting knowledges: (non-biological) psychiatry and psychology, on the one hand, and sociology/ anthropology on the other. The latter was more influential in the United States than in Europe: social research in general enjoyed more respect and better funding in the United States. This specifically American orientation, in which somatic explanations of alcoholism gave way to such research projects as studying how Jewish or Italian *culture* – not a certain physiognomy or genetic makeup – promoted moderation, stands in stark contrast to the much more medicalized discussions of alcoholism and addiction in the British Society for the Study of Addiction.[18]

The marginalization of psychiatry within American alcohology may also have been facilitated by the fact that there were other medico-social problems of greater interest to psychiatry.[19] The sexual problems of the 1940s, for instance – homosexual men, frigid women, sexual psychopaths – were overwhelmingly psychiatrized. American alcohology was unusual, therefore, in that it succeeded in creating a realm of interdisciplinary social research that had a significant treatment component, while maintaining autonomy from medical institutions. This victory, symbolized by the naming of a sociologist as the head of the nation's first specific alcoholism ward (as distinct from detox centres and psychiatric wards), did not suffice, however, to guarantee its long-term success.[20]

Some alcohologists felt that the lack of long-term success was rooted in the same feature that made early alcohology innovative and successful, namely its wide-ranging interdisciplinarity. Selden Bacon, the most rigorous thinker among the early experts, was to later bitterly accuse the diverse bodies with a policy interest in alcohol of retarding the progress of alcohol science. Without acknowledging that it was these very groups that legitimated and helped to fund the university-based research projects, Bacon complained that the data used by alcohology had been generated in the course of practical work and were therefore of poor quality.

> Data for the development of a mature discipline to describe alcohol 'use' or alcohol 'problems' remain largely in the hands of others. Tax collectors, policemen and penal authorities, worried parents, mental hospital functionaries, coroners, a variety of religious officers, many artists, individuals who have suffered from this or that problem believed to arise from alcohol, those in the alcohol beverage business, and many others have provided the data. And a fascinating body of data it has been.
> But it is not *disciplined* data [emphasis added].[21]

Bacon's anger about alcohology's lack of control over its data did not stop with practitioners, however. He went so far as to denounce one of the founding texts of alcohology, Jellinek's study of the phases of alcoholism, for its poor research design:

> A small group of members of AA had decided to 'study themselves'. They could not be accused, even remotely, of possessing professionally academic theories of 'study'.[22]

A perusal of the forty or fifty theories of alcoholism listed in Jellinek's 1960 compendium, *The disease concept of alcoholism*, bears out Bacon's complaints. Contrary to what one might expect from the title, Jellinek's review of the field gives the impression of complete theoretical anarchy, with experts in total disagreement about whether alcoholism is a disease and, if so, of what kind. But it could also be argued that, if alcohology eventually lost its impetus and became much less important than such programmes for social research and policy as criminology, it was not because of scientific deficiencies but rather for reasons rooted in the social organization and discursive elaboration of alcohology's central object, namely drinking.

From the 1950s to the 1970s, one can trace a marked instability in the way in which alcohol was constructed as an object of study and action – what Paul Veyne would call the mode of objectivation of alcohol.[23] This general instability was at the root of the institutional troubles of alcohology. A comparison may be useful. While crime, a scientific object constructed in the second half of the nineteenth century, remains alive and well today as an object of both scientific inquiry and popular interest, the question of alcohol underwent a drastic transformation that threatened the very existence of alcohology. Excessive drinking became, in the 1960s and 1970s, absorbed into the fuzzier and larger question of addiction. This transformation involved the abandonment of the temperance ethos' construction of alcohol as a dangerous and unique social/moral/physiological object by a new objectivation through which alcohol lost its specificity and became just another drug. While alcohology has not ceased to exist, it has in many locations been subsumed under addiction. The United States is unusual internationally in that alcohol research continues to be funded separately from drug research, but medically run treatment programmes tend to be carried on under the general banner of addiction.[24]

But the field of addiction into which alcohol was merged has not remained static: it has itself been shaken up considerably in recent years. With the official (medical) abolition of addiction and its replacement by the less fearful and less pressing category of dependence,[25] the problems that were managed under the banner of alcoholism in the 1940s and 1950s have come to be minor sub-issues within a quasi-medical field that has come to be characterized by theoretical anarchy, shaky support from medical knowledges, concerns about the ethnocentrism of all diseases of the will, and a political profile in which drug trafficking and law enforcement issues vastly overshadow research and treatment. Like so many other chapters in the history of alcohol, the story of American alcohology in the 1940s and 1950s is a tale of insightful and innovative people with access to resources who somehow never managed to succeed. Criminology, and addiction studies to a lesser extent, have succeeded; by comparison with them, alcohology has been a failure. But what is a failure from the standpoint of the institution itself can nevertheless be an excellent object of study, since the ambitions of the project, the efforts of its promoters, and the contradictions and obstacles that impeded a smooth development often reveal a great deal about the spirit of the age – specifically, an age in which the relation between desire and consumption was profoundly reorganized in a shift involving major changes in alcohol's gender and class ascriptions. The rest of this chapter will examine some of the themes of American alcohology, locating them in broader questions of postwar social governance.

PERSONALITY, DEPENDENCY, AND MASCULINITY

In alcohology, in psychiatric and psychological circles, and in spheres of popular culture borrowing from the psy sciences, alcoholism came to be defined in the 1940s as a problem of "the personality". An early statement of this approach was made by a British physician in 1939:

> Not long ago a variety of nervous disorders were attributed directly to the effects of excessive alcoholism [alcohol poisoning], but as our knowledge of nervous disorders has improved, we have grown to regard over-indulgence in alcohol as a symptom rather than a causal factor in mental disorder.[26]

Chronic alcoholism is here explained, in a formulation that would be repeated throughout the literature, as "an attempt to overcome certain personality disorders".

The link between alcoholism and personality was taken for granted not only among psychologists and physicians but in many other sites. Even Selden Bacon, in the 1960s a proponent of a social–cultural explanation of alcoholism, was sufficiently immersed in the postwar discourse of maladjusted personalities that he wrote in 1949 that "maladjustment" often leads to excessive drinking. It was said that people attempt to counteract shyness or insecurity – which in the compulsively social 1940s to 1950s were regarded as indicators of dysfunction – by drinking; and even those who are not seriously maladjusted but who drink excessively are characterized by the fact that "the personality assets are weaker".[27]

Some psychiatrists with a psychoanalytic orientation focussed on repressed homosexuality as the fundamental cause of alcoholism. This unicausal theory was rejected by most experts, however. More common was the view that alcoholism was "a symptom of an underlying personality disorder",[28] but that this disorder was not reducible to any one intrapsychic conflict. The Yale summer school taught its students

that they should not believe the rumours about repressed homosexuality, because alcoholism was caused by different personality defects
in different individuals. "Personality" was then defined as "the dynamic
organization within the individual of those psychophysical systems that
determine his unique adjustments to his environment".[29]

The vagueness of this definition was an asset rather than an obstacle,
since it usefully translated the old concerns about the will into the
postwar belief that mental health consisted of individuals "adjusting" to
the social status quo or, as it was usually put, "adjusting to *reality*". In the
first volume of the *Quarterly Journal of Studies on Alcohol*, the old theme of
alcohol as weakening the will was rather transparently decked out in the
new clothes of personality theory:

> There is little doubt that alcohol is a destroyer of adjustments and
> sublimations . . . [A] man is an alcoholic when he cannot bear to face
> reality without alcohol; his adjustment to reality is impossible as long as he
> utilizes alcohol.[30]

In this way, alcoholism, whose etiology remained fuzzy, was explained by
being subsumed under the more general claim that mental disorder was
closely linked to eccentricity, inadequate sublimations, and social
dysfunction. To again quote from Selden Bacon's early work:

> The social adjustment aspect of the alcoholic is closely related to the
> psychological aspect . . . his range of socially approved behaviour is
> narrow . . . He has no deep and abiding interests, whether in a hobby, his
> job, other persons, world affairs . . . The overwhelming part of the social-
> adjustment picture, however, is one of underparticipation in and minimal
> activation of the culture and society in which the alcoholic is situated.[31]

"Maladjustment" – a hybrid term connecting minor social eccentricities,
such as refusing to have hobbies, with the beginnings of psychological
dysfunction – was therefore a very useful term for early alcohology.
Jellinek's highly influential study of the "phases in the drinking history
of alcoholics" typically included a subsection entitled "indications of
prealcoholic maladjustment",[32] even though unlike other experts he
never believed in the existence of a single alcoholic personality.

It is indicative of a general shift toward more strictly sociological,
often functionalist explanations that, by 1960, Jellinek had largely given
up the language of maladjustment in favour of an approach that defined
both the (for him) very broad category of alcoholism and the narrower
category of alcohol addicts in terms of experiences and observed facts,
not in terms of any theory of the deep psyche. Bacon's work underwent
a similar transformation. In general, by the 1960s, alcohology came to be
characterized by a tendency to shun maladjustment and other psychic

explanations in favour of socio-cultural methods with a certain flavour of critical sociology. Increasingly, the focus was not on the drinker's soul but on questions of damage and harm.[33]

Despite the rapid rise and fall of the maladjusted personality in the postwar period, there was a consensus that, whatever the etiology of alcoholism or even its definition, few alcoholics were genuine psychiatric cases. Alcoholism was more of a social or a psycho-social problem than a specifically psychiatric one. Even in the United Kingdom, physicians expressed a certain skepticism about psychiatrizing alcoholics, going so far as to point out that the inevitable frustrations and delays of psychoanalysis in many cases led alcoholics to "revert to the comforting bottle".[34] In the United States, the alcoholism clinics that proliferated during the 1960s to serve a primarily middle-class, white male clientele only had part-time psychiatric consultants, with most of the actual treatment being provided by social workers.[35] A mid-1970s survey of US physicians showed that, while most doctors thought that alcoholism was indeed a disease, nevertheless the best treatment was to refer patients to AA.[36]

It was often pointed out, however, that depsychiatrization did not mean absence of regulation. The British psychiatrist David Stafford-Clark, in a paperback widely read in the 1950s and 1960s, wrote that

> ... it is probably true that [only] something under 5 per cent of major mental disorder is directly and solely due to alcohol, but it is equally likely that alcoholism is one of the most potent single causes of unhappiness among families, of broken homes, of minor and major crime, and particularly of violence and homicidal attacks, and that not a few of the behaviour disturbances seen in children and the character disorders which may cripple the lives of adults owe a great deal to alcoholic addiction ...[37]

The classification of alcoholism as a form of usually non-psychiatric social/mental maladjustment had a particular gender and sexual organization that is never made explicit in the literature itself but that provided the figure of the alcoholic with much of its content in the postwar period. It was pointed out in the previous chapter that habitual inebriety was associated with masculinity in most countries, but closely linked to deviant, sexually promiscuous femininity in the United Kingdom. By the 1940s, however, this English peculiarity had disappeared, and alcoholism was gendered masculine everywhere,[38] in such a taken-for-granted fashion that Jellinek's study of the phases of alcoholism was based on a set of questionnaires filled out only by men; the ones filled out by women and collected by AA were excluded from the study by Jellinek (and possibly thrown out, since no specific study of women alcoholics was later carried out). But if masculinity was the silent background of postwar alcoholism, this did not mean that it was stable or unproblematic. The constant, usually denied, rumours about the centrality of homosexual urges in the etiology of alcoholism are significant precisely because they were regarded as in need of denial.[39]

Perhaps the reason why homosexuality was simultaneously evoked and denied was that, although there was no evidence that alcoholics were practicing homosexuals in disproportionate numbers, or vice versa, nevertheless alcoholism came to be associated with gender deviation. An excellent example of the way in which gender and sex issues worked to make postwar alcoholism a disorder of the masculine identity is found in the 1944 novel *The lost weekend*, popularized around the world in the 1945 Hollywood movie of the same name.[40] In this account of a few days in the life of a middle-class Manhattan alcoholic, Don Birnam, much is made of the fact that the protagonist's father abandoned the family when the boy was 10 years old. The implication is that alcoholism is due at least in part to the absence of a strong male figure. The adult alcoholic of the novel is portrayed as much weaker than, and indeed as constantly leaning on, the stronger, more virile, fully employed woman who would have been his wife if he had been less dysfunctional. To compound this picture of deficient masculinity, the novel suggests – without ever mentioning the word 'homosexual' – that Birnam's downward slide into complete social dysfunction began when, in a drunken spree, he wrote a love letter to a high-ranking male in his college fraternity.[41]

Homosexuality, suppressed or not, is not usually found in the plots of alcoholic novels, plays, and movies of the time. But the more general point that alcoholism has to do with the attempt to deny and overcome deficiencies in the masculine ego is made in many other sources. Don Birnam spends his days drinking and nurturing fantasies about the great novels that he will never write and the brilliant symphonies he will never conduct, behaviour generally regarded by the experts as integral to the alcoholic personality. A Rorschach test study of (exclusively male) alcoholics at New York's Bellevue Hospital typically revealed the following:

> The Rorschach test picture of the alcoholic, as derived from the protocols of these 47 [male] subjects, may then be summed up as follows. He is a maladjusted, immature individual who has developed few techniques for alleviating his feelings of discomfort. Actually, his attitude implies that he will not recognize limitations or inadequacies in his personality, will not admit them . . . There is a certain 'grandiosity' . . .[42]

In this regard, the *Lost weekend* hero is the perfect embodiment of the postwar American alcoholic. But while in the 1940s grandiosity and self-deceptive dreams of grandeur were regarded as immature, unmasculine, and contemptible, the 1960s' critique of traditional masculine self-control enabled a more sympathetic portrayal of male weaknesses. This is developed at length by the Harvard psychologist Howard Blane in his 1969 book *The personality of the alcoholic: guises of dependency*. A long chapter on "dependency and masculinity" argues that alcoholism (assumed to be a paradigmatically masculine affliction) begins with a feminine tendency to need others, a tendency which males are culturally forced to suppress and deny. Drinking sometimes helps to generate 'Dutch courage'; but Dr Blane suggests that it also provides overly sentimental, needy men with permission to become maudlin and to show their feelings. As was typical for the 1960s, Blane himself does not pathologize these men or condemn them for their weak will: he simply states that "Western culture" does not tolerate male dependency or allow men to show their neediness.

Dr Blane points out that dependency has several meanings, since the physical dependence on alcohol itself is mirrored in and reinforced by the peculiarly masculine dilemma of being unable to ask for, or even acknowledge, one's profound dependence on the love and support of others.

> Psychological dependence in Western society is complicated by the fact that our social values sanction open expression of dependent behavior among men only in special circumstances ... Consequently, man in Western society has had to develop ways of satisfying dependent needs without seeming to be dependent, or, alternatively, to force underground wishes to be dependent, to behave as if they didn't exist ... Dependency, and difficulties with it, has been noted by many observers to play a crucial role in the personality of alcoholics.[43]

Dependence/dependency[44] is also a crucial theme in the famous 1940 play about alcoholics by Eugene O'Neill, *The iceman cometh*.[45] Although set in 1912, and meticulously documenting the physical, legal and social features of the homosocial, working-class urban world of pre-Prohibition saloon culture, *The iceman cometh*'s psychology belongs fully to the postwar. All the men featured in the play – and the one female character who is also an alcoholic – are portrayed as collectively engaged in a silent conspiracy to support each other in what AA would call denial. They spend their lives nursing excuses and pipedreams and avoiding responsibility for what they have done and what they have failed to do, and only begin to be stirred into taking up pursuits appropriate to their sex when a recovered alcoholic comes back to play the role of truth-teller. The denizens of Harry's bar are not men enough to face up to what both psychologists and popular writers of this time always called "reality".

Alcoholism was thus regarded as a disorder of the masculine identity, a gendering specific to the 1940s and 1950s. O'Neill's play projects backward in time the specific psychological views about masculinity and consumption popular in 1940, giving them an air of timeless truth. A 1912 saloon in a poor section of New York was more likely to have constituted excessive drinking as rooted in an excess of masculine animal spirits; it is only in 1940 that men's drinking can begin to be regarded as a symptom of dependence, of feminized weakness. This reconstruction of the gender and sex features of alcoholism is closely linked to the new emphasis on middle-class alcoholics, seen not only in *The lost weekend* but in countless other classic Hollywood films about alcoholic ad men, journalists, and writers. The low dives and pubs documented by the temperance movement and by turn-of-the-century novelists of the slums give way, in the 1940s and 1950s, to the middle-class alcoholic who drowns his inability to get on with the life of a male breadwinner by drinking either at home or in cocktail lounges.[46]

The feminization of male alcoholics, while enabling both expert and popular psychological theories to incorporate alcoholism into their existing paradigms, posed a strategic problem for alcohology: if ordinary American taxpayers became convinced that alcoholics were a bunch of weak-willed daydreamers of questionable virility, they would be unlikely to support publicly funded research and treatment programmes. The leading Yale alcohol sociologists, Selden Bacon and Robert Straus, were well aware of this dilemma, and addressed it by attempting to isolate a subpopulation of redeemable, socially "valuable" alcoholics presented as sharply separate from the skid-row "social drifters".[47] Bacon, who had started his research career precisely by studying skid-row men, actively participated in the project of making alcoholism treatment respectable by developing outpatient clinics (the 'Yale plan' clinics) catering largely to middle-class, employed, white male alcoholics. Straus later acknowledged that there was a gentrification of the alcoholic, but presented this as a fact discovered rather than produced by alcohol science:

> The characteristics of the first 2023 male patients seen in nine outpatient clinics, as studied by Bacon and myself in 1950, were so different from the prevailing stereotypes that we called our report 'Alcoholism and social stability', and used the term 'occupational integration' in the subtitle. Numerous subsequent studies picked up the emphasis that a majority of alcoholics were not fallen skid row, jail, or mental patient types, but men and women who were struggling to maintain family and job stability and integrity.[48]

There is little doubt, however, that if Bacon and the other alcohologists had tried to focus on the skid-row population (or on African-American or Native drinking issues), alcohology would have been consigned to oblivion, as had happened to the struggling medical treatment facilities for drug addicts that were created in the 1930s.[49] Thus, the combined gender, race, and class bias of treatment facilities, and of the very definition of alcoholism that was constituted by social and psy scientists in the postwar period and which is still very much in evidence in today's array of facilities, is by no means attributable to an act of will on the part of alcohologists as individuals. Like the eventual collapse of most alcohology projects into addiction studies, the gender and class bias of alcoholism treatment facilities was not the product of deliberate choices by alcohologists themselves.

## JELLINEK: THE VIRTUES AND PERILS OF ECLECTICISM

E.M. Jellinek was by no means the most rigorous social scientist associated with the Yale Center and its successor at Rutgers, but he was certainly the most influential. Selden Bacon, who as we have seen was rather contemptuous of some of Jellinek's scientific methods, nevertheless stated in an interview with the *British Journal of Addiction* that "this man came very close to being what I would call a genius . . . He was an extraordinary academic character."[50] Bacon's protégé Robert Straus gave a perhaps more honest appraisal in his own interview:

> I have mixed feelings about Jellinek. He was brilliant, but he loved to play intellectual games and I have long felt that his report on phases in the development of alcoholism, which had a very significant impact on the field, was taken far more seriously and was popularized much more than Jellinek intended. The phases became so well known, that for a long time, when other investigators asked alcoholics to describe their drinking histories, they tended to get a recitation of the phases.[51]

But if Jellinek's model of the phases of alcoholism,[52] which as Bacon pointed out was originally based on the dubiously scientific data collected by AA members, turned out to be so influential, it was perhaps because the AA questionnaire was in keeping with the experience of white, male, middle-class alcoholics in the 1940s. In accordance with the first-person narratives that form the bulk of the *Alcoholics Anonymous* Big Book (first published in 1939), the questionnaire used by Jellinek arranged such experiences as blackouts, morning drinking, missing work, and so forth so as to suggest a slippery slope down to the bottoming-out point at which most alcoholics who became AA members in fact turned to AA. Most AA members, especially in the early days, were indeed men who had gone down a similar path: losing jobs, a wife, friends, and all self-respect until they hit a point – often in a public hospital ward or detox centre – at which they decided that they had to never drink again in order to regain their identity as men and as human beings. Therefore, the AA/Jellinek questionnaire, while based on no scientific theory of alcoholism and having no regard for the niceties of survey research, did speak to the experience of many self-described alcoholics. It was thus no surprise that alcoholics around the country would find it easy to use Jellinek's list of progressively worse experiences to describe their lives.

Jellinek was originally a biostatistician: if he decided to go with the AA questionnaire, it was not likely that this was because he was unaware of its unscientific status. This episode, and the way in which some of his colleagues used it against him, sharply demonstrates his willingness to be eclectic, to engage with AA as well as with any and all theories of alcoholism. And it is precisely his wilful eclecticism that distinguishes him from most of his colleagues.

The AA-initiated study of phases provided Jellinek and his over-lapping audiences in the United States and at the World Health Organization with a time line. People could now look up the chart and see how many years elapsed, on the average, between the beginning of weekend binge drinking and the onset of daily morning drinking (morning drinking being regarded, in American popular culture as well as in medicine, as particularly pathological, regardless of the amount consumed). They could try to compute how many years Uncle X might have before he too went from occasional blackouts to full-blown hallucinations. But the phases tended to homogenize all alcoholics, as was undoubtedly AA's purpose, and this made Jellinek's study liable to objections.[53]

In order to differentiate alcoholism not just diachronically along a time line but also synchronically across groups of people, thus distinguishing *types* of alcoholics in a way that ran quite counter to the AA emphasis on the unity of all alcoholics, Jellinek came up with the idea of grouping different drinking patterns and naming them by giving each a Greek letter. One might think that the purpose of such a classification is to expand the range of alcoholism and include as many people as possible under the "disease concept"; but, contrary to what the title suggests, Jellinek's 1960 magnum opus in fact tries to limit the scope of "the disease concept", stating that most of the types described may be alcoholics, but they are not diseased – because they do not suffer from "loss of control".[54]

Alpha alcoholism, he says, is drinking that breaks the social norms and creates social and personal problems, such as upsetting the family budget or causing absenteeism. This kind of alcoholism is equated with 'problem drinker', the term that had become popular at this time. While some alcohol experts regarded problem drinking as alcoholism by a less stigmatizing name, for Jellinek it is a social and a personal problem, but it is not a disease. There is no loss of control. These people could stop if they really wanted to.

111

Beta alcoholism is characterized by even heavier drinking, perhaps to the point of causing cirrhosis of the liver. (Jellinek may here be thinking of such countries as France and Scotland, in which it is normal for men to drink very heavily nearly every day.) But there are no withdrawal symptoms and hence no physical addiction. These alcoholics too, therefore, are not diseased.

Gamma alcoholism, apparently the main form of alcoholism in the United States and Canada, is what AA calls alcoholism. It is characterized by binge drinking and a slow downward slide into helplessness, a process which the alcoholic vainly attempts to stop – vainly because, unlike other types of alcoholics, gamma alcoholics do really suffer from "loss of control".[55] They may not drink for weeks or months, but if they go out on the town they are sure to come home in a terrible state.

This classification, which Jellinek presents without any particular set of data to back it up, is obviously arbitrary. It was nevertheless very useful to alcohology because it recuperates the traditional emphasis on the will, on "loss of control", while simultaneously limiting its scope, since loss of control is typical only of a certain type of alcoholic, not of all alcoholics. In this way, a small group of alcoholics can be sent off to medical or psychiatric treatment for their deficiencies of the will without alcohology giving up its project to 'socialize' alcohol. In this way, too, the scientific study of alcohol can be prioritized and funded without fundamentally challenging the general norms of the postwar period about the harmlessness of legally regulated heavy drinking. As Jellinek had stated some years earlier, "only certain forms of excessive drinking . . . are accessible to medical-psychiatric treatment"; other forms are a matter for "applied sociology, including law enforcement".[56]

While Jellinek's classification draws a clear (if arbitrary) line between the garden-variety alcoholic and the truly diseased alcoholic, it does not draw such a clear boundary between alcoholism in general and normal drinking. This is Jellinek's Achilles' heel – and it is indicative of a certain systematic weakness in postwar alcohology. By relying on cultural norms to define several of his types, he implicitly gives up the project of providing a single, objective, universally valid clinical definition of alcoholism, and opens the door to anthropological nominalistic definitions along the lines of 'whatever is normal drinking in that particular culture *is* normal drinking'.

Other alcohologists would go on to pursue culturalist research projects in the 1960s and 1970s,[57] but the definition that Jellinek reluctantly provides for alcoholism in general does not follow that culturalist, nominalist path. His definition takes a different route out of the dilemmas caused by the failure of the project to clinically define alcoholism: a harm-based route. Foreshadowing later medical definitions of addiction and dependence in focussing not on the drinking itself – and certainly not on the drinker's motivation or personality structure – but rather on objective consequences, on what might be called collateral damage, Jellinek begins the process of re-objectivizing alcohol and drinking as *epidemiological* rather than as clinical objects. "Alcoholism [is] *any use of alcoholic beverages that causes any damage to the individual or society or both.*"[58] In keeping with this anti-psychological approach, Jellinek's later work paid much attention to documenting changes in cirrhosis death rates.

In a few short years, Jellinek went all the way from the functionalist social psychology current in the 1940s to a skeptical rejection of all psy inquiries. Although it is difficult to say whether his new interests and approaches constituted rejections of the old or simply additions, it is not unfair to characterize his approach to alcoholism as a successful combination of the risk-management approach of the "damage" definition with the experiential, AA-based approach of the definition of addiction as "loss of control".[59] Combining risk-based, proto-epidemiological approaches with the subjective experience of alcoholics themselves was a unique and original idea. Other alcohologists, more wedded to particular disciplinary and theoretical approaches than Jellinek, tended to study either one aspect or the other, working either as epidemiologists and measurers of aggregate consumption *or* as ethnologists of drinking behaviour.

Jellinek's synthesis – or eclecticism – was not just a combination of two approaches current in his own time: it also effected a union of tradition and modernity, old and new approaches to drinking. While the damage definition introduces a harm-based approach to *alcoholism* foreshadowing research and policy developments in the late twentieth century, the loss-of-control definition of the *disease* aspect of alcoholism placed Jellinek almost in the nineteenth century, alongside the inebriety writers who wrote about palsy of the will. Thus, separating alcoholism in general from the disease of alcoholism allowed Jellinek to be the heir of the nineteenth century inebriety writers while simultaneously pointing toward a future marked by risk and harm.

In respect to loss of control, however, Jellinek does more than simply inherit the loss-of-control paradigm from the nineteenth century. He inserts a new, typically modern and perhaps typically American element in the long history of worries about loss of control. That element is the *experience* of the alcoholic, an element which could only be acknowledged by the inebriety writers in offhand remarks, asides, and untheorized case notes. Clearly influenced by AA, Jellinek acknowledges that alcoholics are, even while they are still drinking to excess, actively engaged in a powerful struggle against their own desires.

Alcoholics are keenly aware of the fact that they are powerless, so that, even if nobody is there to institutionalize them, diagnose them or otherwise medicalize them, they dare themselves, as it were, to drink moderately. The process of becoming addicted is therefore not simply a process of losing control and lacking in self-government: it is also a process of governing oneself, however unsuccessfully:

> The question of why the drinker returns to drinking after repeated disastrous experiences is often raised. Although he will not admit it, the alcohol addict believes that he has lost his willpower and that he can and must regain it. He is not aware that he has undergone a process which makes it impossible for him to control his alcohol intake. To master his will becomes a matter of the greatest importance to him ... He now attempts to control his troubles by changing the pattern of his drinking, by setting rules about not drinking before a certain hour of the day ...[60]

Jellinek ends up characterizing this internal struggle as a form of self-delusion rather than as a valid practice of the self. But he goes further than any other alcohol specialist in acknowledging that addicts may be engaged in a form of self-government, contrary to the popular myth that addiction consists precisely of having no self-government. Setting rules for oneself about when and where one will drink, for instance, which has been considered since Jellinek's time as one of the many potential symptoms of alcoholism, is certainly an indication of the existence of some form of self-government and self-control.

Jellinek's eclectic approach to alcoholism has perhaps come as close as is possible to creatively synthesizing – or, more accurately, juxtaposing – quite incompatible approaches. His eclecticism, however, was his downfall as well as his virtue. When attempting to elaborate his notion that only "loss of control" over drinking constituted a disease, he ended up making the radical, for 1960, claim that "a disease is what the medical profession recognizes as such. The fact that they are not able to explain the nature of a condition does not constitute proof that it is not a disease."[61] The claim that alcoholism is not a real disease, that it is constructed as such by physicians who need not be able to explain anything about it to claim jurisdiction over it, must have made Jellinek highly unpopular at the World Health Organization, a body which undoubtedly believed in the physiological reality of disease. But he typically makes that comment as a throw-away line, without reconciling it with other statements he made about the reality of addiction, or without fully exploring its implications.

While Jellinek managed to juggle several incompatible theoretical balls at once, alcohology as an institution did not pursue his eclecticism. Instead, different currents went their separate ways. The epidemiology approach pursued by scientists with a strong policy interest in reducing alcohol-related damage began to develop quite autonomously from the anthropological approaches pursued by scholars who were by and large more hedonistic, or at least more willing to study the ways in which drinking played an integrative, socially useful role in both traditional and modern societies.[62] Neither the epidemiological studies nor the socio-cultural studies sufficed, however, to build a new foundation for alcohology, since within epidemiology alcohol's specificity was lost in the larger domain of drugs and health risks, whereas within critical studies of culture drinking became just another area of consumption.

## THE JEWS VS. THE IRISH: ALCOHOLOGY'S SOLUTION TO AMERICA'S POSTWAR DILEMMAS OF ETHNIC DIVERSITY

It was mentioned earlier that Selden Bacon, an old Yankee, had made an attempt to break the close cultural connection between American patriotism and temperance by invoking the easy drinking patterns of the early republic as a possible model for the mid-twentieth century. While this particular approach was not followed up, either by Bacon himself or by other alcohologists, a different but convergent strategy to re-define American identity in relation to drinking was pursued by a number of alcohologists. The tools used were those of the sociology of culture and ethnicity, well developed in the United States by this time.

Insofar as alcohology sought to develop a new identity for postwar Americans aiming at enlightened hedonism (rather than puritanism), it was to non-English European cultures that the social scientists of alcohol generally looked. Americanness was now to be defined in cosmopolitan, post-Puritan terms. The conclusions of the widely read 1967 compilation *Alcohol problems: a report to the nation* are representative of this approach:

> Neither a disapproving attitude, as held by some Protestant groups, nor an excessively permissive one, as among the French, appears to be effective in preventing alcoholism. Instead, cultural patterns with built-in restrictions and taboos against inappropriate drinking – Italian and Jewish practices, for example – are better as models.[63]

Although little reference was made in the drink studies to developments in the ethnic food business, the underlying assumption made by alcohology was that foreign patterns of consumption were no longer to be regarded with universal suspicion. Italian ice-cream parlours and Chinese restaurants, for example, had been regarded as morally dangerous and potential sites of 'white slavery' in the 1910s and 1920s; but by the 1940s Italian ice-cream and pizza, and Americanized Chinese food, had lost their dangerousness and become commonplace, not only in large cities but even in small-town America.

115

Drinking presented specific problems, for if one could Americanize specific commodities such as pizza or even red wine, the alcohologists admitted that to Americanize drinking *customs* and *styles* was a more challenging project:

> It is unrealistic ... to think that traditional Italian drinking practices – emphasizing wine [rather than whiskey] and restricting drinking primarily to meals – could suddenly replace current American drinking patterns. On the other hand, the very diversity of drinking patterns may make it easier to bring about changes in the United States than in a more homogeneous society.[64]

The alcohologists' research on ethnicity and alcohol consumption showed rather marked biases in favour of some cultures and against others. The Chinese-American community, while praised for its contribution to American eating patterns, was rarely mentioned in alcohol studies, although this community could easily have become a model of moderate drinking.[65] But while Americans could consume chop suey without feeling culturally inferior to the Chinese, drinking customs, which necessarily involve cultural and ethical practices more deeply than specific food items, were not to be borrowed from the Chinese. For similar reasons related to white supremacy, American alcohology showed a remarkable lack of interest in documenting differences between African-American and white American drinking patterns. On the whole, then, the cosmopolitanism of American social science in the 1950s and 1960s had its limits. The limits were basically those of white European cultures, with Jews defined as European.

Although Italians were often touted as a good model, particularly in contrast to the more alcoholic but otherwise culturally similar French, it was in the end Ashkenazi Jews who provided the main reference point in alcohology's discussions of culture and ethnicity. The first research project that used alcohology as an avenue for promoting (Ashkenazi) Jewish culture as worthy of general imitation at least in regard to drinking was Robert Bales' 1944 Harvard PhD thesis, summarized in an article published in 1946 that would be repeatedly cited in alcohology circles. In keeping with the enlightened hedonism project, Bales argued that high rates of alcohol consumption do *not* correlate with high rates of alcoholism, and that high rates of alcoholism are in fact found in cultures that generate a great deal of anxiety and repression and have few outlets for the primitive passions.[66]

In the 1950s, Bales' study was followed up by Charles Snyder, a Yale sociologist, who undertook a large-scale survey-based research project that documented in fine detail the drinking patterns and alcoholism rates of American urban Jews. He concluded that Jewish drinking patterns compared very favourably with those of traditional Protestant Americans, insofar as young men from fundamentalist Christian families, if they drank at all, were much more likely to become alcoholics than were Jews.[67]

While Jews provided the model or paradigm of moderate, integrated, family-based drinking, Snyder stated as a well-known fact that Jewish mothers were particularly prone to anxiety about their children's consumption of food, and hence had a tendency to produce "addictive" and "compulsive" eating.[68] Bales' earlier study had also reproduced, in an even more explicit manner, the stereotype of the Jews as a neurotic race: he had argued that the high prevalence of neurosis among Jews was an excellent indication that their moderate drinking was rooted not in overall good mental health, but in a specific culture of drinking that constituted a healthy feature in an otherwise not admirable culture. Both Bales and Snyder thus reproduced anti-Semitic myths while praising Jews for their custom of consuming small amounts of traditional drinks as part of the Sabbath meal and other rituals.

Jewish drinking patterns were not only compared with those of WASP Americans, but were also routinely contrasted to the unhealthy drinking customs of another traditionally stigmatized minority ethnic group, namely the Irish. Snyder claimed that, although American Jews and Irish-Americans have the same level of psychoses and neuroses, the Irish have much higher rates of alcoholism.[69] Bales' study, which had also set up the Jews and the Irish at opposite poles of the drinking-patterns spectrum, elaborated the theory (based on three secondary sources) that Irish culture in Ireland promoted very heavy drinking because it repressed youthful male sexuality in the interests of economically sound late marriages:

> The culture [in Ireland] was such as to create and maintain an immense amount of suppressed aggression and sexuality. Both of these suppressed tensions found their outlet in drinking.

After emigration to America, Bales argued, Irish families became even more dysfunctional, since the poor job opportunities for Irish-American men meant that fathers became weaker within the family and sons became overly attached to their mothers.[70]

Paradoxically, then, the project to cosmopolitanize America's drinking customs by learning about and even emulating some non-Protestant patterns of drinking perpetuated racist stereotypes at the same time that it undermined the claims to cultural superiority of Yankee WASPS. Alcohologists, like many other postwar Americans, no longer believed that all things foreign were morally dangerous; but, while eager to borrow some ethnic foods, ethnic drinks, and even some ethnic drinking customs – restricting their borrowing to the domain of white European 'ethnics' – the borrowing amounted to a recuperation of commodities and customs understood and valorized according to racist criteria. The neurotic Jewish mother overfeeding her child and the aggressive drunken Irish male were stereotypes reproduced and amplified, rather than challenged, in a social scientific literature priding itself on its enlightened cosmopolitanism.[71]

Alcohology's fascination with ethnicity had, in the long run, mixed effects. On the one hand, the study of cultural differences in alcoholism rates made alcohology interesting and relevant to many writers on social issues. On the other hand, emphasizing ethnic/cultural differences generated a risk for alcohology itself, namely the risk that it would become subsumed under ethnic and urban sociology and lose its connection to psychology and to treatment policies. Perhaps because of a fear of losing their turf, many alcohologists continued in the 1950s and 1960s to write about alcoholism in a culturally undifferentiated manner, refusing to turn the problem of alcoholism over to the sociologists of culture and ethnicity. (This was particularly true for the social psychologists, who continued to study the alcoholic personality without making any reference to ethnicity or culture.)

In the 1960s and 1970s, the sociologists and anthropologists of drinking cultures became increasingly critical, often refusing to valorize certain cultural features over others or to make any normative claims about drinking or any other consumption differences between cultures. This move – best represented in the work of Joseph Gusfield – enabled later studies to increase the level of critical rigour, at the expense of connections to policy and treatment. If alcoholism was a mere social construct, as was argued implicitly by Gusfield and explicitly in the influential book *Drunken comportment*,[72] then the rug of the disease model was pulled from under alcoholism treatments.

Those alcohologists who wanted to remain alcohologists rather than become cultural anthropologists or sociologists tended to turn, in the 1960s, to the tools of epidemiology. Led by the studies of national consumption rates done at Toronto's Alcoholism Research Foundation (later Addiction Research Foundation), alcohology sought now to influence policy not so much in regard to treatment for individuals – since alcoholism as a disease had conspicuously failed – but in regard to public-health measures to reduce aggregate drinking. These studies of aggregate figures tended to assume that alcoholism and/or alcohol problems vary directly with availability: in other words, instead of tackling the alcoholism of the minority, the best tactic was to reduce aggregate consumption, a move that would automatically, without heavy-handed medicalized intervention, reduce alcoholism. And aggregate consumption rates were, for epidemiological and statistical researchers, real in a way that the contested construct of alcoholism was not. In fact, alcoholics do not even exist within epidemiology.[73]

The epidemiological studies, increasingly influential within the World Health Organization but not generally influential at the level of national governments, repositioned alcohol as an issue of the management of statistical risk factors. This severed the longstanding close link between drinking and the management of individual souls and individual wills. It is a remarkable paradox in the history of social science that alcohology, initially built on the idea that the problem of drink was a problem of discovering and treating *alcoholics*, would so rapidly disown and abandon the alcoholic. By the 1970s, alcoholism and addiction centres did exist and did provide more or less medical treatment: but alcoholics are rarely seen in expert discourses on drink. And as will be seen in chapter 8, even expert advice to governments on questions of intoxication can now dispense with the alcoholic identity altogether. Neither anthropologists nor epidemiologists nor pharmacologists are interested in, or perhaps believe in, the existence of individuals who feel that they are indeed alcoholics. It is perhaps not surprising, then, that despite the considerable resources mobilized by postwar alcohology, the treatment of individual alcoholics – other than the bandaid treatment provided in detox units – would basically fall, from the postwar period to our own days, to a resource-less organization whose foundation was precisely an unshakeable faith in the existence and distinctness of the individual alcoholic: AA.

CHAPTER 5

# THE POWER OF POWERLESSNESS: ALCOHOLICS ANONYMOUS' TECHNIQUES FOR GOVERNING THE SELF

Although generally ignored by social science, Alcoholics Anonymous has been the subject of a number of studies. Some of these, written by addiction specialists, attempt to evaluate AA's success rate. Others, less policy-oriented studies, use data from AA to illustrate quite general, pre-existing theories – about the domination of psychotherapy in contemporary life and/or about the use of personal narratives to construct an identity.[1] This form of philosophical idealism, so common in sociology, can be avoided by paying close attention to the specificity of AA practices for governing self and others. This chapter therefore attempts to study AA in a loosely anthropological vein, describing rather than evaluating, and paying much closer attention to the techniques used by AA groups and individuals than to the theoretical claims made in its literature. The analysis of some of AA's rich storehouse of techniques for sobriety will occupy most of the second half of this chapter, but it may be useful to state at the outset that the most striking feature of these techniques, taken as a whole, is that, despite the organization's basis of unity in alcoholism, the governance of alcohol is not the main focus of AA. It is the soul of the member that is the main object of AA's innovative approach to ethical governance, an approach relying primarily on *self*governance rather than on advice or exhortation. Insofar as the liquid consumption of the member is being governed, drinking is governed for the sake of the soul.

BETWEEN ETHICAL WORK AND CLINICAL PRACTICE:
AA AS A HYBRID TECHNOLOGY

Alcoholics Anonymous describes itself not as a movement but as "a fellowship", and it positively refuses to engage in political and social change, to lobby for or against legislation, or to participate in the public arena in any way.[2] This explicit refusal of a public image, unusual in the context of American philanthropic or spiritual organizations, is best explained as a reaction to the old temperance movement. Despite possessing complex organizational forms, successful fundraising techniques, and powerful lobbying tools, the North American temperance movement had become, by the 1930s, ridiculous: a symbol of everything that was either wrong or simply impractical in the American tradition of moral reform. AA was founded very shortly after the repeal of Prohibition in the United States, and the Protestantism of its founders was markedly more modern, more non-denominational and much less proselytizing than that of their parents. They thus sought to consciously distance AA from temperance; and there was no more effective way of doing this than refusing to participate in public debates, perhaps especially debates about liquor legislation.

AA's early success thus owed a great deal to its insistence that individuals, even individuals collected together in cohesive groups, could and indeed should confine their ethical work to changing themselves and, at most, supporting others who had also made the decision to change.

Paradoxically, the very success of AA contributed to normalizing the heavy drinking that became common in the 1940s and 1950s across class and gender boundaries, in North America and in other developed countries. AA shared the view held by social and medical scientists in the 1940s and 1950s that the problem of alcohol was not to be located in alcohol itself, but rather in the souls of that minority of drinkers who could not control their drinking. Much as today's legalization of gambling casinos is implicitly validated by the sudden discovery of "the pathological gambler"[3] for whom treatment has to be provided even as governments open up more gambling venues, so too the popularization of the alcoholic identity likely legitimated increasingly high levels of alcohol consumption for the (non-alcoholic) public at large.[4] This historical paradox is not discussed within AA circles, probably because one of the few dogmas they adhere to is that the distinction between alcoholics and 'normies' (normal drinkers) is an ontological one, not one produced by legal or cultural regulation.

Thus, the interests of AA are not necessarily opposed to those of the liquor industry: AA did not challenge the general post-World War II project that earlier in this book has been called 'enlightened hedonism'. And indeed, if AA had set itself squarely against the liquor industry or against consumerism in general, it probably would have melted into oblivion, given the historical defeat not only of temperance but of what became disparagingly known as 'puritanism'. Thus, although AA is in

121

some ways an anti-consumer organization, and certainly challenges the project of American entrepreneurs of the soul to develop a for-profit psychotherapy market, it does not explicitly challenge either liquor advertising or the more general cultural inducements to drinking that were always denounced by temperance activists.

If AA has a contradictory relationship to the practices of the consumer marketplace, it has a similarly ambivalent relationship to the other major institution governing drinking and eating practices in Euro-American cultures, namely medicine. This ambivalence with respect to medicine is precisely what makes AA an excellent site in which to study the complex ways in which the powers of various medical gazes (the clinical gaze, the epidemiological gaze, etc.) are simultaneously amplified and challenged in extra-medical circles. There are certainly other practices and social sites upon which a variety of contradictory medical and scientific gazes converge, but if we are interested not only in complexities and contradictions *within* medicine but also in the ways in which non-professionalized forms of expertise have challenged the authority of physicians and scientists, few sites could be as fruitful as AA. Today we have AIDS activism, breast cancer survivor self-help groups, and other situations in which 'consumers' and activists seek to wrest control of health problems from traditional institutions, but none of these is as old or as rooted in working-class life as AA. And indeed, purposively or not, most of the consumer/survivor mutual-help organizations that exist today owe a major debt to AA. It was AA, not women's health or anti-psychiatry activists, that invented the mutual-help, leaderless group; it was AA that came up with the notion that physicians should not have the monopoly on disease; and it was, to my knowledge, AA that first succeeded in turning a disease into a full-fledged, lifelong social identity. The reflections on AA's practice offered in this chapter are thus written both to do justice to an organization that has been generally dismissed or ignored by both medical and social experts *and* to open up avenues for studying the complex interactions of medical, spiritual, psychological, and 'commonsense' means for understanding and changing one's own life, in the hopes that other researchers also interested in the formation and circulation of non-professionalized knowledges may continue the task.

Insofar as the men who started meeting together to help one another stop drinking had a theory of their situation, the basis of that theory was the statement that 'alcoholism is a disease'. The insistence that alcoholism was neither a sin nor the inevitable result of alcohol availability, but was rather a condition afflicting a specified minority of drinkers, would appear to bring AA into the domain of the medicalization of deviance. But, although AA was certainly borrowing some of the prestige of medicine when it chose to define alcoholism as a disease, it was by no means a puppet of the medical profession. Indeed, it could be argued that AA's peculiar definition of alcoholism as *a non-medical disease*, while at one level amplifying the authority of the medical model by labelling the vice of alcoholism as a disease, is nevertheless, at another level, one of the most successful challenges to the authority of medical and psy experts that this century has seen – a challenge that is particularly significant because it was unique for its time.[5]

On the one hand, then, alcoholism was defined as a disease; and, to corroborate this claim, a physician was asked to write an authoritative preface for the first edition of the Big Book endorsing AA's curative powers, a preface still reprinted in the current edition. Official AA discourse is uniformly conciliatory toward medicine and physicians. For instance, the 1996 survey of its North American membership carried out by AA itself notes, with implicit pride in its good relations with medicine, that "73% of members' doctors know they are in AA", and that "39% of members said they were referred to AA by a health care professional".[6] But this conciliatory stance is somewhat misleading. Although AA as an organization has always sought to cultivate good relations with all health professionals, the fact is that it casts all professionals in a supporting role. Physicians and other health system workers are supposed to support AA and to refer patients to the organization: they are not allowed to diagnose alcoholism or to treat anything other than severe physical problems.

In sharp contrast to the official AA project of building cooperative relations with physicians, many members, particularly blue-collar men, freely vent their anger at the superciliousness of male physicians, seeing their allegiance to AA as a form of resistance against medical power. A 38-year-old auto worker who dropped out of high school, when asked if he had ever sought help for his drinking problems from the health system, said:

> I never used no other method – I don't believe in doctors, they're full of shit. What do they know about alcohol addiction? I never went to no detox place because I heard stories about guys that go in there and climb the walls – I didn't want to be locked up like no animal so I stayed clear of that shit. No . . . I did it the tough way. I faced it head on. I knew I was in trouble and I knew where to get help – from other guys who knew where I was coming from – who had been where I had been. Not some rich snotty doctor who never done hard time in his life.[7]

Within AA, alcoholism is said to be a disease, or an illness,[8] but it cannot be defined by absolute quantities of alcohol consumed or by any specific clinical criteria. Alcoholism is defined as a *subjective* experience of lack of control: being unable to stop drinking when one truly wants to stop. And since only *you* know whether you really want to stop, only you can diagnose yourself.[9]

One might conclude that AA's self-diagnosis abolishes medical expertise by universalizing it, in a move paralleling the Protestant Reformation's laicization of priestly authority. But AA goes further than simply rejecting the authority claims of physicians and priests: the organization has levelled a profound challenge not only to the qualification process but even to the techniques taken for granted by those professionals. The nineteenth century clinical/disciplinary techniques described by Foucault – hierarchical observation, classification, and so forth – are overtly refused. In AA, there is a positive refusal to collect information about anyone but oneself. Similarly, the twentieth century techniques that have, within the field of alcohol studies, largely displaced the clinical gaze – epidemiological measures and predictions – are also refused. Members do not observe others, and neither do they collect aggregate information about their groups for purposes of risk management. There is a membership survey that AA carries out in the United States and Canada, but it is done only every three years and it provides only the most basic demographic information, and it is devised and administered by AA itself, not by sociologists or survey specialists.

Although organized around alcoholism as a disease, the gaze of AA is first and foremost an ethical one. It observes and judges, but what is being observed, judged and transformed is one's own spiritual progress, not the body of medicine or the mind of the psy sciences. This spiritual progress has a positive, if somewhat vague, content; it is not reducible to the behaviour of not drinking. The ultimate goal of AA is not the already ambitious one of helping people stop drinking; it is the even more ambitious one of helping people achieve inner peace. That is why members sometimes speak of "dry alcoholics" – people who no longer drink but who still have the old behaviour patterns (typically, egoism, boastfulness, and a misguided feeling of power). There is even a term – the "dry bender" – to designate the sort of emotional turmoil that, in AA discourse, indicates that one has become dry but not yet *sober*. Sobriety is thus more than the absence of drinking: it is a difficult to define but nevertheless positively existing state.

This explicitly spiritual rationality of self-government might lead one to classify AA with the religions and hence outside of medicine, as Paul Antze's insightful anthropological study does.[10] But if we are interested in analyzing, rather than pigeon-holing, the myriad ways in which various types of knowledges coexist and interact in the practical world, we may want to describe AA's internalized gaze as a hybrid one. For instance, while in most ways opposed to clinical practices, AA sometimes legitimates its knowledge with the same manoeuvre used by clinicians against the knowledge of scientific research. Just as GPs sometimes invoke their years of experience to generate a clinical judgement that is at odds with statistical studies or textbook definitions,[11] so too do members of AA often appeal to a quasi-clinical criterion of 'what works' in order to further a rationality of self-governance that is primarily spiritual.[12]

The hybridity[13] of AA's approach to knowing and managing alcoholism is apparent in its ambiguous use of the term 'disease', as explained above. It can be further illustrated by looking at two terms that help to operationalize the general notion of a non-medical disease and that recur constantly both in texts and in group and individual discussions: one is 'self-control' and the other is 'recovery'.

Self-control acts to constitute the hybrid zone between the clinical and the ethical. It is primarily an ethical term, rooted in spiritual practices of self; but it also appears in some medical discourses, for instance in case descriptions and diagnostic criteria for drug dependence or obsessive-compulsive disorder. Self-control is a wonderfully useful term precisely because it is a hybrid, partly moral, partly physiological, as Roger Smith has pointed out in respect to the closely related term 'inhibition', which has been used to denote both a neurological fact and a moral/cultural process.[14] In AA talk, the Protestant overtones of self-control tend to prevail over the scientific or psychiatric ones: God is often invoked and it is common for AA group meetings to end with the Lord's Prayer. Thus, the analyses of self-control and its perils provided in meetings and in conversation by individual members are inevitably tinged with religious meaning. Nevertheless, it is not a question here of classifying AA's discourse as *either* scientific or spiritual, medical or moral. AA makes full use of the rich semantic resources of terms such as 'self-control'. When members discuss their efforts to use the Higher Power to regain self-control, the history of scientific efforts to locate and measure the will and map the dysfunctions of inhibition and control, while remaining in the background, is not rejected. Members are no more aware of the long and complex genealogy of addictive and compulsive disorders than anyone else, but nevertheless this genealogy had already shaped alcoholism before AA was invented. The developments outlined in previous chapters thus contributed significantly to the meaning and effectivity that words such as 'self-control' have, both for the speaker and for the audience, in today's AA group meetings.

Another key term involved in the constitution of AA's hybrid terrain is 'recovery'. Recovering alcoholics are not on the way to being cured: AA firmly believes that 'once an alcoholic, always an alcoholic', and the

North American 1996 membership survey tells us that almost half of the 7,200 respondents are still active in the organization even though they have been sober for over five years.[15] In contrast to medical usage, then, recovery does not mean getting healthy or becoming normal. It means learning to live with one's dysfunction as peacefully as possible. The concept of recovery that has spread beyond AA to a myriad other self-help groups, and indeed to the general population, giving rise to such joking terms as "a recovering Catholic", constitutes a hybrid terrain on the borderlands of medicine. On the one hand, the term 'recovery' is drawn from medical usage, and hence implicitly appeals to or evokes the paradigm of disease; but it simultaneously undermines that paradigm by breaking the medically created link between cure and recovery, since AA members believe they can be healthy without being cured, happy without being normal.

How, then, does one set out to recover? AA's pragmatic eclecticism allows its members a wide latitude in choosing remedies that work, including drugs or psychiatric care. But it is stressed that neither medical treatments nor religion on its own will work in the long run. The only lasting solution lies in the "twelve steps" – not in *believing in* the twelve steps, but in *"working"* the twelve steps.[16] Members speak of "working the program"; and by this they mean first and foremost the twelve steps, with activities such as church attendance or seeing a professional counsellor regarded as options that individual members might include in their programme, but that never substitute for any of the twelve steps. And, although members sometimes express personal discomfort with one particular step, they cannot pick and choose: the steps are a package. In AA literature, the steps are always reprinted together, without any emphasis on some to the detriment of others, and in every group meeting the twelve steps are read as a single text. Group meetings (particularly those designated as 'closed' meetings, that is, meetings excluding observers and meant only for those who already see themselves as alcoholics) do often concentrate on one step or on a group of steps. But the group will move through all of the steps at various points. A group that wanted, for instance, to exclude the twelfth step (which is a promise made to other alcoholics to go out and help them) could not be an official AA group. There is wide latitude given to both individuals and groups to interpret the steps (and the accompanying slogans that form much of the material for group reflection) as they see fit; but the text of the twelve steps is treated as fixed for all time.

Drinking itself, as noted at the outset, is barely mentioned in the twelve steps. The first step is acknowledging one's individual powerlessness over alcohol: "We admitted that we were powerless over alcohol – that our lives had become unmanageable." This then leads to letting one's decisions be guided by the personalized counsel of one's divine entity, the Higher Power (steps 2 through 4). Alcoholics are told to assume responsibility for harm they inflicted on others (steps 5 through 9); and finally, the last few steps stress that this new relation of self to self has to be followed by the traditional ethical work of helping others, the lifelong activity known as 'twelve-stepping'. Activity is the key term here: although driven by beliefs and dogmas to an extent perhaps not recognized by most of its members, AA is nevertheless an anti-intellectual, and particularly an anti-scientific, organization. Its knowledge is always justified by reference to the subjective experience of its members, not to either scientific logic or factual truths. Stepping is an activity, and the steps are something one *works* on; the steps as a whole are a programme for governing one's life, a programme that, as they always emphasize, is compatible with a large (although not infinite) number of belief systems.

The twelve steps are complemented by the "twelve traditions", also read at most AA meetings, which specify the practices to be followed by the organization in the same way that the twelve steps specify the techniques for individual ethical practice. Most of these have to do with internal democracy, anonymity, refusing the temptations of money and fame, and avoiding political controversies that might either divide the organization or alienate potential alcoholics. Compared with the twelve steps' strongly spiritual, even religious flavour, the twelve traditions are prosaic and businesslike, but they too have a quasi-sacred status within the organization. People might debate how to interpret this or that tradition, but they do not seek to revise the basic text.

If despite the obviously religious flavour of much AA talk (including the repeated mention of God in the twelve steps) I still see AA as fundamentally different from established religions, it is because it does not attempt to universalize its ethical techniques. That is why it does not, as an organization, preach from pulpits or from our TV screens; neither does it solicit money nor tell anyone that they should join. Members may suggest to friends who drink that they might find AA useful, but they are expected to let each alcoholic make his/her own decisions. While cultivating a hands-off, when-you-are-ready stance toward people who admit having drinking problems, AA members are even less interested in changing the behaviour of those who do not report problems with drinking. In sharp contrast to most ex-smokers, AA does not seek to change the behaviour of normal drinkers – for example, they do not necessarily advocate alcohol-free social occasions.[17] They believe that it is up to alcoholics themselves to become either sufficiently strong to manage occasions in which drinks are served, or wise enough to avoid such situations. AA provides a design for living that is presented as an absolute necessity for those who are alcoholics – 'AA saved my life' is a comment frequently heard in AA circles. But although their zealous enthusiasm for the twelve steps, particularly when expressed to researchers who do not appear to have a drinking problem, suggests that they believe that the twelve steps are more like vitamins than like medicine, that is, good for everyone, they nevertheless do not explicitly make universal claims for their programme.

A key feature of the programme is that it manages to articulate the once-in-a-lifetime experience of "spiritual awakening" or rebirth,[18] the extraordinary features of evangelical conversion, with the humdrum, non-sacred, even banal practices of self-management of everyday life. An early leader of AA expressed this two-edged character of the programme as follows: "AA is first a way back to life, and then a design for living.[19] The 'way back to life' trope connects with the evangelical discourse of 'I once was lost and now I'm found' that resonates so powerfully even with secularized Christians; while the 'design for living' encompasses the little techniques of self-management that AA shares with such non-spiritual programmes as advice on smoking cessation. Putting them together in one sentence, and in a single programme that is simultaneously spiritual and practical, is AA's brilliant stroke.

Let us now go on to analyze in some detail a few of the techniques that make up AA's sophisticated toolkit of devices for caring for oneself in such a way as to change one's whole life. This will form the bulk of the chapter; by way of conclusion I will offer a few remarks regarding the conceptual resources available for this study – resources which, to anticipate the conclusions, are simultaneously too many and too few.

POWERLESSNESS

The first and most important of the twelve steps begins: "We admitted that we were powerless over alcohol . . ."

Many therapy and self-help groups are geared to empowering their members. Such groups as Codependents Anonymous fit very well with the general culture of neoliberalism, as argued in chapter 1. The aim of the self-esteem industry is to foster individual capacities so as to constitute individuals who will make a successful enterprise out of their lives: helping other people or creating a collective consciousness is not on the self-esteem agenda. When a woman at her first meeting of Codependents Anonymous states: "I don't know what I'm powerless over, yet, but I'm sure I'll find out",[20] she means that powerlessness is a bad state, one caused by the effect of a dysfunctional family on the primeval innocence of her inner child.[21] Such a woman would typically use the group to first define and then overcome this powerlessness. But when an AA member speaks of powerlessness, he/she means that alcoholics are by definition forever powerless over alcohol. For AA members, therefore, powerlessness is not something to be blamed on one's parents and overcome with the help of experts and books: it is a permanent feature of one's self that cannot be eradicated, but can be managed with the all-important support of the collective.

To this extent, AA indirectly subverts the neoliberal discourse of personal entrepreneurship and perpetual improvement.[22] Members are perpetually in recovery, always working on their souls, but they do not imagine they will ever re-make themselves from scratch, in contrast to the neoliberal illusion that the poor can become business executives by sheer willpower. AA goes so far as to challenge American individualism by regarding exaggerated views of one's power as part of the very illness of alcoholism. Alcoholism is, some AA texts tell us, born out of a delusion that we can indeed stop drinking when we want to or otherwise control our behaviour. "In our drinking days, we believed, we had such control. In sobriety, we realize that we didn't have control. We learn that we can make choices about what *we* do and little else."[23] The statement made by one member of AA that "people with low self esteem can have very big egos" is, in its own low-key way, a telling critique of some assumptions of neoliberalism.[24]

ANONYMITY

The requirement that AA members remain anonymous, particularly in their relation to the media, is also at odds with the culture of enterprise. Initially, anonymity was crucial in recruitment, since the stigma of alcoholism was such that few people would attend a group unless there was an iron-clad guarantee of confidentiality. This aspect of anonymity is still important for many people. But anonymity is perhaps less essential now to protect the individual – in some circles, being a recovering alcoholic is no longer stigmatized, and may even bring some cachet – than to ensure that the group does not succumb to the temptations of money, fame, and power that have crippled other organizations. "Anonymity nurtures humility", writes an AA member, in a book that will not contribute to his personal fame, since he does not use his last name. "Anonymity keeps us focussed on principles rather than personalities. There are no 'stars' in AA."[25] External anonymity is thus closely linked to one of its key traditions, namely the refusal to own property.[26] The tradition of "corporate poverty"[27] is so sacred that the worldwide AA organization recently refused to exercise any sort of intellectual property claim over their symbol – the triangle inside the circle – even as recovery entrepreneurs were making large sums of money selling trinkets with that symbol.[28]

Anonymity is one of a panoply of AA techniques enabling members to maximize the democratic potential of the organization by exercising a certain self-denial – a despotism not so much over one's own desires, as in traditional Protestant ethical forms, but over some dominant trends in contemporary culture.

NO CROSS-TALK

AA groups work partly because potentially hurtful opinions about other members are firmly repressed. If any newcomer is tempted to make judgemental remarks on other people's comments, he/she is told that "cross-talk" – editorializing or judging – is not allowed. The groups observed followed the 'no cross-talk' rule to a remarkable extent, even when some people's accounts of their drinking miseries teetered on the edge of bragging about drunken exploits. Members, particularly women, will make disparaging remarks outside of meetings about "drunk-alogues";[29] but the meeting itself tolerates an extremely wide range of speech forms and emotional contents, and judgemental comments about others are kept to a minimum.[30] Since the success of AA in attracting a wide variety of people of all classes, ages, and socioeconomic conditions clearly depends on its ability to remain, if not non-judgemental, at least more non-judgemental than the main alternatives – religion and medicine – it is clear that the prohibition on cross-talk is a crucial mechanism for the perpetuation and growth of AA.

The prohibition on judging others may be particularly crucial in attracting to the organization older, white working-class or lumpen males, who at least in our local study make up the majority of group membership and take up more than their share of talk time at open group meetings.[31] Men who have in the past felt judged by doctors, or who for class-specific reasons reject "psychobabble",[32] are pleased to find that AA does not expect newcomers to have the sort of middle-class cultural capital that is routinely assumed in therapy groups and in feminist or left-wing organizations. Indeed, AA actually encourages the sort of plain English – peppered with homey folk sayings, somewhat trite metaphors, and the occasional four-letter word – that reminds the observer of the institution inhabited by many AA members in their previous life, namely the bar or pub. Unlike most voluntary organizations in civil society, which tend to level upwards and systematically privilege those with professional backgrounds, AA tends to level downwards.

TELLING ONE'S STORY

AA is one of the many movements in today's world that rely heavily on autobiographical narratives. First-person accounts of the movement from alcoholism to sobriety form a large part of the Big Book, and open group meetings have at least one or two autobiographical segments.

It would not be very helpful, however, to simply impose the paradigm of confession on AA. First of all, the telling of one's story is not always confessional. It approaches the confessional in step 5 work, the one-to-one discussions between members and their sponsors about the harms done by the alcoholic member to others. Even in that more private context, however, the sponsor is unlikely to monopolize the power to interpret or the power to forgive, as is the case in the confessional practices found in the institutions of the church, the criminal law, and psychoanalysis.[33] In group meetings, the key feature distinguishing 'telling one's story' from confession is that the people listening do not either interpret or judge the speaker. There is, of course, a certain element of catharsis and forgiveness, but the interaction between group members differs from the hierarchical confessional practices studied by Foucault.

Storytelling in AA more closely resembles the 'coming out stories' that are basic building blocks of the gay movement, or the narratives of violence and abuse that constitute various survivor groups. In those contexts, as well as in AA, the storytelling functions as much to bind the group together and create a sense of commonality as to build up individual identity. But the role of storytelling in AA is more limited than in it is elsewhere. Such practices as reciting the Lord's Prayer and reading out the twelve steps and the twelve traditions, which most groups perform, function as supra-individual rituals, closer to the format of a church service than to the free-for-all practices of most self-help groups.

It is also important to note that some group meetings discourage personal storytelling altogether, and organize themselves around the process of moving through the twelve steps. Such meetings can focus either on a single step or on a related group of steps. Either way, the step meetings effect a different sort of unity than the more autobiographical ones. The steps provide members with a long-term sense of direction and progress; and, since it applies to members who no longer struggle with drinking on a daily basis, the twelve-step process unifies the organization by keeping newcomers and oldtimers together. While members might well tell anecdotes about themselves in the course of step meetings, the purpose of the meeting is not to solicit unique narratives but rather to forge an alcoholic identity whose common features are regarded as more important than that which distinguishes individuals. Although AA has certainly felt the pressures of identity politics, making some limited room for groups that describe themselves as catering largely to women, to gays, or to aboriginals, no group that excludes people on the basis of identity can call itself an AA group and be listed in the directory that phone volunteers use to direct interested callers. Those aspects of one's life that distinguish one from other alcoholics are to be kept firmly in the background:

> Whenever, wherever, one alcoholic meets another alcoholic and sees in that person first and foremost not that he or she is male or female, or black or white, or Baptist or Catholic or Jew, or gay or straight, or whatever, but sees rather another alcoholic to whom he or she *must* reach out for the sake of his or her own sobriety – so long, in other words, as one alcoholic recognizes in another alcoholic first and foremost that he or she *is* alcoholic and that therefore *both* of them need each other – there will be not only *an* Alcoholics Anonymous, but there will be *the* Alcoholics Anonymous that you and I love so much and respect so deeply.[34]

These days, however, AA members belonging to groups with strong identity politics have to constantly justify their solidarity with alcoholics of all (other) identities. An urban aboriginal man who finds AA useful reports being criticized by his aboriginal friends: "They tell me I'm selling out to the white man because some of my friends now are white. They say that the white god won't hear me, but I don't listen. I know what I know."[35]

Storytelling in AA, then, bears little resemblance to a psychoanalytic inquiry into the deep self. Storytelling functions rather as a way to enlist individuals in AA's pre-existing narrative of alcoholism. Sexual escapades, drug addictions, domestic violence, and other events that feature prominently in many members' lives are left firmly in the background, not only in group meetings but even in interviews (in which more time was available).[36] The sometimes rigid emphasis on alcohol, or rather on AA's prior views on alcoholism, to the exclusion of other problems in people's lives may be doctrinaire, but it probably helps to explain why so many AA groups survive for decades. By contrast, the Adult Children of Alcoholics groups observed by Elayne Rapping, which give their members encouragement to engage in free-ranging and usually self-serving autobiography, tend to self-destruct.

Younger people, more influenced by both psychotherapy and the practices of identity politics, can be seen at group meetings highlighting certain features of their life other than alcoholism: they might make more of their ethnic identity or their addiction to substances and behaviours other than drink, for instance. They are also more likely to focus on psychological causation, mentioning their dysfunctional family of origin, whereas the oldtimers tend to speak about alcohol itself, not about their parents or their own psyches, as having caused their problems. But even the younger generation only rarely seeks to form groups that are only for a certain type of alcoholic. They too – and this is something that is palpable when observing a meeting – share and help to reproduce AA's custom of backgrounding differences in favour of fostering the solidarity of all alcoholics with one another.

Stories about the self can and do function in very different ways, and help to enact different outcomes. Telling one's story is not a single technique with an invariable meaning and effectivity, even within a single organization. It is a very flexible technique that can be deployed in contradictory ways. It can solicit individual uniqueness, or it can create group solidarity; stories about oneself can be deployed to validate the authority of the analyst, or, on the contrary, to replace analysts with self-help groups; storytelling can be used to elicit sympathy for one's pain, or simply to gain approval for one's abilities as an entertainer.

THE HIGHER POWER

The explanations given in the Big Book and in semi-official histories of AA suggest that the term "Higher Power" was chosen in order to refer to the Protestant God without offending non-Christians or agnostics. Alcoholics were and are exhorted to give themselves up to the Higher Power, or, synonymously, to "God as we understood him"; this power is that which will make up for the alcoholic's admitted lack of power over alcohol. The chapter addressed to agnostics in the Big Book explains that it does not matter what precise content one gives to the term 'Higher Power'; the point is simply to provide the alcoholic with a name for that supra-individual source of strength that can be drawn upon to effect what the individual's willpower had not managed to accomplish.[37]

AA members today justify the Higher Power language in the same terms as those used in the Big Book, as if the concept had remained the same over the years. But there are indications that the deistic notion of the Higher Power that the original members constructed has quietly given way to a different technique for transcending the limits of ordinary human willpower. In meetings, people talk not about "the" Higher Power but rather about "my" Higher Power – as in the phrase heard at a meeting, "my Higher Power must have a sense of humour . . .".[38] The vaguely divine force acknowledged by many agnostics and lapsed Christians and Jews is difficult to define; but whatever it is, it is singular. The proliferation of individualized higher powers would suggest that today's AA members believe in guardian angels without believing in a God that guarantees the truth of angels, a development in keeping with today's tendency to liberalize religion to the vanishing point. This tendency is visible in the advice given in a recent AA book: "It has been suggested that we simply pray 'To whom it may concern'."[39]

Through their work on the first few steps, AA members develop a sense of a powerful and protective force that is always available, always beside them. As Paul Antze shows, AA's divinity is unusual in being purely benevolent: the judgemental, wrathful aspects of the Judeo-Christian God have been expelled and ascribed solely to the demon alcohol.[40] But this benevolent force does not rule over the world, or even over all alcoholics. Its power is strictly limited to acting through and with that particular individual. While in some ways AA bucks the dominant cultural trends, then, in respect to the God term it appears to be converging with New Age spirituality, with its emphasis on syncretism and individual consumer choice in religious beliefs.[41]

Consumer choice in imagining one's Higher Power is not free of all determinations, however. The origins of the alcoholics' Higher Power in the Protestant God often break through the discourse of choice and autonomy. A woman who was marginalized within her AA group, particularly by the women members, because she was known in her small town to earn money through prostitution, explained that when she was told that it was up to her to define the Higher Power, she told her group that she didn't want to imagine a masculine deity.

> I had trouble with facing god and this old guy stood up and started yelling at me and telling me that if I didn't turn myself over to my Higher Power I was never going to make it. But I just kept thinking – god is a man, and my whole life I have been turning myself over to men. So I said, well, my Higher Power is going to be a woman – and they all laughed and said I wasn't working the program, I wasn't taking it seriously.[42]

The insistence on visualizing the Higher Power as masculine is a feature not of AA in general but of the Protestant culture within which this particular woman (living in small-town Ontario) found AA. In Mexican-American AA groups, men as well as women are encouraged to imagine the Higher Power in the image of the Virgin Mary or of a revered patron saint, such as Our Lady of Guadalupe.[43] But insofar as AA has been largely shaped by white Protestant Americans, the Protestant image of the Higher Power as a deity whose masculine powers are unmediated by female saints has become the hegemonic definition of the Higher Power. Catholics, women who refuse to deify any male figure, aboriginal people, and others who have different religious traditions can exercise some personal control over the specific features of the Higher Power, as individuals, but they are certainly not encouraged to band together with others of similar background in order to develop a counter-spirituality.

Differences in religious and spiritual practices, then, are largely confined to the individual realm. The famous phrase in the twelve steps, "God *as we understand Him*" (underlined in the original), acknowledges differences among AA members, but the 'we' is a group of individual alcoholics, not a coalition of distinct cultures.

The fact that there is no communication among the different Higher Powers, or any way of adjudicating disputes between them, may look like a schism waiting to happen; but, paradoxically, the 'many guardian angels, no god' situation may contribute to AA's stability rather than undermine it. If the divine power is purely personal, and if the divinity exercises no power to judge and punish, there is nothing to fight about. 'Different higher powers, same steps' is not among AA's numerous slogans, but it could be.

"ONE DAY AT A TIME": SLOGANS FOR DAILY LIVING

Most AA group meetings take place in rooms that are borrowed for the meeting, rather than owned or controlled by AA. Generally speaking, little is done to decorate or rearrange the room, other than moving the chairs; but an almost constant feature of the process of turning a room (most often a church basement) into an AA meeting room is the hanging up of a few hand-made, usually tattered placards with AA slogans written on them.[44] "One day at a time" is one of the most popular slogans; and those words are often repeated by members.

The old temperance movement had its own technique for sobriety, namely the temperance pledge. This was a piece of paper signed by the prospective member, a paper typically committing the signer to abstaining from alcoholic beverages *forever*. Thus, if somebody who had signed the pledge drank, even once, this represented a complete failure.

AA meetings are full of people who drank for some time, stopped for a while, went back to drinking, back to AA, and so forth. Rather than rejecting these people as backsliders, as the temperance movement would have done, AA provides them with two techniques with counter-vailing effects. One is the custom of celebrating months or years of sob-riety with commemorative tokens, a round of applause, and sometimes even a party – a technique that rewards long-term abstention. But the other technique, embodied in the "one day at a time" slogan, counter-acts the tendency of oldtimers to feel superior. Although long-term abstention is prized, AA members sometimes say that the person with the longest sobriety is "whoever woke up the earliest that morning".[45] The focus on the 24-hour cycle thus tends to equalize everyone. Short of coming to a meeting with alcohol on their breath, all alcoholics are equally sober.

The 24-hour focus is a technique for managing oneself that is used in other aspects of living. For example, people who are mourning are often told that they should focus on getting through one day at a time, a bit of homey advice that counteracts the tendency to depression caused by the prospect of a whole life without one's loved one. This effect is useful for people quitting drinking, since many report feeling that they fear that a life without alcohol will be a life without fun and without sociability. But in the specific context of drinking, the one-day-at-a-time technique has added power: the power to forgive lapses. Of course, if one goes back to drinking, then one has to recalculate the length of sobriety; but one has not become an outcast or a failure. Since failure to remain dry has historically carried powerful connotations of moral failure (especially in countries with a tradition of temperance), and since guilt feelings about going back to drinking figure very prominently in the lives and autobiographical accounts of self-diagnosed alcoholics, it is very important for the success of AA to provide its members with a relatively guilt-free way to reconnect to the organization immediately after any lapse. While rewarding members for staying sober for long periods of time, AA thus manages to simultaneously validate the efforts of those who do not quit once and for all by providing them with a technique through which they can feel good about themselves simply for having stayed sober for that day.

The moral of this story, as far as social theory is concerned, is that the admittedly inane, even vacuous slogans posted around AA meeting rooms ("Keep it simple", "Easy does it", "One day at a time") are not so vacuous. They have little semantic content, but as crystallizations of AA's homegrown collective wisdom they are full of practical meaning and power. The little slogans on the placards – repeated in self-help books and in the words of AA members – may appear to be beneath the notice of the social scientist, especially the social theorist; they are the very opposite of the serious texts favoured by academics. And yet, perhaps precisely because they have so little inherent content, they play a very important role in the practical management of people's lives. This power is not due to any feature of the text itself: their power to enable people to manage their lives has been shaped in and by the ongoing practical work of an organization, for without the practical work of AA, the slogan "one day at a time" would have little effect.

In Greco-Roman ethics, there was a theoretical term for collections of practical wisdom put together from fragments and given new life through constant re-reading and reflection: *hupomnemata*. These were guides for conduct consisting of borrowed bits of wisdom. Plutarch and his peers, as Foucault points out, sharply distinguished these collections of past wisdom from the genre that is better known to us today, "intimate journals or narratives of spiritual experience".[46] Scrapbooks rather than serious books, collectively rather than individually authored, reflecting the ethical work and wisdom of the past rather than one's personal relation of self to self, *hupomnemata* are precisely *not* constitutive of individual identity. Today, similar scrapbooks are sometimes put together by hand by individuals who scavenge through spiritual guides and self-help psy books; but they are more likely to take the form of small-format hardbacks with inspirational bits of prose and poetry. A common format is the 365-page little book with one inspiring thought for every day of the year. The popularity of the "Meditations for women who do too much" type of literature may be an indication that the discursive resources of popular North American culture are not as monopolized by narratives of victimization and/or individual heroism as critical sociologists of popular culture would have it. Attentive to the needs not fulfilled by novels, tabloids, or confessional literature, AA has been instrumental in revitalizing the *hupomnemata* genre, keeping alive the time-honoured social practices of borrowing and adapting bits of collective and/or anonymous wisdom for one's own purposes.[47]

## BETWEEN IDENTITY AND HABIT: AA'S AMBIGUOUS PRAGMATISM

One could easily study AA from the point of view of discipline and nor-malization, stressing the ways in which AA constitutes and reproduces the alcoholic *identity* as a master status. And this would not be inaccurate: within AA, drinking – or, rather, the drinking of those who regard themselves as alcoholics – ceases to be considered as a series of discrete acts and becomes instead a series of symptoms of an underlying identity. Indeed, one could take this analysis further to demonstrate how AA's non-expert knowledge of the alcoholic identity has served as a sort of prototype for the proliferation of identity-based forms of self-governance in the last decades of the twentieth century. Twelve-step groups (Narcotics Anonymous, Sex Addicts Anonymous, Codependents Anonymous) formed themselves by extending the AA paradigm of alcoholism as a disease around which to organize an identity to other conditions. But even groups and networks that are not based on the twelve steps, such as the new identity of 'people living with HIV/AIDS', use a number of techniques pioneered by AA, perhaps most sig-nificantly utilizing a disability, injury, or disease as a source of social identity. Although there have of course been some major changes, including the rejection of AA's apoliticism by groups focussed on either sexual victimization or on disability, it was nevertheless AA that historically opened up the possibility of identity-based forms of power and knowledge not controlled by established professions and bodies of expertise.[48] That lay organizations and consumer groups – not just experts – have the capability and the will to normalize their own members and constitute identities, turning disabilities, abuses, and injuries of all sorts into powerful mechanisms for acting politically and ethically, is something that we tend to take for granted today, especially in the United States, but which was a great novelty in the 1930s.[49]

While a major, if not the chief, force in the historical emergence of diseases that function as mechanisms for identity-building and even 'empowerment', AA is nevertheless not the sort of organization that functions through a single mode of governance. Although it contributed in a major way to the formation of new forms to govern drinking as rooted in an alcoholic *identity* rather than as a series of discrete acts, AA was also shaped by a different sort of American cultural tradition, that represented theoretically by pragmatism.

AA's founders paid some homage to Carl Jung and to the psy sciences more generally, but they also acknowledged that the book most widely circulated among the early members was William James' *Varieties of religious experience.* This work elaborates the position that religion – like all other knowledges, including theology and philosophy – ought to be evaluated pragmatically, in terms of its practical effects. Focussing on religious *experience* rather than on religious belief or theological theory, this work stressed the empirical diversity of the *varieties* of such experience in ways that challenged the conventional ways of thinking about religion. James pursued the unorthodox project of putting Thomas Aquinas and Luther on exactly the same plane as Madame Blavatsky and spiritualist healers, arguing that theological controversies were meaningless unless they could be shown to have real-world consequences. In a statement foreshadowing Foucault's work, James stated in the conclusion to his lengthy documentation of various forms of religious practices that "God is real since he produces real effects".[50]

Although James' targets were philosophy, intellectual history, and theology more than medicine or psychiatry, pragmatism was profoundly opposed to the emerging psy sciences' project to posit deep identities lying underneath phenomenal appearances. James was a professional psychologist, but in his context that meant he knew about the sciences of the brain and the nervous system. Although he was persuaded by the argument that much experience is determined unconsciously, he was quite scathing toward psychoanalysis' efforts to construct itself as a general theory, arguing that the privileging of sexual experience and sexual trauma as causal factors shaping human individuality was quite arbitrary.

For both James and his compatriot John Dewey, the emerging scientific project to replace the act-based governance of traditional (liberal) law and religion by the identity-based governance of the psy sciences was fundamentally misguided, because it re-enacted rather than transcended the old philosophical battle between empiricism and rationalism. Are human beings a series of distinct acts and sensations, as

Hume argued, or are we characterized by an underlying essential soul or by its scientific modern equivalent, an underlying psychic identity? John Dewey's pragmatist framework sought to displace this binary by deploying the in-between, hybrid category of habit. As mentioned in chapter 1, Dewey deployed habit to deconstruct the old theological battle between the advocates of free will and the believers in determinism, since habits are precisely those patterns of action that are neither fully willed nor utterly determined, occupying that space in between perfect autonomy and utter necessity.

If habit can be used, as it was by the pragmatist philosophers, to deconstruct the fundamental binary opposition of the whole field of alcoholism and addiction – freedom vs. determination – habit can also be used to deconstruct a related binary, that between act and identity. The deconstruction of the act vs. identity opposition that grounds Foucault's well-known views about the replacement of the act-based apparatus of sovereignty by the normalizing, identity-constituting tools of discipline was not explicitly carried out by either James or Dewey, but all the elements for such a deconstruction are present in their work, particularly Dewey's.

In an argument that validated the low-status spiritual practices of his day (such as the 'mind cure' of Christian Science) and that was very agreeable to the early AA pioneers, James critiqued the assumption made by Protestant religious thought of his time that moral goodness was to be found in the deep structures of the soul. But if moral goodness is for James not identity-based, neither is it composed of isolated virtuous acts (as other religions claim). As Dewey notes, acts are never as discrete as empiricist philosophy claimed. Acts are in their vast majority not willed one at a time, but rather are rooted in and caused by habitual patterns. The testimony of AA members suggests that it is extremely difficult, if not impossible, to suddenly will ourselves into a new identity; and neither can we suddenly perform an act that has no precedent in our biography (refuse a drink, say). The pragmatist conclusion that we must, if we seek to work on the self, change our *habits*,[51] is thus in excellent agreement with the practical wisdom of AA and of many earlier projects to treat inebriety.

Unlike identity-based governance, which totalizes the self, habit-based governance decentres and fragments the self. If we think of alcoholism as an identity, we are territorializing the self. But the opposite project – the attempt to manage heavy drinking as a series of isolated acts, as if we were free to begin each day and each evening anew – has also been notoriously unsuccessful, as countless addiction-autobiographies testify. The practical failure of this intellectualist type of recovery project has a theoretical correlate: attempting to govern drinking as if each drink were an isolated decision perpetuates the fiction of an autonomous will that decides on each action from scratch. Repeatedly getting drunk, or repeatedly using alcohol to soothe emotional wounds, builds up certain grooves and patterns. In William James' work, these grooves are presented as physically existing in one's neurons; in Dewey's work, habitual patterns are presented, less somatically, as partly physical and partly ethical. It is Dewey's explicitly hybrid interpretation of habit that best reflects the experience of most recovering alcoholics.

Now, AA's *theory* of alcoholism as a disease fits the familiar Foucaultian pattern of identity-based governance. Foucault analyzed the transformation of the discrete series of acts known as sodomy into the full-fledged identity of the homosexual; similarly, AA believes that, although the drinking of normal people is indeed just a series of acts, the drinking of alcoholics is the effect or result of an underlying alcoholic identity.[52] AA's techniques for sobriety, however, are somewhat at odds with its own theory. Slogans such as "one day at a time", "easy does it", and so forth, do not make any presuppositions about identity: as argued above, they are more accurately interpreted as a modern-day version of the ancient scrapbooks for daily ethical meditation, the *hupomnemata*. And *hupomnemata* were one of a variety of ethical techniques designed to build up virtue not through cleansing the transcendental soul (neither the Greeks nor the pre-Christian Romans had such souls) or through mapping the essential identity of particularly psychic types, but rather through the slow accumulation of good habits on the purely superficial level of habit.

While AA's theory of alcoholism as an identity is rooted in the double intellectual heritage of AA's founders – religions and medicine/psy sciences – AA's techniques can without injustice be regarded as rooted in a much more ancient tradition of ethical work on the self. Pierre Hadot has pointed out, in an argument that has many parallels with American pragmatism, that in Greco-Roman culture the binary opposition of mind and body, thought and nature, freedom and necessity had not yet occurred. Ethical reflection at that time unified rather than separated thought and the body: spiritual exercises did not then involve, as they did later for Christians, a struggle *against* the body. Pre-Christian spiritual exercises were a project to simultaneously shape and govern bodily conduct and mental habits without separating the self into ontological levels (body vs. soul, symptom vs. underlying cause, acts vs. identity).[53]

AA's techniques for governing the soul use neither medical tools (objectivist observation, diagnosis, etc.) nor the tools of the psy sciences. Its practical techniques bear a strong resemblance to Hadot's spiritual exercises: they constitute a a cobbled-together, low-theory, unsystematic system for habit reform. These techniques do not separate symptoms from disease, incidental or trivial acts from underlying structures: the most apparently trivial situation can be fraught with ethical significance, and it is up to the alcoholic him/herself, not to any authorized observer, to arrange the incidents and experiences of his/her life as they please and to give them meaning. Marriage, for instance, regarded by psy experts as a sign of emotional stability and maturity, appears in the narratives of AA members both as a good sign and a bad sign, sometimes as a symptom of being overly dependent and at other times – even in the same narrative – as an indication that one is finally able to achieve intimacy.[54]

If there is no standard list of symptoms, there is similarly no sacred list of treatment techniques. In AA, the point is not to generate a system of knowledge about alcoholism, but rather to provide members with an array of practical examples and suggestions among which the member will choose whatever works. This is why the techniques need to be taught primarily in group meetings and in one-to-one conversations, with books taking a definite second place. Each member will find some slogans meaningful and others not helpful, and be inspired by some of the stories heard at group meetings while being put off by others – just as James argued that it did not matter whether one gained one's spiritual wisdom from Saint Teresa of Avila or from a streetcorner astrologer, as long as it worked.

In any case, the texts, whether they be stories heard at a meeting, the twelve steps, or the meditations for every day not authorized by AA but bought and used by many members, are not so much texts as mnemonic devices. When an AA member thinks of a particular phrase, slogan, or story, he/she is meant to think not of intrinsic meaning but of the particular context in which that statement was first heard or read. When hearing a slogan being repeated, listening to an audiotape of an AA conference, or reading over one's favourite part of the Big Book, an alcoholic is reminded of the ways in which his or her soul became rearranged, as it were, on contact with that story or phrase. This is true, in the pragmatist sense of 'it works', even for non-members: as I think about the meaning of "one day at a time", I do not think about theories of temporality. Rather, I call to mind the working-class, middle-aged woman in bargain-basement clothes who at one particular AA meeting stood up and, somewhat haltingly, described to the group just what sort of effects that phrase had on her conduct. She did not say, as the priests of my childhood would have said, that X or Y is the *true* meaning of the text. Instead, as if heeding the pragmatist thinkers' advice to focus on effectivity and practical effects, she simply outlined how exactly the text had helped *her* to persevere in sober conduct at a difficult moment. The people listening were thus not told what to think, or even what to do, but simply encouraged to reflect on the ways in which they could define for themselves how to appropriate and use the same text.

The discussions about habit formation that are found not only within AA but in virtually all of the literature on alcoholism recovery written by those with practical experience are nevertheless rarely consistently pragmatist. The language of identity rarely disappears completely. AA members describing in detail how they worked to re-shape the behavioural and ethical grooves of their soul, for instance by pushing themselves to attend an AA meeting every time they felt like going to the pub, will easily switch into comments that classify certain behaviours, such as working too hard, as symptoms of an underlying alcoholic identity.[55] The alcoholic identity, like all contemporary identities, tends to unify and centralize the set of habits that converge or are folded into an individual. While, if we remain strictly on the level of habits, there is no necessary link between drinking and other habits, positing an identity tends to territorialize habits and turn them into parts of a system. People both in AA and outside of it often say: I smoke because I am an alcoholic (or an addict); I work really hard to please the boss because I am an alcoholic; and so forth. This way of externally forcing a unification of the multiplicity of habits that make up one's conduct forecloses the possibility – envisaged by Dewey – of managing oneself consistently, not as a bundle of sensations (as Hume famously said) but rather as a bundle of semi-willed habitual patterns that are not necessarily unified from beneath by a single master identity. Having developed in the dual shadow of disciplinary governance and the American politics of identity, AA shrinks from considering the possibility that, if some people tend to drink when they are tired or angry, this may be a matter of habit, similar to pacing the room when one is nervous, biting one's nails when waiting for something, or pulling on one's hair while reading. While such habits are not completely automatic, in the sense that it is possible to become aware of them and change them, the habits were never deliberately chosen.

The coexistence of habit and identity within AA, therefore, is not a peaceful one. The theory of the alcoholic identity – that alcoholism is for those who are alcoholic not a matter of conduct but a matter of identity – does not do justice to AA's own practical wisdom, and prevents both AA and those who study it from developing the more novel possibility of a fully habitual ethics. Such a possibility, glimpsed several decades ago by John Dewey, has not been consistently articulated at the level of discourse – although, as has been shown not only in this chapter but in the preceding ones, there is much evidence from the field of alcoholism treatment to suggest that this theoretical avenue is well supported by the practical experience of inebriates and alcoholics.

# CHAPTER 6

# THE LIQUOR OF GOVERNMENT AND
# THE GOVERNMENT OF LIQUOR

Thus far we have considered a number of medical, religious, and hybrid strategies for governing drinking that share one fundamental assumption, namely that the prime site of investigation and governance is the individual who drinks too much. Because of their focus on the individual, these diverse projects tended to concur that strengthening the drinker's capacity for individual freedom – the will – is the best way to address the psychological and social problems associated with excess drinking.

Governing through *persons*,[1] however, is only one dimension of the governance of drinking. Drinking has also been regulated, controlled, and stimulated through a number of programmes that have acted on drinkers only indirectly. Curtailing pub opening hours; instituting general prohibition or specific prohibitions (e.g. banning aboriginals from buying alcohol); developing systems for restaurant and hotel licencing that regulate the relationship between food, drink, and times of the day; calculating the ways in which alcohol consumption interacts with heart disease or other health risks ... these and many other governmental activities do govern drinkers, but only indirectly, and they proceed without making any distinctions between alcoholics, abstainers, and moderate drinkers. A book that only documented the rise and fall of the alcoholic as an identity, as a kind of person, would be limited in its ability to shed any light on our present. As this and the following two chapters will show, alcohol continues to be a highly problematic substance both for individual consumers and for various authorities; but, while people continue to describe themselves and their relatives and acquaintances as alcoholics, the construct of the alcoholic has become increasingly irrelevant in most formal systems of governance.

Like sex, alcohol has been a site on which the governance of individuals has been historically intertwined with the governance of the health and the morals of national populations. The present chapter will examine a few of the large number of legal and administrative strategies that have been deployed to reduce the risks associated with excessive drinking through the multifarious and little-understood technologies of liquor control and liquor licencing, including prohibition. Although these techniques have many parallels with those used to maximize the health of national populations, it will be seen that the apparatus of liquor regulation, even in jurisdictions with government monopolies, does not seek to maximize health but rather to organize and regulate consumption, producing orderly, disciplined drinking. This chapter and the subsequent one analyze the governance of alcohol under the sign of risk, although as we shall see, liquor licencing uses old notions of disorder and danger more than calculations of risk factors. The governance of alcohol does not on the whole support the thesis that our societies are moving away from a disciplinary model of governance toward the impersonal management of statistically calculated risks. The availability of impersonal strategies, from liquor control laws to risk management strategies, has not prevented what I shall call, in the concluding chapter, 'the resurrection of the free will'.

The sheer size and complexity of the network of organizations and knowledge systems that regulate the consumption of alcohol and indirectly shape the activities of drinkers precludes any attempt at comprehensiveness. The mechanisms studied here, which are in turn largely examined through case studies, are representative of generalized strategies, but are not exhaustive. There are other projects and strategies designed to govern populations through alcohol. Taxation, tariffs, excise policies, subsidies to wine producers, and other measures located in the realms of fiscal and economic policy form a very important dimension of alcohol regulation. The economic dimensions of the political governance of alcohol would be well worth studying – but this must be left aside for the present.

This chapter will cover several of the most commonly used political/ administrative strategies for regulating the sale of liquor in English-speaking societies: liquor licencing, liquor control, and prohibition. Of these three, prohibition may seem like an outdated despotic project of little theoretical interest, particularly from the Foucaultian point of view of the genealogy of freedom; but, although *general* prohibition has been largely abandoned outside of officially Islamic countries, *specific* prohibitions – most notably concerning people under a certain age – are very widely used in the English-speaking world. As a strategy that reflects and reproduces some of the fundamental historical exclusions of

144

liberalism, the specific prohibition will here be studied not in the context of age exclusions but in the context of aboriginality. This admittedly incomplete study of aboriginal prohibition is important for the book's overall argument because, like the study of British inebriate women in chapter 3, it reminds us that a genealogy of freedom needs to include the experiences of those who have not been deemed worthy to use their own wills to govern their desires and their acts.

## THE STATE AND CONSUMPTION: THE CONTRADICTIONS OF LIQUOR CONTROL

Liquor licencing and control systems, whatever their particularities, all share the difficult position of having the regulation of personal consumption as their objective – an objective rather out of keeping with the logic of liberalism. Absolutist states experienced no legitimation crises in drawing up sumptuary laws:[2] they did not in any case recognize a sphere of private freedom, at least not outside the walls of one's house. But liberal states have greater difficulties in enacting systems to control the habits of consumption of their citizens. One of the preconditions enabling liberal regimes to enact liquor control mechanisms is the differentiation of alcoholic drinks from other drinks and foodstuffs.

Alcohol is not everywhere differentiated or singled out as an inherently problematic substance requiring government regulation. I grew up in Barcelona, and as a small child I was occasionally sent to the shops to get a bottle of wine, something which would be quite shocking as well as illegal in other contexts. In Spain as in other Southern European countries, the absence of specific mechanisms to separate out alcoholic drinks at the level of sales results in an organization of public space and of leisure time that is quite striking to many foreigners. Usually described in the vaguely culturalist language of ambience and atmosphere, this organization of space and of consumption is often regarded as flowing naturally from the essentially hedonistic character of Latin peoples. But what is experienced by both locals and foreigners as the result of a specific national psyche or culture is at least in part the effect of administrative and legal practices that are largely invisible to the people involved.[3] If one is going for a walk with a friend in Barcelona, one does not have to decide – as one does in the United Kingdom or in most of North America – between going for a drink or going for a coffee. One speaks rather of going *a tomar algo*, to consume something, with the something being indeterminate. By contrast, in jurisdictions with regulations separating drinking from other activities, the terms 'drink' and 'coffee' act to divide and label urban spaces and types of personal interaction. It is this separation of having a drink from other activities that is the fundamental precondition, and also the effect, of all liquor control projects, including prohibitions.

There is little doubt that the dual forces of European unification and public-health concerns about levels of drinking hitherto considered normal will tend to soften the historic differences in the regulation of alcohol consumption that one finds within Europe.[4] Nevertheless, the field of alcohol provides little or no evidence for claims about globalization and increasing uniformity. In marked contrast to substances that are internationally problematic and generally subject to outright criminalization – cocaine, heroin, cannabis – what is striking about alcohol policy is the incredible variety one finds in regulatory strategies.

These differences are often attributed to culture. The culture argument is generally circular: one observes Italian people drinking wine at family outdoor picnics, and this is counted as evidence of a particular cultural attitude towards wine and towards pleasures in general. But the culturalist analysis does not ask whether the culture that is regarded as causing behaviours can be considered instead as a series of *effects* produced by certain, often trivial, mechanisms.[5] These mechanisms are not necessarily unique to any specific field or object. For instance, the lack of differentiation of alcohol from other commodities in Southern Europe is mirrored in the lack of differentiation of times and spaces for smoking. State apparatuses, like individuals, have habits that sometimes result in a certain way of controlling a problem being chosen without any real deliberation – just out of habit. If no-smoking spaces are often provided even in rooms where there is no barrier to keep the smoke in the smokers' section, it may be that such spaces are not rooted in any health knowledge but are unthinkingly modelled on the legal, non-medical distinction between licenced and unlicenced spaces. Instead of linking the regulation of cigarettes to the regulation of drinking by tying both to some underlying culture or national psyche, this chapter suggests that a better approach to the regulation of consumption would be to study the *horizontal* linkages that create partly chosen and partly habitual assemblages of regulatory practices.

Institutional habit may be one reason why liquor regulation strategies – with the exception of general prohibition – have been under-theorized even by those implementing them.[6] In addition, it is difficult to study alcohol control strategies comparatively because the means used to regulate, and the general values and objectives of regulation, have dramatically shifted both historically and across jurisdictions.[7] A case in point is the very different role played by time as opposed to space in different systems. In the United Kingdom, in Australia, and in New Zealand, the history of licencing has been largely a debate focussing obsessively on pub opening *hours*; whereas, in the United States, a major 1936 study of liquor control states that the strategy of severely restricting tavern hours is not an option because it is "unenforceable".[8] But, while deeming time to be inherently unregulatable, American authorities regulated the space of public drinking much more closely than did the United Kingdom or Australia: the bar, for instance, was eliminated in most states despite its venerable place in working-class masculine history. In Finland, by contrast, the liquid itself is thought to be the prime target: authorities there have endlessly debated the merits of beer vs. spirits.[9] The debates about the pros and cons of specific drinks are paralleled at a more scientific, less experiential level by debates about the significance of alcoholic strength. In North America, the 1930s saw heated policy debates on the alcoholic strength of beer, with the Attorney General of Ontario leading the way in 1925 with a learned hours-long exposition in the legislature on the scientific differences between proof spirits and percent alcohol as measures of the strength of beer.[10] Later on, in the 1950s and 1960s, when the strength of beer had been standardized long enough that 5 per cent had become the 'natural' strength of beer, the emphasis in North American liquor control shifted to the regulation of the furniture, decor, and entertainment possibilities of drinking establishments.[11] To make the study of liquor licencing and control even more complicated, although one can indeed discern certain preferences and fashions in what the problem is thought to consist of, nevertheless in each situation a large variety of regulatory strategies operate simultaneously. That is, although pub hours have in the United Kingdom and Australia been the main topic of debate, the space of pubs is by no means unregulated, as is the alcoholic strength of beer and a number of other regulatory targets.

There is very little evidence of any governmental effort to bring together these multiple coexisting regulatory targets and rationales into a coherent system with a clear rationale. While in other fields, for instance the criminal law, authorities labour constantly to generate general principles, in the field of alcohol control they have proceeded purely pragmatically. Judges and Supreme Courts have rarely pronounced upon the fundamental principles or the key issues of alcohol control; and the discourses of psychiatry, epidemiology, and (more surprisingly) public health have been excluded from policy decisions. The decisions of provincial liquor control boards in Canada, for instance, have not generated nearly as much meta-discourse as other policies bearing on the health of the nation; and, on the legal side, they have not drawn even the modest interest shown in better-known areas of administrative law, such as social assistance law. Regulatory problems have been dealt with in an ad hoc manner, and there has been little or no effort to produce an overall rationale. The study of alcohol control systems thus reveals not only a rich variety of practical solutions but also a profound incommensurability in the questions asked, in the dilemmas felt to be inherent in alcohol sales and consumption.

This lack of a sense of what the field is about is characteristic of what Michel de Certeau wisely called "minor" practices: the low-status knowledges that do not reach the organizational critical mass necessary to distribute authority and organize inter-professional debates.[12] The officials managing liquor control systems have rarely if ever been professionals. They have been and still are very low-level public servants, and – in contrast to probation officers and judges – they are not required to even listen to the advice of psy and social experts. Despite the fact that alcohol controls intersect with the concerns of law, psychology, sociology, fiscal policy, and several branches of medicine, the administrative law of liquor control and licencing has not been guided by any of these experts.[13]

Taking for granted the intellectual standards and the rhetorical practices of the major practices has led the few scholars who have studied the regulation of alcohol sales to complain about administrative tyranny and political irrationality. Such complaints have done little to help us understand what liquor policies actually *do*. Just as the alcoholism treatments described in earlier chapters were said to constitute a hybrid and humble realm of ethical governance, so too the administrative practices that are the empirical focus of this chapter are pragmatically assembled sets of techniques that have never aspired to the rigour and coherence of either law or science. Liquor control systems are bizarre from the point of view of law, and downright ridiculous from the point of view of biomedicine; but the minor practices of governing have their own 'minor' logics, and these are worth studying in their own right.

In the scanty literature that exists on liquor control, a major distinction is made between jurisidictions that allow private shops to sell alcoholic drinks by the bottle and those that have state monopolies. This distinction between free enterprise and socialism is rather illusory, however, since, despite their name, state monopolies usually confine themselves to monopolizing *off-site sales*, and, most commonly, only off-site sales of hard liquor. In any case, whether off-site sales are carried out in ordinary grocery stores or in state stores, so-called state monopoly jurisdictions have more in common with non-state monopoly jurisdictions (such as the United Kingdom) than is apparent from the accounts of liquor control experts. The commonalities shared by the two supposedly distinct types of system (control and licencing) are obscured by the custom of using the phrase 'liquor control' to refer exclusively to state-owned liquor stores, reserving the term 'licencing' –

as if it were ontologically distinct from control – to designate the complex administrative system for the regulation of public drinking, that is, *on*-site sales. First of all, the state monopoly jurisdictions – including Finland's, which is as monopolistic as they come – do not simply monopolize: they also regulate, through the licencing of on-site private facilities. But the key commonality shared by control and licencing systems is that the sale of alcoholic beverages has historically provided legislatures and state bureaucracies in liberal states with an opportunity to exercise disciplinary powers rarely seen outside of totalitarian states.[14] For instance, the detailed records kept by the Ontario government's liquor inspectors as they entered pubs incognito to record the behaviour of the patrons, regulate the character of the music, draw maps of the precise location of every table and chair, collect information about the family fortunes and misfortunes of the licencee, respond to neighbours' complaints, and accumulate a mass of detail about every disturbance that took place in or near licenced establishments have few parallels in the official records of most liberal states.[15]

Now, it would be easy to examine the mass of regulations about licenced premises with a view to documenting the persistence of what Foucault called surveillance, the power to normalize through hierarchical observation.[16] In keeping with the rather wild logic of liquor control, however, visibility – subjection to the panoptical gaze – is not consistently regarded as a good thing: it could just as well be bad, from a governmental perspective. In some Canadian provinces, the "beer parlours" legalized in the 1920s and 1930s were forced to permanently cover their windows so that passersby were not offended by the sight of drinking, whereas in neighbouring provinces regulators decided – in keeping with American practice – that public morals were best served by the opposite technique, namely requiring that unobstructed windows be placed such that passersby could observe the interior.[17] The 1970 Commission of Inquiry that called for the modernization of British Columbia's licencing laws did take official notice of the contradictory theories of the relation between visibility and morality assumed by various provincial regulations. But the commissioners did not question the deeper assumption that there is indeed a moral architecture of drinking establishments, a direct causal relation between how the building is constructed and furnished and the subjectivity of the customers. In a subsection entitled "Public viewing of interior of public house", the commissioners wrote:

> We see no harm in constructing a beer parlour which permits passersby seeing patrons enjoying a glass of beer. However we think it is much more important to encourage owners to design an establishment not only

> functionally attractive but worthy of viewing from either inside or outside.
> Further, we believe that there is a direct relationship between tasteful
> decor and exemplary deportment.[18]

The moralistic phrase 'exemplary deportment' might lead one to conclude that bar patrons were being constantly and intensely disciplined
and moralized by the Liquor Control Board and its inspectors. This,
however, would be inaccurate. The beer parlours of mid-twentieth
century Canada were fundamentally unlike the asylums, prisons, and
schools that have come to represent the powers of surveillance and
discipline; most importantly, the drinkers were paying customers, not
inmates, and the logic of state inspection and licencing was shaped by
the fact that the beer parlours, however closely regulated, were
nevertheless located firmly in the marketplace.

In keeping with other state mechanisms for regulating private
enterprise affecting consumption (e.g. laws against the adulteration of
foodstuffs), the primary target of the complex structure of liquor and
beer licencing was not the individual drinker, but rather the
entrepreneur who had the licence, and her/his business premises. In
Ontario, the person holding the licence was heavily and very personally
disciplined by the board, with their name and family circumstances
known personally not only to inspectors but even to the members of the
board in the provincial capital. But, contrary to the panopticon image,
the person "enjoying a glass of beer" in a licenced bar was not handled as
a potentially immoral individual. Individual knowledge and moral
regulation of the drinkers was not absent from the aims of the
authorities, but it was primarily effected through a system that disappeared by the mid-1960s requiring individual permits to buy alcoholic
drinks for *off-site* (private) consumption. Unlike pub licencing, the
individual permit technique, which indeed named and disciplined
individual drinkers, has been deployed in a limited number of jurisdictions.[19] While the individual liquor permit constitutes a classic tool for
exercising discipline over named individuals, systems for licencing and
inspecting public drinking establishments are not classic disciplinary
mechanisms: the inspectors and the authorities issuing licences
generally leave the disciplining of tavern patrons to the owners and
employees of licenced establishments.

Subcontracting the discipline of drinkers, as it were, to the very
people with an economic interest in promoting drinking is an internally
contradictory project. Nevertheless, it was the route taken by nineteenth century Britain, as well as by twentieth century North America.
This allocation of authority happened with little explicit discussion, out
of regulatory habit, as it were. In the United Kingdom, pub licencing

had been one of the important prerogatives of the local JPs long before the central government decided to create a new category of beerhouses that depended on the central government, not local worthies, for their licence.[20] And in North America, when public drinking was re-legalized after the repeal of prohibition, there was already a long tradition of municipal licencing of restaurants and drinking establishments.

If the licence holder had to please the customers but also discipline them, the premises themselves also had to play the dual role of stimulating drinking but regulating its consequences. In Canada, and in some American states, the interior decor of licenced premises has been historically heavily inspected and regulated, along with extra-alcoholic amenities such as food and music. In Ontario, the Liquor Control Board waged a decades-long battle to keep food and drink sales separate, even when the same establishments (hotels) served both. And the board used its musical discretion to differentiate the respectable hotels, which were allowed to have tasteful trios playing on weekend evenings, from rough hotels such as Toronto's Brunswick House, whose requests to be allowed to have live music were repeatedly denied during the 1930s.[21] Some adornment and extra-alcoholic pleasures were thus allowed, but only to a very limited and highly regulated extent.

Licencing and inspection, therefore, are disciplinary strategies to be sure, but they do not by and large act directly on individual consumers: they act on that legal/physical space known as 'the establishment'. Significantly, the Liquor Control Board of Ontario demanded a "Monthly Conduct Report" not from potential alcoholics but from the establishment itself.[22] Even prostitutes, longstanding targets of the most intrusive forms of direct personal regulation, have not been personally apprehended by government inspectors but rather indirectly excluded. In several Canadian provinces, this was done for some decades through the environmental technology of segregating "ladies and escorts" from men on their own. Separate rooms with separate outside entrances enabled the same establishment to serve the traditional homosocial working-class male crowd while minimizing the risk of prostitutes soliciting by making it illegal for women on their own to enter the men's side.[23] Women on their own – always thought to be more tempted by heterosexual sex than by drinking – were not allowed to enter the men's side, although in many establishments they could see into it through a saloon-type half door or through a doorway.

In general, licencing enacts a subcontracting of many functions of governance. The regulation of drinking premises, which is significantly located in the world of private enterprise rather than in the more sociologically familiar world of professional expertise, shares some of the features of professional licencing structures, but in addition it provides a rich field in which to study the complex articulation of legal authority and administrative discretion with the spheres of private enterprise and consumer conduct.

It would be plausible to characterize the long-term history of liquor control as a shift from the direct disciplinary governance of individuals and spaces of drinking to the governance of populations through risk-management and risk-minimization strategies. While the liquor control systems set up in North America in the 1920s and 1930s had as part of their mandate "to inhibit vicious or excessive drinking",[24] by the 1980s officials and legislators spoke the language of risk factors, not the discourse of morality. The thesis that the government of deviance has tended to shift, in the twentieth century, from disciplinary techniques aimed at normalizing individuals to less direct and less intrusive, more actuarial measures aimed at reducing opportunities and controlling risks, a thesis developed in an extensive literature across subfields of sociology, would therefore seem to be perfectly adequate to understand changes in ways of governing alcohol.[25]

The risk thesis does shed light on the liquor control field. It certainly helps to explain why research on the effects of beer-worker strikes on aggregate consumption would suddenly become thinkable and valued, whereas in earlier decades the focus would have been on the soul or the psyche of the individual inebriate or alcoholic. And yet, the risk-society thesis does not explain everything. While doing research for this chapter, I was called upon to perform the routine academic duty of chairing a PhD dissertation defense. I did so, and a couple of weeks afterwards the School of Graduate Studies sent me a sharply worded letter reminding me that, as the chair of the event, I should have acted as a liquor authority:

> It has recently come to our attention that in celebration of the successful oral examination of Mr K— on December 5, a bottle of wine was consumed on the School of Graduate Studies premises. This is simply a reminder that all alcoholic beverages to be served on the St George campus must be ordered through the University of Toronto Campus Beverage Service and that the School of Graduate Studies is responsible for ensuring this at 63/65 St George. Thank you for your future cooperation.[26]

A copy of the university's policy on liquor control was helpfully attached to this letter.

This situation illustrates several of the general features of liquor licencing as a mode of governance. First, it was not the drinkers themselves but rather those responsible for the *space* of drinking – the School of Graduate Studies, and the member of faculty delegated by the school to chair the event – that are being governed through licencing.

Secondly, the concern about liquor consumption simultaneously achieved an unintended regulatory effect in the field of ethnicity/religion: the reason why the PhD candidate's supervisor had brought a bottle of wine to the thesis defense room was that the candidate was an Orthodox Jew and only drank kosher wine, which made the usual practice of repairing to the faculty club for drinks inappropriate.

The risk-society and rise-of-actuarialism literature, insightful as it is, cannot account for the vast amount of time and energy spent not only by official liquor control bodies but even by private organizations (the graduate school, in this instance) in a policing enterprise that has no relationship at all to health or safety risks. The 'rise of risk' literature is insightful, but in drawing attention to the modernizing, risk-management aspects of contemporary regulation it systematically underrates the persistence of highly moralized techniques that are not efficient from the point of view of managing populations or maximizing health but which are nevertheless qualitatively and quantitatively significant. Obversely, the risk-society literature tends to produce in scholars a tendency to notice only the moralism of our ancestors, while neglecting to document their innovations in risk management. In order to correct this tendency, this chapter attempts to utilize conceptual tools such as normalization and risk management without automatically periodizing them. Discipline and risk are analytical entities, not separate systems. In the real world there are many mechanisms (such as liquor control boards) and specific techniques (such as prohibiting the sale of spirits by the glass) that are not easily classifiable as either risk techniques or disciplinary techniques.

Let us now turn to two case studies of the intertwining of discipline and risk in the context of the repeal of North American general prohibition laws. The repeal of general prohibition[27] is an obvious choice of empirical site for our purposes, since it gave authorities a chance to start from scratch, as it were, free from the historical baggage and vested economic interests that have always weighed down the licencing debates in countries that have never gone through general prohibition. The next section will examine the licencing debates of the post-repeal period. This will be followed by an analysis of a set of specific prohibitions that existed before, during, and after Prohibition: aboriginal prohibitions.

## DISCIPLINING THE OWNERS, RISK-MANAGING THE DRINKERS: THE IMAGINARY SALOON IN THE POST-REPEAL PERIOD

Contrary to the stereotypes of the worried Puritan and the happy-go-lucky advocate of prohibition repeal, American historians have shown that the pro-repeal (wet) forces were as full of anxiety about the future as their puritanical opponents. Could drinking be legalized without bringing in its wake all the social evils of the demon rum? Would bootleggers come to dominate the liquor trade in the new era? Would liquor control laws be disregarded and disobeyed just as prohibitory laws had been? The multifarious anxieties of the repeal period converged, and indeed condensed into, a single image: the saloon.

The saloon had been a central, perhaps even the central, institution of masculine working-class culture, as Roy Rosenzweig's well-known study, among others, has shown.[28] As Joseph Gusfield notes, "In the long effort of middle-class America to cope with the moral disorder it attributed to urban growth, the saloon was imagined as the home of the dangerous classes and the vivid symbol of a popular culture that spawned immorality".[29] By the late 1920s, when some liquor sales began to be legalized in Canadian provinces and repeal became a probability in the United States, the Holy Grail of alcohol policy was the following question: how could governments legalize some sales of alcoholic drinks, restore the legality shaken by bootlegging, and raise some much-needed tax revenue, without bringing back the unpleasant features and dreaded consequences of the saloon?

Was the saloon a particular type of place? Was it the presence of particular people that made the saloon what it was? Was the saloon characterized by a particular kind of drink? Or by extra-alcoholic features such as the presence of loose women and of lewd music? Both wets and drys agreed that they did not want the seamy saloon to return; but what exactly made a drinking establishment a saloon? That the question facing authorities engaged in the emotionally charged task of re-legalizing alcohol sales was a thoroughly technical one was recognized by some of the participants. A study commissioned in 1935 by John Rockefeller of the first few years of American states' efforts to begin the government of alcohol from scratch made this point. Luther Gulick, director of the Institute of Public Administration and major New Deal figure, stressed in his introduction to this volume that alcohol control was not about solving the ideological battle between wets and drys, but was rather a *technical* issue:

> The major questions of public policy and the questions of administrative policy are intimately intertwined. 'The saloon shall not return' is an excellent illustration of this fact. As a policy, this statement is widely endorsed, by the President, by governors, by the press, and by most articulate groups. It was undoubtedly the mandate of the people in most areas. But how? Through what administrative devices? Here was the rub.[30]

The first technique to ensure the non-return of the saloon was, not surprisingly, the abolition of the word saloon. "Beverage rooms", "beer

**Saloon in the Waterloo area, *c.* 1900. Note the spittoon on the floor and the absence of tables and chairs, in contrast to the more genteel atmosphere of most drinking establishments later in the twentieth century. (Courtesy of the Seagram Collection, University of Waterloo, Ontario.)**

parlours", "hotels", "cocktail lounges", and other terms proliferated in the post-repeal management of licenced establishments. The words that never appeared – the repressed terms lurking under the discourse, as it were – were 'saloon' and 'bar'.

This censorship of those two words seems to have been the most popular, most consistently used technique for governing alcohol in the post-repeal period, in the United States and in Canada. But the authorities were well aware of the fact that banning a word was not sufficient. Thus, they quickly undertook the more difficult task of specifying which spatial and time arrangements, which bits of furniture or types of conduct were constitutive of the saloon and as such subject to prohibition in the new, non-saloon establishments.

The techniques devised and implemented by liquor regulators to address this overriding question of post-repeal policy are far too numerous and heterogeneous to list. This is not surprising, since no definition of the essential, as opposed to the accidental or contingent, features of the saloon was ever produced. But a sense of the rich regulatory imagination of the anonymous officials of the new state liquor agencies can be obtained by briefly discussing two topics that generated much regulatory interest: 1) food; 2) the stand-up bar.

In respect to food, one technique widely used in many states of the United States to legalize public drinking without legalizing the saloon was to confine licences to restaurants. This clever idea was quickly proven to be unenforceable, however, since no authority ever devised a legally actionable definition of a meal (as any anthropologist might have predicted). Publicans could easily dispense free sandwiches or put out snacks, but the result was then not a restaurant but a saloon with some food lying about. The authoritative Harrison and Laine study of American post-repeal regulations stated: "In New York, to cite only a single example, there are scores of licenced premises which by no stretch of imagination could be called bona fide restaurants."[31]

The linkage between the saloon and food was sometimes reversed. In a number of Canadian provinces, for several decades after the end of prohibition, the only drink that could be consumed in public was beer (rather than the whisky favoured by saloon patrons), and beer could in turn only be had in hotels. Although the hotels of course had dining rooms, the beer business was strictly segregated. Whether to save the moral sensibilities of middle-class hotel guests or to prevent the mixing of the pure pleasures of food with the impure pleasures of alcohol, food and drink were rigidly kept apart.[32] In Toronto, hotel proprietors vainly requested permission from the Liquor Control Board to use dining rooms to hold the overflow crowd during the beer rush hour, but the board held firm to its theory about the incompatibility of food and beer.[33] In western Canada, when beer parlours were legalized, food was banned, as in Ontario, rather than mandated, as in the United States. The food category also included soft drinks: as Robert Campbell's detailed study of British Columbia licencing states, when the Liquor Control Board allowed beer parlours to open in March of 1925, "parlour operators sold only beer; they could not stock soft drinks, food or cigarettes". In 1954, British Columbia beer parlours were finally allowed to sell sandwiches, but not meals, while the establishments in the legal category of dining rooms could serve alcoholic drinks with meals but not without, with the definition of meal being left to the inspector's discretion.[34]

The general rationality of moderation and disciplined enjoyment that underpinned the 'no to the saloon' sentiment and also grounded the alcohology project documented in chapter 4 was, therefore, as difficult to operationalize as Luther Gulick had predicted in 1936. The American attempt to force people into Southern European patterns of drinking by giving liquor licences only to restaurants was quickly foiled by the creativity of licence holders and by the customers' persistence in not eating even when food was free. The opposite tactic of removing all food from the beer parlours and taverns, a tactic sometimes said to be justified as a measure to force working-class men home for their meals, did not necessarily achieve the desired effect, and was indeed criticized as forcing people to become drunk through drinking on an empty stomach.[35] No generally accepted solution to the question of how to link food and public drinking was ever found.

If the linkage between food and the objective of disciplined, orderly drinking was never defined to general satisfaction, there were by contrast few differences regarding the key physical embodiment of the saloon, namely the stand-up bar. Long associated in North America with urban workingmen drinking their paycheck away, as well as with cowboys having bar fights and shoot-outs, the bar was generally banned in the new, post-repeal drinking establishments. California, Indiana, and a handful of other states did allow for what was euphemistically described as "counter service", but most other states specifically prohibited this particular fixture, as well as the associated behaviour of walking toward the bartender when entering the room and asking for a drink. Some jurisdictions combined the regulation of furniture with other projects: in Massachussetts, for instance, "women are not allowed in taverns, and must be seated while drinking in other establishments".[36]

Now, as in the case of meals, it was impossible to generate a legally tight definition of a bar, for it was never clear whether the problem lay in the physical design of the counter, in the workingmen's practice of standing up to drink, or in the across-the-counter sociability of bartender and patron. Given the lack of agreement on the ontology of the bar, there could be no specific rule banning the bar itself; what there was, instead, was a positive demand that patrons must be *seated*, often specifying that they must be seated *at tables*. In Ontario, and also in British Columbia, "no bar was permitted; patrons could not stand and drink. They sat at tables where waiters served them draft or bottled beer."[37] Western Canadian beer parlours continued to enforce the table service rule into the 1970s, as did "beverage rooms" in Ontario.

The obsession with the imaginary saloon was likely at work in other practices that have no discursive elaboration but would appear to have been designed to abolish the easy sociability of men standing at a bar. In early Ontario beverage rooms, for instance, the beer was dispensed into glasses in a separate taproom not accessible to customers, and then brought to the seated patrons by a waiter. This disposition of space made chatting with the barman as he poured beer, a traditional saloon activity, physically impossible.

Beer parlours and beverage rooms were not allowed to serve anything other than beer, a prohibition which could be and was sometimes read as a positive injunction to consume beer. As time went on, however, the demand that beer be drunk was moderated, as the total ban on the public consumption of spirits by the glass was modified and eventually repealed. The highly indirect and complex way in which this was done, however, suggests that Luther Gulick's and Joseph Gusfield's insight about the centrality of the saloon in post-repeal liquor governance remains valid for the later period, the more hedonistic post-World War II environment. The physical bar and the sale of whisky by the glass were legalized only after being thoroughly cleansed of saloon connotations: enter that innovation in drinking history, the cocktail.

It was the establishments legally known as 'cocktail lounges', created mostly in the post-World War II period, that were for the first time after many decades allowed to bring back the bar. Cocktails were not a postwar invention: they became popular in the 1920s, figuring centrally, for instance, in the American classic novel of that time, *The great Gatsby*. But it was only in the 1940s that cocktails emerged from middle-class living rooms and illicit Harlem dives into the legal light of day.

In the new establishments serving mixed drinks, the fixture allowing patrons to stand and drink was called a "counter" rather than a bar, as if to invoke the respectable institution of department-store shopping. The department-store connotation was not accidental. Class, sex, and gender had to be simultaneously reorganized in relation to spirits drinking in order to make the cocktail lounge possible. In respect to sex and gender, heterosexuality in the context of public drinking, which in the era of beer parlours had been associated with prostitution, was now revalorized and made central to the new legal category of the cocktail lounge. But this was a new, historically specific form of heterosexuality, namely the postwar heterosexuality associated with middle-class consumerism and early marriage,[38] a sexual mechanism that was as far removed from the loose women of the saloon as the cocktail was from nineteenth century grog.

Cocktail lounges (created in 1947 in Ontario and in 1954 in British Columbia) were innovative in no longer being compelled to segregate the sexes as the beer parlours had done. Indeed, in keeping with the dual logic of prohibition and compulsion of liquor licencing, cocktail lounges were forbidden to segregate patrons by gender. In some cocktail lounges, male patrons who did not come with a female companion were provided with a temporary partner who would chat with them and encourage them to buy more drinks (as in the Manhattan bar immortalized in the 1945 alcoholism film *The lost weekend*). Mixing the sexes, therefore, went hand in hand with mixing the drinks. In sharp contrast to the straight whisky favoured by saloon men, the liquor contained in cocktails was diluted with other liquids and aesthetically embellished with coloured drinks, paper umbrellas, olives, plastic stir sticks, and so forth. If the cocktail, the drink of choice of American middle-class consumeristic heterosexuality, was not the descendant of the pre-prohibition bar whisky but rather its symbolic opposite, so too the cocktail lounges were not the descendants but rather the polar opposites of the saloon, in the minds of officials as in popular representations. Having performed the symbolic labour of resignifying and cleansing spirits drinking, cocktail lounges were allowed – indeed, were compelled – by law to have a bar. But, to discourage working-class men from using these bars to socialize with each other and drink standing up, as was their time-honoured custom, the bars – or, more accurately, counters – were forced, in both Ontario and British Columbia, to have stools.[39]

The triumph of the cocktail in the 1950s could be read as a disguised return of the saloon, insofar as it involved the legalization of public spirits drinking and of the bar/counter, after forty or so years. But it could equally plausibly be argued that it was only with the legalization of cocktail lounges that the very rich historical experiences associated with the North American saloon were finally buried. A whole world of working-class male experience – the world of the saloon – was gone, never to return. The shiny counter and the leatherette stools of American 1960s bars were of course used by workingmen out for a beer or a whisky, as well as by respectable couples consuming martinis; even today, wine bars for yuppies have not totally eliminated the working-class bar. But the class and gender meanings of spirits drinking dramatically shifted in the post-World War II period.

This admittedly sketchy study of the spectre of the saloon in post-repeal practices shows that, after the legal repeal of prohibition, the war against intemperance did not so much end as continue to be waged by other means. Indeed, there is evidence to suggest that the post-repeal period, usually interpreted as the replacement of draconian prohibition by enlightened regulation, was in fact characterized by a mad prolifera-tion of prohibitions. In Canada and in many American states, food and music were prohibited, heterosexuality was prohibited unless men and women already came as couples, drinking whisky was for many years prohibited, serving drinks to intoxicated patrons was prohibited. And, apart from these and other general mini-prohibitions, the immense discretionary powers of liquor inspectors could and did generate a constant stream of micro-prohibitions that were specific to the licencee.

But if the post-repeal period, during which contemporary North American systems of liquor control and liquor licencing were built up, can with justice be characterized as the multiplication rather than the retreat of the sovereign strategy of prohibition, it should also be noted that the post-repeal period is also characterized by a proliferation of *imperatives* to consume alcohol. The banning of all activities except beer drinking from beer parlours had the effect of *forcing* everyone to drink heavily, for lack of anything else to do.[40] And cocktail lounges caused respectable women, who had formerly tended to stay away from public drinking establishments, to drink, and to drink not wine or beer but hard liquor, disguised under sugared mixers. The obsessive concern with the cleanliness of the premises and the conduct of the patrons coexisted with a remarkable lack of concern about the total amount of alcohol imbibed either by each individual or in the aggregate. As long as patrons did not sing, dance, transgress the spatial boundaries assigned to them, or infringe the food regulations, they could drink all they wanted; and indeed the system assumed that the *only* valid reason for entering a beer parlour or tavern was to drink.

Liquor inspectors did look at bathrooms and fire escapes as well as at drinking behaviour, but in doing so they were not engaged in pure actuarialism.[41] Unlike insurance inspectors, liquor officials were charged with the management of *moral* risks: the unclean bathrooms were evaluated from the point of view of the moral atmosphere of the establishment. Moral risks are more like old-fashioned dangers than like actuarial figures or statistical correlations.[42] The management of moral dangers has often been handled through illiberal and highly intrusive techniques, and in this respect liquor licencing has more in common with the regulation of prostitution and gambling than with insurance or epidemiology.

Precisely because the risks of drinking were not actuarial or epidemiological but rather moral and cultural, no expertise was thought to be required to measure them. Officials used their own commonsense rather than sociological studies or morbidity calculations to determine both policy and individual discretionary decisions. Actuarial studies relevant to liquor licencing policy can be imagined, and indeed a few such studies have been done. (One such study showed that, contrary to the saloon image of male-on-male violence in bars, "drinkers observed in bars were twice as likely to kiss and hug than to behave aggressively".)[43] But liquor licencing and liquor inspection have remained even to this day virtually unaffected by social or medical science. Risk discourses and measurement techniques generated at other sites (e.g. epidemiology) sometimes now flow through the space of the bar, for instance in warnings printed on bottle labels and in the signs warning pregnant women about drinking that one finds in some licenced premises. But liquor licencing itself, as distinct from other modes of governing alcohol that also traverse the space of the bar, remains the domain of commonsense – proving that risk management is not always dependent on either professional expertise or on numerical calculations.

In North America, liquor licencing developed at a time when the grand temperance project to individually reform drinkers had been largely abandoned as a result of the failures of prohibition, and the psychological projects to diagnose the alcoholic personality that developed in the 1940s and 1950s had not yet developed. Liquor licencing is, at one level, a machine for circumventing the age-old problems of governing drinking behaviour by simply shifting the target of governance *away* from the individual drinker. And yet, liquor licencing does not abandon the goals and techniques of discipline: on the contrary, it provides the state with a tool to exercise intense moral regulation over the licence holders. But, perhaps because of its origins at a time – the 1930s and 1940s – when there was little interest in 'alcoholism' at the clinical level, the proliferation of prohibitions and compulsions acting upon proprietors coexisted with a positive refusal to use state resources, for instance, inspectors, to govern drinkers. Presented with the perennial problem of public drunkenness, the Liquor Control Board of Ontario never asked itself whether the drunks were lacking in willpower, whether they should be medically treated, or whether they should be punished. It simply asked whether the publican was entitled to use force to eject the drunks into the streets, or whether other means for dealing with drunks should have been devised.[44] Individual drinkers and their medical or psychological problems were thought to be beyond the scope of state governance.

Disciplining environments and publicans, then, through mechanisms heavily laden with the most prohibitory tactics of sovereign governance, liquor licencing is an innovative system for managing the risks of drinking without touching the individual drinker, in a type of risk governance characterized by moralization and commonsense. The ability to combine such diverse techniques of governance in a single bureaucracy may be what explains the taken-for-granted persistence in our own times of byzantine systems of state regulation of individual consumption that are neither economic nor health-promoting. The coexistence of such different vectors and objects of of governance within the same apparatus suggests that it may be fruitful to undertake further case studies of governance that do not a priori periodize forms of power/knowledge or make assumptions about the character of specific techniques.

If discipline and risk management are intimately intertwined in licencing strategies, forms of governance that are older and more coercive than either risk management or individual discipline are also found in the field of liquor control. One strategy for liquor control that starkly reminds us of the persistence of sovereign despotism consists of what I call 'specific prohibitions'. Today, the most important one of these is age-related. That specific prohibitions are closely related to the exclusions of liberal citizenship is perhaps most clear in the case of aboriginal people, who, very much like children, have often been considered unfit to even attempt to develop practices of self, such as moderate drinking.

ABORIGINALITY, ALCOHOL, AND THE FEAR OF EXCESS

In Papua New Guinea, in Australia, in the United States, and in Canada, the sale of any alcoholic drink to aboriginal people was prohibited during long periods of time, in many cases until the 1960s. Like age-related exclusions, race-related liquor laws define maturity, citizenship, and responsibility. The repeal of aboriginal prohibition was in many jurisdictions linked, either directly or merely temporally, with the granting of suffrage.

Specific prohibitions use alcohol as a means or a site for the gover-nance of 'problem' subpopulations. Specific prohibitions separate those whose drinking has to be controlled externally through a simple ban from those (the 'general population') whose drinking patterns are thought to be subject to self-control and the exercise of one's own will. The problem subpopulations are not allowed to develop a relation of self to self in the practices of drinking – or in the usually intertwined practices of citizenship.

Where it exists today, aboriginal prohibition is generally justified by reference to the susceptibility (either cultural or genetic) of certain 'races' to the disease of alcoholism. But this association was not always made by alcohol experts. The late nineteenth century experts discussed in chapter 2 made a link between aboriginality and excess: but the link was in terms of drunkenness, not in terms of inebriety or alcoholism. Aboriginal peoples, and non-white races more generally, were thought to be like children in a number of ways; and, like children, they could not control their intake of alcohol because they had a very low innate ability to defer gratification and regulate their own pleasures. Thus, they got drunk easily and recklessly, but they did not suffer from the neurasthenic weakness of inebriety.

Thomas Jefferson, who was responsible for the first American prohibition of alcohol sales to aboriginals, stated that Indians could not withstand the cultural impact of white settlement, including the whisky trade, because "the Indian could only be considered a child".[45] This view was repeated by missionaries who wanted to protect natives from the white liquor traders, and reiterated by alcohol experts on both sides of the Atlantic. A British physician expressed this view as follows:

> Some people and nationalities are in the 'infantile' stage – the 'bout and orgie' stage – the state of External Control ... Others are in the 'adolescent' stage ... All savage races are without toleration [for alcohol] for the same reason that children are. They live in the 'bout and orgie' stage ... It is pure ineptitude to ask the New Zealander or the Dahomian to control his appetite for liquor while both are devoid of control in every other matter.[46]

The American physician who did the most work propagating the idea of inebriety as a disease entity, Dr Thomas Crothers, specified that, although black people certainly get drunk, they are not inebriates: they lack the sensitive neurological mechanism whose difficulties lead both to neurasthenia and to inebriety.[47] Another American physician stated, as a matter of well-known fact, that the "blonde races" are more prone to alcoholism than other races, while another reported that Mexico's traditional alcoholic beverages were being supplanted by Anglo-Saxon drinks with the result that "alcoholism" was spreading: "It is an unfortunate fact that wherever the northern races go they carry their vices with them."[48]

That North American aboriginals are of course more northern than most Europeans, in the geographical sense, did not upset this view of northern vs. southern vices: the north–south dichotomy so commonly deployed in the psy sciences around the turn of the century was an imaginary geography, not a matter of latitude. Africans, Maoris, and Australian Aborigines were lumped together with the Blackfoot, the Cree and the Kwaikutl in order to preserve the belief that, as the noted Edinburgh psychiatrist Sir Thomas Clouston put it, "there is an essential difference in the power of CONTROL" between "northern" and "southern" races.[49]

Since the bouts and orgies of aboriginals were not rooted in individual psychic defects but in the essential, ahistorical features of their race, there was no effort made to govern aboriginal drinking through the individual, either through discipline or through pastoral reform. Natives were to be physically prevented from consuming intoxicating liquors.

In Australia and in the United States, where native people learned to drink alcohol from the 'rough' white males with whom they had the most contact in the colonial period, it became possible to develop a paternalistic myth of the primal innocence and purity of all aboriginal peoples. This often paternalistic association of aboriginality with pristine temperance was less plausible in Africa. Rather than attempt to separate aboriginal people from alcohol, the colonial strategies pursued there generally involved confining them to whatever drinks were thought to be traditional, while restricting or prohibiting access to European drinks. For instance, the colonial powers agreed in 1919 to ban trade spirits in sub-Saharan Africa – with 'trade spirits' referring to the distilled drinks produced in Europe specifically for African customers, most notably the 'Dutch gin' and American rum that were widely sold in West Africa.[50]

Alternatively, a strategy pursued in Africa at other times involved banning the *native* rather than the imported liquors. This was effected in South Africa by the dual strategy of using the police to suppress African women's alcoholic drink business, while simultaneously pushing African men into consuming the official beer dispensed in municipal beer halls.[51] In Ghana, a British colonial governor justified his government's support of the new brewery built specifically to supplant the local palm-wine trade by invoking the image of the archetypal English glass of ale:

> What is the secret of England's greatness? Certainly not lime juice. Anyhow beer is not as bad as gin, and not nearly so bad as the liquor which is manufactured by certain enterprising persons of this country by means of two old petrol tins and a piece of copper tubing.[52]

The question of liquor and race, therefore, did not always give rise to systems for preventing aboriginals from touching *all* drink. The authorities handled the question in a variety of ways, sometimes instituting prohibition but at other times enforcing rules about which liquids were prohibited, which ones were allowed, and which ones were compulsory. The missionaries generally sought to align colonial rule with both specific and general prohibition projects,[53] but the political authorities of colonialism pursued a number of different projects in different places, some in conjunction with missionaries but many in opposition to them. In nineteenth century North America, the liquor trade served a number of very important economic functions for certain groups of whites and for some Indians;[54] and elsewhere liquor trading issues created major rifts between different colonial powers, most notably in Africa, but also in the South Pacific.[55]

But even in the United States and Canada, where aboriginal prohibition was pursued with relative vigour at least at the level of official policymaking, it is clear even from the sketchy evidence available that liquor laws governed racial status as much as, and perhaps more effectively than, they governed drinking. And the particular effect that liquor laws had on racial formation was to institute a binary distinction between Indians and whites that did not reflect existing

**Men drinking in South African liquor shop. (1877 engraving, unknown source, courtesy of Wellcome Institute Library, London.)**

patterns of intermarriage and cultural hybridity. To make matters more complicated, the binary racial opposition created by liquor laws did not necessarily follow other legal definitions of Indian status. Let us first turn to the Canadian situation.

The federal Indian Act defined Indians narrowly and legalistically, making "Indian" coterminous with those aboriginal people who signed treaties with the Crown and their direct descendants on the male line only. Such groups as the Dene and the Inuit (Eskimo) were never official Indians, since they never signed treaties. The federal Indian Act defined the relation between official Indians and alcohol quite precisely, by making it an offence to sell, barter, or give alcoholic drinks to Indians. It is interesting to note that unlike in nineteenth century American law, which only prohibited whites selling to Indians – a more clearly paternalistic rationale – Canadian law prohibited Indians as well as whites from selling alcoholic drinks to Indians.

A foreshadowing of the problems inherent in these statutes is contained in the wording of the legislation itself. The law stated that both white and Indian liquor providers break the law if they give drinks to "any Indian or non-treaty Indian, or any person male or female who is reputed to belong to a particular Indian band, or who follows the Indian mode of life . . .".[56] The liquor provisions of the Indian Act thus opened the door for a legally questionable broadening of the definition of Indian. People who did not get the benefits of band membership, and who had to pay taxes like white Canadians instead of being exempt like treaty Indians, were nevertheless to be governed as Indians for liquor purposes if they "followed *the* Indian mode of life". This undefined phrase was no dead letter: in one of the few reported cases relating to these issues, a judge instituted an inquiry into the identity of a drinker and determined that although "his father was French and his mother a squaw", since he had voted in Indian band elections although he claimed to have given up the Indian mode of life, he was an Indian for the purposes of liquor laws.[57]

Provincial and municipal police forces had been enforcing, or not enforcing, these federal laws for years by the time that provincial liquor boards were set up. But the new liquor boards established parallel mechanisms for policing alcohol sales, quite independently of police forces: archival records of the first few years of the Liquor Control Board of Ontario provide evidence that, at the level of government-owned liquor stores, aboriginality was an important dimension of regulation.

In the first year of its operation, the Ontario Board issued at least two circulars to all store managers around the province to guide them on this issue. The first was a response to a situation in a small town, where the liquor store manager had reported on an Indian attempting to get an individual liquor permit. The board stated that, even though the Indian did not live on a reserve but rather in town, and paid taxes there, nevertheless he should not be granted a permit.

> There are a few persons in most Indian bands who for one reason or another are not on the membership list of the band although they were born and brought up on the reserve . . . The fact that an Indian pays taxes and votes in the municipality in which he resides does not of itself change his status.[58]

This circular was misleading in that it did not clearly tell store managers that Indians who gave up Indian status were indeed allowed to buy alcohol.[59] But the board was not alone in moving the boundary of indianness back and forth: the federal Indian Act and subsequent judicial interpretations had helped to confuse the issue by regarding lifestyle (for instance, wearing moccasins) rather than genetics as determinative of Indian identity, so that the board's quasi-legal determination that the category of potentially intoxicated Indian was broader than the category of legally acknowledged Indians was not altogether mistaken.

166

This circular did not produce the desired effects. A year later the board sent around another circular commenting on "unfortunate cases" of Indians obtaining liquor for off-site consumption from the new government stores. The board now seemed aware of the legal fact that Indians who gave up their status were allowed to drink on the same basis as whites, but it showed a great reluctance to allow these legally white people legal rights: "Even in the case of enfranchised Indians who may have established their exemption from the provisions of the Indian Act, caution needs to be exercised, *for obvious reasons* [emphasis added]."[60]

It was not until the 1960s that the "obvious reasons" began to be questioned, and legal challenges to aboriginal prohibition began to appear on the Canadian legal landscape. The myth of Indians as lacking control over drinking was as strong as ever; but, despite the persistence of this representation, it was no longer thought to be legally acceptable to make specific laws for aboriginal people other than those arising from treaty issues. The precedent-setting case was *R. vs. Drybones*, decided by the Supreme Court in 1967. Using the Canadian Bill of Rights, the court struck down section 94 of the Indian Act, which made it an offence for an Indian to be intoxicated outside of a reserve. The singling out of racial identity in this manner, such that conduct that would no longer be prohibited for a white person was prohibited for Indians, was said to be no longer tenable.[61]

Many Canadians are under the impression that the *Drybones* case ended the special liquor regime for aboriginal people, but in fact the special regime was continued through geographically specific rather than identity-specific distinctions for almost two more decades. The 1971 *R. vs. Whiteman* case decided that, although it was impermissible to single out Indians as a group, it was not a problem to make intoxication *on a reserve* an offence. The fact that few white people would ever be found consuming anything on a reserve was not thought to make the law unconstitutional under the *Drybones* principles.[62]

It was only in 1985 that special liquor offences concerning aboriginal people and aboriginal spaces were removed from the Indian Act, probably because the government feared a challenge under the then relatively new Charter of Rights. Nevertheless, during the many decades that they had been in effect, the intoxicant sections of the Indian Act had helped to constitute the image of 'the drunken Indian', and had connected this image not to official legal Indian status but to the cultural category of the Indian mode of life. The existence of these special laws had also given legal and judicial authorities support to institute quasi-anthropological inquiries into culture and lineage that insisted on drawing a clear line between whites and aboriginals, failing to recognize the cultural and genetic hybridity of a significant percentage of the Canadian population. This sort of anthropological jurisprudence is visible in the following excerpt from a judicial decision:

> Daignault, who was present when Pepin got the liquor, swore that he never knew that Pepin took treaty [i.e. obtained official Indian status], although he knew that he was a half-breed. Pepin himself was examined before me, and he swore that he never dressed like an Indian, . . . that he never wore moccasins . . . As a matter of fact Pepin speaks English fluently, and dresses better than many ordinary white men, and there is no indication whatever in his appearance, in his language or in his general demeanour that he does not belong to the better class of half-breeds.[63]

Given the persistence of alcohol-related illnesses and violence among Canadian aboriginal people to this day, there is little evidence to suggest that the specific prohibitions set out in the Indian Act actually protected them from the risks of drinking and alcoholism.[64] But this brief survey of the cases suggests that the prohibitions certainly had effects, even if they did not prevent drinking. First, by making most drinking by aboriginals illegal and by banning them from licenced premises, they excluded aboriginals from many of the circuits of sociability, employment contacts, and so forth, that were important for the white working class, particularly men. An aboriginal World War II veteran, interviewed in 1996, stated that he had never obtained information about veterans' benefits because this information circulated through the Canadian veterans' organization, the Legion: Legion halls generally consisting of bars and little else, as an official Indian he had never been allowed to enter Legion premises.[65] Secondly, aboriginal prohibition had the effect of instituting various legal inquiries into issues of race, kinship, lineage, culture, and manners, in such a way as to maintain the fiction that aboriginal people have unchanging traditions instead of history, as well as the related fiction that people had to be either Indian or white.

In the United States, a somewhat similar federal prohibition of alcohol sales to aboriginal people worked in slightly different ways. Unlike the Canadian provisions, American law selected only treaty Indians for inclusion under the alcohol prohibition statutes, thus saving judges from having to carry out anthropological inquiries into cultural identity. And also unlike the Canadian provisions, for most of the nineteenth century American prohibition concerned not only a people but also a semi-fictional, semi-legal place: 'Indian country'.[66] Indian country was a negatively defined region, referring to land that was neither designed as a reservation nor part of a state of the United States. It was a liminal region, neither American nor Indian, in which few laws operated, but which was curiously constituted by liquor laws, since the attempt to define and enforce aboriginal prohibition was a major way in which Indian country came to be defined, as William Unrau's study has shown.

In 1862 the federal government attempted to make the law somewhat more specific and enforceable, by removing the vague phrase "Indian country" and specifying the meaning of "Indian" persons. However, "Indian country" reappeared in the 1874 revised federal statutes – an anachronistic move, since by then most Indians in the midwest had been confined to reservations and the no-man's-land of "Indian country" had been therefore much reduced. This did not last, however, since in 1876 a federal judge made a ruling that invalidated the 1874 law.[67]

The phrase "to an Indian in Indian country" was therefore struck from the statutes as of 1876. Eventually, in 1892, Congress passed a new law enforcing aboriginal prohibition, this time including beer, wine, and bitters as well as the traditional spirits. This meant that aboriginals (aboriginal men, by and large) now obtained liquor in the black market, paying bootleg prices and being excluded from the saloon, that public space of male working-class sociability.

In Canada, enforcing the specific prohibitions regarding aboriginal people led to inquiries into the cultural constituents of racial identity. In the United States, liquor prohibitions regarding aboriginal people gave rise to a number of judicial inquiries into the *place* of Indianness, a place that was a space within law as much as a social space or a cultural creation.

The workings of aboriginal prohibition are thus theoretically as well as empirically interesting. It has been difficult in most societies to govern race directly, but race has certainly been governed. Liquor laws are one of the sites in which this indirect regulation has been constituted, often in ways not determined by the workings of better-established legal categories, such as official Indian status. This is a specific instance of the more general argument made in this chapter to the effect that the complex machineries of liquor control and liquor licencing that exist in all English-speaking countries and many non-English speaking ones have had, and continue to have, a number of quite heterogeneous effects in many areas of social life not obviously connected to alcohol. Governing through alcohol is everywhere an ad hoc, unsystematic, non-professionalized 'minor' practice that takes very different forms and is articulated with all manner of extraneous objectives and habits of governance. Its study may be informative, therefore, for those who are interested in complicating the picture painted by many contemporary sociologists of living in an expert-dominated risk society. That risks have been managed without expert knowledges, that disciplinary control over minute details coexists with hedonistic consumption, that regulation is not necessarily the opposite of prohibition, and that governing *through* an object such as alcohol may often involve governing all sorts of activities, spaces, and identities without doing much to govern drinking itself, are conclusions arising from this specific study of liquor laws but potentially useful across a wide range of fields. In addition, the study of liquor control, liquor licencing, bar inspection, and aboriginal prohibition serves as a useful reminder that the more liberal and/or pastoral modes of governance deployed in respect to adult, white, male alcoholics are not the only ways in which alcoholic 'excess' has been governed.

# CHAPTER 7

# REDUCING RISKS, REPLACING FLUIDS

The state bureaucracies of liquor control, licencing, and prohibition are by no means the only mechanisms regulating the risks of drinking. This chapter will examine a few of the numerous other ways in which this is done. The first section of the chapter will cover a diverse group of programmes that seek to manage either drinking itself or some of its collateral effects – programmes gathered under the twin banners of risk and harm. It will be argued that, although projects to regulate and minimize the risks of drinking at the level of collectivities can indeed be characterized as forms of neoliberal risk management, the harm-reduction programmes aimed at individuals are often nothing but miniaturized and personalized systems of liquor control. And if harm reduction programmes designed to enable individual drinkers to control or moderate their drinking are only partially neoliberal, the targetting of pregnant women under the rubric of 'harm to fetuses/ babies' is even less liberal. Governing through risk factors does not always take the form of impersonal risk management, as a brief discussion of 'fetal alcohol effects' will show.

The second section will explore, in a suggestive rather than exhaustive fashion, some of the strategies that have been deployed to replace alcoholic drinks by liquids that have very different meanings.[1] Some of these, most notably coffee, act in most cases as the polar opposite of alcohol: if alcohol represents the pleasures and the dangers of indulgence, coffee represents the sober virtues of hard work. But the case of the history of Coca-Cola shows that temperance can be detached from puritanism: sobriety can also be promoted by inciting consumers to enjoy rather than deny themselves. While, in the nineteenth century, non-alcoholic drinks were often consumed under the banner of virtue, thrift, and hard work, Coca-Cola managed to escape the connotations of dull, health-conscious domesticity that are still attached today to drinks such as Ovaltine and herbal tea. Perhaps "Coke is the real thing" because, although it started out life as a health drink, it quickly became a symbol and a technology of American consumerism, a vehicle for an "enlightened hedonism" through which Americans could enjoy all the pleasures that in Europe would have required alcohol, but without any of alcohol's risks and harms.

## HARM TO THE SELF: CONTROLLED OR 'MODERATE' DRINKING

Many people today, ranging from addiction experts to consumers of alcohol and other problem substances, reject all treatment strategies that are based on the notion of alcoholism or that are in other ways rooted directly in the diseases of the will tradition. These people often show more interest in programmes seeking to provide drinkers with non-moralistic counselling that does not divide the population into distinct identity categories and that enables individuals to define their own problem and set their own reform goals. This type of counselling, however, is, in the field of drinking, rarely non-directive. In other fields, there are some harm-reduction programmes that manage to avoid stigmatizing the activity or the person, and that confine themselves to helping the user to control or minimize the collateral effects of using the substance. Needle exchange programmes provided under the rubric of HIV prevention are probably the best example of such innovative approaches.

With respect to drinking, there are a number of privately and publicly initiated programmes for regulating alcohol consumption that employ neoliberal risk-management techniques that carefully avoid value judgements about drinking itself. In the province of Ontario, a jurisdiction with a long history of openly moralistic laws controlling both alcohol and other pleasures, both the liquor control board and manufacturers of alcoholic beverages now suggest, in impersonal advertising, that drinking is not necessarily harmful, and that the main risk to be avoided is *driving* under the influence. "If you drink, don't drive" is a message widely disseminated in billboards and signs. Along similar lines, the plastic bags in which clerks at Ontario's government liquor stores put wine bottles bear a legend commemorating the liquor control board's seventieth anniversary – "70 years of serving you responsibly". This legend suggests that there is nothing wrong with drinking as long as the distribution of liquor is in responsible hands.

A similar logic is at work in the recent changes in the governance of undergraduate beer drinking by American colleges and fraternities. As

Jonathan Simon has documented, alcohol is still regulated, but now under the rationality of safety, not temperance. In other contexts the issue of safety, particularly when articulated to fear of crime, has converged with neoconservative moves to re-stigmatize drinkers and drinking: the clearest example of this is the decline of the intoxication defense documented in chapter 8. But in the context of college life, safety appears more as a matter of consumer protection than of crime. Students are all treated as consumers in need of basic protection, without heavy drinkers being targetted. Simon writes:

> Much as the consumer movement has more broadly emphasized the need to regulate the context of consumption in the name of consumers by intervening in marketing, sales, and even the production of goods and services, the new rationality of government in higher education seeks to regulate the environment in which student choices are made. It emphasizes the risks rather than the moral stigma of various disfavoured behaviours, and seeks to manage comprehensively the environment in which behaviour takes place, in the name of reducing risk.[2]

In contrast to the risk-management logic of corporate harm-reduction plans, most programmes designed for individual drinkers amount to personalized liquor control systems that tend to act more on the drinker's soul than on the environment, for that is the only space within the jurisdiction of the drinker. Colleges may govern the time and place and consequences of drinking, as do pub proprietors, but individual drinkers are rarely (in fact, never) organized into consumer groups to change the environment of drinking. Instead, the relevant health or psy authorities enlist the drinker in the project of constituting an orderly life and a well-regulated soul, in which – as in the well-run pub – the enjoyment of pleasure does not disrupt the prevailing ethical order.

Unlike state liquor control systems, programmes promoting what is known in Europe as "controlled drinking" and in North America as "moderate drinking" assume that drinking *less* is an important (although not necessarily the main) objective. This is related to health concerns; but it is also related to the persistence of the notion that self-control is an inherently desirable state.

Controlled/moderate drinking programmes do not, therefore, support the thesis that we now live in a post-disciplinary society. A Canadian article laying out guidelines for such programmes states that total abstinence needs to be imposed as a goal by the counsellor in many cases, since those people who have in the past purposively gone out to get drunk are not suitable candidates for controlled/moderate drinking programmes. For these people (the alcoholics, though the word is carefully avoided), moderation is "an unattractive goal and is discouraged by the therapist".[3] Counsellors are told to inquire into the drinker's history to see if he/she regularly drank *for the sake of getting drunk*; having objectively determined the state of the drinker's subjectivity, the counsellor is then to actively discourage these people from choosing 'moderate drinking' as a goal. This reflects the AA theory of alcoholism – 'once an alcoholic, always an alcoholic' – more than the logic of risk management.

In North America as a whole, and in the United States more than in Canada, the development of harm-reduction programmes for individual drinkers has historically been handicapped by the fact that Alcoholics Anonymous has strenuously opposed such programmes, and by the related fact that, as much of the literature on treatment programmes makes clear, most treatment practitioners are heavily influenced by AA ideas. Indeed, the term "controlled drinking" is rigorously absent from the American literature on alcoholism treatment. Medical authorities who believe in the existence of alcoholism, addiction, or dependence have their own reasons to oppose controlled drinking programmes, but their voices are not heard. The opponents feared by promoters of cognitive therapy and the self-control approach are those in AA, who firmly believe that for alcoholics there is no such thing as control over drinking, and that harm reduction only encourages the fallacy of personal power.[4] This alliance of the psychiatric project to label certain drinkers as addicts and the AA project to create a community of recovering alcoholics has resulted in a situation in which harm-reduction programmes designed to allow drinkers to minimize harm to themselves are routinely referred to as "controversial", even in countries that do not have such a significant AA influence as the United States.[5]

Thus, harm-reduction programmes offered to drinkers who themselves feel the need for help or who are referred by others to get help do not fit the elegant neoliberal logic of the risk-management, harm-reduction model. Neoliberal projects involving client-initiated definition of risks and objectives, as Tom Osborne has pointed out, entail an abandonment of universal entities such as morals and health in favour of more discrete and more measurable objects – "determinant strategies, targets, and specifics".[6] But North American programmes designed for alcohol consumers seldom even attempt to leave behind the disciplinary logic of medico/moral power. Most harm-reduction programmes available to drinkers, as opposed to those enacted at the level of populations, are not strictly neoliberal because, although they do work through and upon the individual will, that will is not a value-neutral, rational-choice will. Cultural values about work, family, sex, and pleasure are clearly constitutive of what counts as self-control.

And yet, today's moderate drinking programmes are not the same as last century's inebriety cures. The harms of drinking are discussed *both* in the risk-management language of health and safety *and* through traditional discourses of self-control, responsibility, and desire. In keeping with this hybrid rationality, missing work and sexual promiscuity are frequently mentioned as indicators of harm, without any clarification of whether the harm involved is to society's values, to the safety of third parties, or to the self's freedom. The pamphlet on alcohol that is most easily available in Toronto, through doctors' offices and other outlets, typically separates "sensible" drinking from "problem" drinking, in a faint echo of the normal person vs. the alcoholic dichotomy; but it carefully eschews any terminology that might be experienced by the consumer as alarmist, melodramatic, or psychiatrized. Its approach to questions of desire is particularly noteworthy in that it manages to give the old stereotype linking drinking to other excessive bodily pleasures a vaguely liberal twist. Instead of saying that alcoholism leads to promiscuity, it states that one of the four indicators of "problem drinking" is engaging in sexual activity that is disapproved of not by society but by one's better self. The second indicator (not labelled a symptom, but acting as one) is "having sex, when you drink, with someone you don't particularly like".[7] This formulation, which constructs morning-after shame as one's true consciousness, nicely manages to combine moralism and liberalism.

If the moralism is visible in the examples and in the referral decisions, the liberalism is often in the techniques. Many of the techniques used in controlled drinking programmes are borrowed directly from the neoliberal arsenal of tools with which consumers/clients can plan their own futures and govern their lives, their consumption, their health, and their risks.[8] The alcohol treatment literature is full of advice on such unwittingly Foucaultian topics as "systematic self-observation",[9] including sample charts to help counsellors train clients to carefully record their intended and their actual alcohol consumption. The lists, diagrams, and charts may have drinking as their subject, but at the formal level they are virtually indistinguishable from such documents of neoliberalism as the kits provided by the financial industry to incite ordinary people to enter the stock market while controlling their financial risks.

Also in keeping with the institutional habit, typical of risk-management systems, of using statistical calculations of the probability of particular outcomes, contemporary alcoholism treatment literature relies on statistical knowledges produced by a small but internationally influential group of alcohol epidemiologists. Epidemiological measures of harm due to alcohol are, however, difficult to standardize. Many studies exist that document the average consumption of a particular group or nation-state, but few people would today dare to suggest that in matters of drinking the average is the norm. And studies that do not normalize consumption but simply measure the influence of changes in liquor advertising or in price on aggregate levels of drinking are only sporadically integrated into the treatment literature. A scientific account of risk factors for alcohol "misuse" in a recent issue of the *British Medical Bulletin* tells us that people drink less if the price goes up, and counsels governments to raise the tax on liquor. But it then goes on to say that, although allowing advertising in jurisdictions that formerly banned it does *not* seem to increase the levels of drinking, liquor advertising should be banned anyway. There is no evidence of epidemiological effects, but the author inventively states that it can reasonably be assumed to counteract the effects of alcohol education.[10]

The cavalier attitude shown by practitioners and even by experts themselves toward the findings of alcohol science is an indicator or symptom of a broader phenomenon, namely that switching to the language of harm does not necessarily help to produce consensus about treatment. In the case of alcohol, there is no general agreement that physical health is what is to be maximized, given that many programmes (especially in North America) emphasize self-control rather than physiological well-being. It is thus difficult to imagine how alcohol epidemiology could directly contribute to treatment. Calculations of past averages or of the probability of future events only become risk measurements once there is agreement about which risks are to be prioritized. Given the fundamental disagreements about the nature and importance of the potentially endless risks associated with alcohol, it is not surprising that statistical knowledges have been taken up very unevenly and very differently depending on the national/cultural context.

While the British Royal College of General Practitioners sets the levels of harm at 21 standard drinks per week for men and 14 for women,[11] those maximum levels – which are quite a bit lower than they were in the 1970s – would be considered unacceptably high in North America. Even more important than this quantitative difference is a qualitative difference about the nature of harm. While British sources tend to focus on daily or weekly amounts of alcohol consumed, in keeping with the more biomedical orientation of alcohol science there, Canadian sources suggest that drinking every single day is bad, regardless of the total weekly amount consumed. For reasons which are never made clear but which are undoubtedly rooted in the theory that alcoholism is a disease of the will, it is consistently suggested that drinkers set aside two or so days a week as abstinence days – as if drinkers had to prove to themselves that they drink out of choice and not out of habit or compulsion. Along the same lines, moderate drinking programmes usually begin with the client being told in no uncertain terms to avoid all drinking for a three-week period.[12]

It is therefore clear, particularly in North America but even in other parts of the world, that harm-reduction programmes made available to drinkers have not freed themselves from the disciplinary spectre of the alcoholic identity – or from the even older spectre of the inherent immorality of drunken excess – even though they usually avoid all mention of alcoholism. A number of moral and disciplinary rationalities, discourses, and techniques continue to be effective in so-called harm-reduction programmes. Their existence suggests that the impersonal corporate techniques for transforming moral problems into safety and replacing discipline by risk management studied by Jonathan Simon and other scholars working on risk have a limited reach. Rules for campus drinking may be produced under the new rationale of risk management, fuelled in part by the need of corporate entities to lower insurance costs and reduce civil liability. But if some of those students decide to become consumers of treatment programmes rather than of beer, they will be very unlikely to be educated on risk-management techniques for maximizing drinking pleasures while controlling risks. The advice on how to cut down or quit may take the form of risk factor evaluation, but, substantively, this is not always very different from the 1890s theory that some places were to be avoided and that some people had a greater physiological or socio-cultural propensity to drink excessively.

There is thus a clear tension between the risk-management logic of such projects as "If you drink, don't drive" campaigns, and the hybrid, semi-disciplinary, semi-liberal logic of most treatment programmes. In more general terms, the relation between the governance of spaces and populations, on the one hand, and the governance of individuals on the other, may be more complicated than most analyses of risk and harm reduction have shown. There are undoubtedly some programmes that manage to translate the objectivist, post-disciplinary logic of population-based risk management into a plan for individual self-governance: HIV prevention programmes developed by gay-positive counsellors come to mind. But many if not most of the available techniques for the government of the self are hybrid. To put this in diachronic terms, what we often see is a piling up of rationalities of governance on top of one another, rather than a shift from one to another.

In situations in which a variety of logics and objectives coexist, it may be difficult to determine the effective meaning of terms that may be closely associated with one mode of governance but may serve in some

**Toucans in their nests agree**
**GUINNESS is good for you**
**Open some today and see**
**What one or Toucan do**

In Britain today, Guinness presents itself as a health drink despite its alcoholic content. In North America, by contrast, it is no longer possible to market any alcoholic drink under the sign of health – although some midwives do recommend Guinness to women who are nursing babies. (Poster by Raymond Tooby, 1957, Guinness Brewing Worldwide Ltd.)

contexts to allow a kind of slippage between otherwise incompatible rationalities. "Harm" and "safety", in particular, are terms that are not monopolized by neoliberal health strategies enticing individuals to align their wishes with the knowledges provided by authorities. As I have shown elsewhere in the context of the judicial project to modernize obscenity law by using "harm" as the test of obscenity, "harm" sometimes means "harm to society's values and morals", and is to that extent articulated with sovereign and disciplinary logics rather than with risk-managerial ones.[13] Not all discourses and programmes that speak of risk and harm, therefore, are necessarily actuarial or risk-managerial, even if they are shaped by risk management to a certain extent.

## HARM TO BABIES: FROM 'MOTHERS OF THE RACE' TO GUARDIANS OF FETAL HEALTH

Chapter 3 documented the ways in which concerns about maternal drinking intersected, around 1900, with British national and imperial worries about the future of 'the race'. It was pointed out there that the scientific debate on whether or not fetuses were affected by maternal drinking was derailed by the much bigger debates on the mechanisms of inheritance and on the relative role of nature and nurture in working-class alcoholism. And, in contrast to our own days, the inebriety specialists talked about "maternal drinking" or even "female inebriety" (since women were rarely distinguished from mothers) without putting any particular emphasis on the fetus as a distinct object or on pregnancy as a distinct site of governance.

After World War I, concerns about maternal drinking abated and, for the next forty or fifty years, little work was done by alcohol specialists or by others on the question of alcohol's effect on babies. The post-World War II paradigm of alcoholism as a *personality* defect precluded any sustained interest in physiological mechanisms. But with the renaissance of biological explanations for social problems, in the 1970s and 1980s, a new object of governance came into being: fetal alcohol. This is not the place to do an examination of the construction of fetal alcohol syndrome (FAS), or of the new and even vaguer condition known as fetal alcohol effects (FAE), but it is possible to gesture toward an analysis of the way in which biomedical research on the risky business of being a fetus is being translated into broad-ranging programmes to change women's drinking practices.

The widespread, international campaign about fetal alcohol effects (FAE) is at one level a risk-management programme. And yet, there are a number of features about this current campaign that make it a very peculiar form of governance. One strange feature of the FAE campaign is that information about risks is presented without any attempt at allowing the relevant audience, that is pregnant women, to define the harms and set their own goals in relation to those harms. While, in other fields within child health, parents do have some discretion (e.g. where I live, parents can exempt their children from supposedly universal vaccination programmes), the mother is presented in fetal health discussions not as a responsible parent but as herself the main source of risk. A second peculiar feature of this campaign is that there is very little room for individualized programmes. The advice given is usually universal; particularly in the United States, but increasingly so in other places as well, there is zero tolerance for drinking while pregnant.

These two features of the FAE campaign – the complete subordination of maternal subjectivity, and the insistence on universal zero tolerance – are effectively enacted in the warnings printed on the labels of all alcoholic beverages sold in the United States:

GOVERNMENT WARNING
(1) According to the Surgeon-General, women should not drink alcoholic beverages during pregnancy because of the risk of birth defects.
(2) Consumption of alcoholic beverages impairs your ability to drive a car or operate machinery, and may cause health problems.

The precise way in which FAE is linked to other alcohol-related risks in this warning is significant. First of all, out of all the possible risks and harms that have been associated with alcohol, only four are listed in this impressive warning. One of these is listed first and is given a whole sentence – a warning to pregnant women not about their own duty to be well but about the danger their drinking poses to the innocent baby. The other three are compressed into the second sentence. Driving is first – and the risk here is obviously also a risk to third parties, since drunk driving is always regarded as a threat to the innocent non-drinkers. Labour productivity and workplace safety are then mentioned; and then, in final place, the health of the drinker rates a qualified mention. The fact that the qualifier "*may* cause" is used only in the context of the fourth priority – the drinker's own health – is noteworthy, since there is as much evidence to support it as there is for the first three governmental objectives.

At a more symbolic level, linking pregnancy more closely to driving and to operating machinery than to personal health suggests that pregnant women are engaged in performing an important and responsible task. Pregnancies today, like so many other human conditions, are supposed to be active states, not passive ones; like workers in the global economy, pregnant women are expected to be always vigilant and ever-rational. One hundred years ago, women were enjoined to do their quasi-military duty as mothers of the race. But today, the product of pregnancy is not 'the race' or the nation: it is the baby. And for the sake of that particular product, the baby, women are to forego *all* drinking during pregnancy, even though no epidemiologist has yet produced figures linking occasional moderate drinking during pregnancy with any negative outcomes.

The Canadian literature addressed to pregnant women sometimes uses the same imperious language of the American government warning. And in some Canadian cities, the warnings about drinking are supplemented by prominent signs in every restaurant and coffee shop proclaiming that second-hand smoke is bad for fetuses, thus doubling women's anxiety about risks. But in the pamphlets produced by 'enlightened' quasi-state agencies, calculations, not absolute prohibitions, are used to entice women themselves to come to the decision to avoid risks. One colourful poster pinned up in many Canadian doctors' offices avoids the American route of imposing zero tolerance:

> Alcohol and pregnancy: If a woman drinks heavily when she's pregnant, her baby could have fetal alcohol syndrome (FAS). The effects could include problems with mental development as well as physical problems such as facial deformities and heart defects. The risk of FAS increases with the amount of alcohol consumed during pregnancy. A woman who is pregnant *or planning to have a baby*, should talk to her doctor about alcohol and other drugs.[14]

What makes this advice less alarmist than the American warning is the stress on "heavy" drinking. And yet, the listed effects of FAS are quite frightening: one would think that all babies born to women who drink are retarded. Additionally, while fetal alcohol as a substance is presented in a less alarmist fashion than in other sources, the scope of the FAE campaign is quietly enlarged. It is not just pregnant women who should watch/stop their drinking: it is now all women "planning to have a baby".

Another pamphlet, this one geared more to professionals than to consumers, does not differentiate between the minority of heavy drinkers and the majority of women. Considering all drinking as risky, it then manages to present zero tolerance as a goal that emerges naturally from the statistics about FAS:

> Pregnant women who drink risk having babies with fetal alcohol effects (known as fetal alcohol syndrome or FAS) . . . While it is known that the risk of bearing an FAS-afflicted child increases with the amount of alcohol consumed, a safe level of consumption has not been determined.[15]

This is, of course, scientifically true – but it is equally true of a myriad other substances, from car exhaust to food preservatives and additives, which also pose risks to fetal health but which have not been the subject of large-scale educational campaigns aimed at health providers and/or at women themselves.[16] Thus, we see that some risks appear as more 'risky' or more worthy of government campaigns than others; and not all subjects of risk governance are regarded as liberal subjects whose own desires and aspirations are to be considered as integral to the way in which they are governed.

REPLACEMENT FLUIDS

From the point of view of alcoholism, there are a number of industries, most notably the soft drink industry, that could be regarded as vast and wonderfully non-coercive harm-reduction programmes. Partly to highlight the need to study private-sector techniques for acting on harms, habits, and souls alongside the better studied technologies developed by professionals, bureaucrats, and philanthropists, an overview of the highlights in the history of replacement fluids will conclude this chapter.

In Britain, a combination of falling prices and lower tariffs meant that by the 1780s tea, hitherto an occasional luxury, became an item of mass consumption.[17] By the 1830s and 1840s, as Indian (rather than Chinese) tea was becoming an everyday staple, a number of major Quaker commercial families (the Tukes, Mennels, and Hornimans, for instance) stopped making beer – which had been the eighteenth century temperance drink – and went into the Indian tea trade instead.[18] Tea was undoubtedly the most successful substitute for alcohol, particularly when it started being consumed regularly in the workplace during breaks (in place of the pot of ale fetched from the pub by apprentices), and temperance was not far from the minds of at least some politicians involved in imperial tariff reform. Prime Minister Gladstone declared in 1882 that "the domestic use of tea is a powerful champion able to encounter alcoholic drink in a fair field, and throw it in a fair fight".[19]

The provision of tea was largely left to the for-profit sector. On their part, organized temperance reformers became involved in providing appealing cold non-alcoholic drinks that could be sold in the place of beer. Philanthropic organizations often set up stalls at public events, selling lemonade, ginger beer, and soda water.[20]

While some cold drinks managed to achieve modest commercial success by the turn of the century (e.g. the Schweppes company), hot drinks associated with imperial trade (first tea, then cocoa and coffee) were at this time more successful as alcohol replacements. Although consumed by some as temperance drinks, they managed to transcend the puritanical connotations of temperance, dissent, and workingmen's improvement associations. Cocoa and chocolate were distinguished precisely because they were marketed as *pleasurable* as well as healthful and sober.

The Birmingham Quaker family firm, Cadbury's, regularly took out full-page advertisements in the *British Journal of Inebriety*. These ads, though clearly associated with temperance through their medium of publication, did not overtly stigmatize alcohol: they simply reiterated that cocoa and chocolate were both healthful and pleasurable. (Today, chocolate is generally marketed under the sign of indulgence: but for Edwardians sugar and fat content were indications of health, not risk.) Apart from these paid advertisements, there were statements from the journal – advertorials, they would now be called – praising cocoa and other drinks both generically and by brand name. Fry's, Cadbury's, and Rowntree received warm endorsements in issue after issue.[21]

Coffee, tea, cocoa, and related brand-name drinks such as Ovaltine continued through the twentieth century to function as replacements for alcoholic drinks in some contexts. Coffee was particularly important in the United States as a replacement fluid. Coffee was and remains the symbolic opposite of or antidote for alcohol. Memoirs of AA members, from its earliest days to today, never fail to mention what AA member Nan Robertson describes as "the ever-present coffee urn". The AA historic tour in Akron, Ohio, includes "a photograph of an icon of sorts, a homey, comforting object" – the coffeepot provided by the woman who brought together the two men who founded AA.[22] An AA saying (anonymous, of course), states that "all you need to start a new AA group is two drunks, a coffeepot, and some resentments".[23]

Coffee differs from cocoa in that it is very often consumed in public and with non-family members. This allows it to function as a replacement fluid for the *Lost weekend* type of drinker that filled the early AA groups, and it continues to be dominant in that organization. But, by the same token, coffee's effectivity is limited in that it is, now, strongly associated with work. Workplaces regularly provide coffee and seldom provide any other drink, and breaks in the working day are, in North America, known as coffee breaks regardless of what is actually consumed at that time. Perhaps because coffee and tea are eminently rational fluids, associated with the work ethic and with duty – though not devoid of their own minor, moderate pleasures – there was room in the twentieth century to re-invent the technique of the temperance movement of the 1830s and 1840s, that is, providing cold liquids that would be consumed largely because of their pleasure value, not because they were healthy or conducive to working.

A number of candidates for that position were available at the end of the nineteenth century. Mineral waters, mostly from France and

Germany, were widely sold around the world. But mineral water, then as now, connoted health more than pleasure. Soft drinks, on the other hand, could fulfil the same functions as mineral water but could additionally be consumed for the sheer pleasure of the sweet flavour. A British nurse involved in caring for recovering alcoholics explained the logic of soft drinks as follows:

> [Alcoholics] should all, also, be encouraged to develop a taste for 'soft' drinks. Water, as a rule, is a horror to them, and as it is most important for them to have plenty of fluids something must be found to take its place. It will be easier for them too, when out on their own again, if they can have something 'out of a bottle' when their friends are indulging in their favourite drinks. One must always try to build up good, safe habits: it is not enough to remove the bad ones.[24]

Out of all the soft drinks developed in the first half of the twentieth century, the most successful one was (and is) Coca-Cola. Around 1890, Coca-Cola was initially marketed, like the mineral waters advertised alongside cocoa in the *British Journal of Inebriety*, for its therapeutic value, including claims that it cured headaches. One of the earliest advertisements displayed in the Coca-Cola museum in Atlanta states: "The ideal brain tonic. A delightful summer and winter beverage. For headache and exhaustion."[25]

One early advertisement sided with the politics of temperance: it featured an endorsement from a baseball player who stated that he

**Distinguishing itself from other late nineteenth century health drinks by appealing to sex and pleasure rather than to sobriety and thrift, Coca-Cola became the most successful brand-name drink of the twentieth century. (Both courtesy of the World of Coca-Cola Museum, Atlanta, Georgia.)**

drank Coca-Cola after games, not beer or whisky. But, early in the twentieth century, the marketing people moved away not only from temperance but even from health.[26] By the 1910s and 1920s, Coca-Cola was being portrayed as consumed in many situations that looked very much like cocktail parties or high-class bars. Rather than challenging the cultural practices around drinking by preaching temperance, then, Coca-Cola managed to borrow the existing associations and pleasures of alcohol for its own purposes. A 1925 painting by Fred Mintzen showed a

bellhop in fancy white uniform solemnly carrying a tray with a bottle of Coke on it as if it were expensive cognac;[27] and many advertisements showed middle- or upper-class women in cocktail or evening dresses, elegantly consuming Coke.

Unlike most other alternative fluids, Coca-Cola was also connected to alcoholic pleasures more directly. Especially in the southern US states, it was used as a mixer. Although this particular way of consuming was not emphasized by the company, and is barely mentioned in the vast exhibits of the Coca-Cola museum, it is worth noting that Coke helped to break down the dichotomy of consumption (alcoholic vs. temperance drinks) that had been created by the temperance movement. Other non-alcoholic fluids can of course also be mixed: in some parts of Europe, for instance, it is not uncommon to put brandy in one's coffee after lunch or dinner. But while other mixers have been very successful, particularly the tonic water that many people never drink except with gin, none has been so closely associated with a particular *brand*, a particular company. People will order a G and T in a bar, without specifying brand, but they will order "a rum and Coke".

Appealing to the temperance crowd and to drinkers simultaneously, Coca-Cola also made sure that it was not associated with any particular *space*, or, rather, it made sure that virtually every occasion and every space was marked as a potential opportunity for drinking Coke. Advertisements show people relaxing at home, taking a break at work, having lunch at a lunch counter, socializing at fancy parties, going out on dates, and slaking their thirst after strenuous outdoor play. They show older and younger people, men and women, people working and people relaxing. Only African-Americans are excluded.

There thus seemed to be a deliberate effort to convince (white) people that, unlike other health drinks, Coca-Cola was not to be associated with domesticity, middle age, or sickness. Perhaps to reinforce its potential as a replacement for alcohol, it was not marketed as a youthful drink until the 1960s.[28] For most of its history, Coke was an adult drink for both pleasure and work, and for both public and private occasions.

While emphasizing its versatility in regard to time and place of consumption, Coke's marketing strategy put increasing emphasis on its national identity. Although, at the beginning, there was nothing particularly American about it – being derived from a French wine containing cocaine[29] – by the 1920s it had firmly associated itself with the United States of America, both domestically and internationally. The Americanization of Coca-Cola reached fever pitch during World War II, when the company signed a contract with the army guaranteeing that every soldier would have access to Coke, and that each Coke would cost only five cents, no matter what the transportation costs. This loss-leader marketing strategy involved transporting bottling equipment across North Africa and large parts of East and Southeast Asia, perhaps in the hope that after the war the local populations, as well as the American troops, would have become used to Coca-Cola.[30]

During the war, a barrage of advertising depicted Coca-Cola *both* as the troops' favourite refreshment *and* as a consumer good that people in far-flung places of the earth all enjoyed. Many of these ads went so far as to feature whole sentences in languages other than English, a highly unusual tactic at the time. Thus, Coca-Cola portrayed itself as symbolizing patriotism *and* internationalism at the same time. The essentially American drink, it nevertheless was represented as helping to facilitate interactions between American soldiers and 'locals' all around the world.

The story of Coca-Cola's marketing suggests that studies of harm reduction and risk management that focus solely on formal pro-grammes developed by health or psy professionals may be missing an important dimension of the governance of risks. From Cadbury's cocoa through Coca-Cola to the mineral water that became popular among health-conscious urbanites in the 1990s, a number of commercially initiated projects have played a major part in reshaping our consuming habits. While some of these have succeeded precisely because they stress that their product is *not* like alcohol – Perrier and Evian water advertising comes to mind – Coke is interesting in that it took up the challenge of selling temperance without losing any of the pleasures associated with alcohol. The longstanding link between sobriety and self-denial was broken by the product that was sold as containing all the pleasures of alcohol (and even more, since it was a family drink as well as an adults-only drink) without any of the associated risks and harms.[31]

In our own day, Coke continues to thrive, but it has been joined by a number of new technologies for promoting sober pleasures. North America and the United Kingdom have both seen an explosion of high-quality cappuccino shops in which one can spend more on a coffee than one would on a beer. These are sometimes marketed as alternatives to licenced establishments, for instance as venues for hot dates, in ways that traditional coffee and tea shops cannot match.[32] In the meantime, mineral water companies are flourishing, and health food stores sell de-alcoholized wine.

Perhaps because of the sheer abundance of drinks that are promoted as healthful but still manage to borrow the glamour and and indulgent associations of alcohol, consuming an alcoholic drink, especially in public, has become increasingly problematized. Pregnant women and anybody who is going to be driving in the near future are subject to extra-legal but often moralistic specific prohibitions; and drinking to

Are you a
SCHWEPPICURE?

A Schweppicure
is a kind of epicure
who expects the presence
of Schweppervescence

Companies other than Coca-Cola have also tried to market non-alcoholic drinks through appeals to indulgence and pleasure, even though they have never matched Coke's success. (Courtesy of the Robert Opie Collection, Museum of Advertising and Packaging, Gloucester.)

excess is less likely to be forgiven as a weakness of the will or as the effect of disease. Although hard evidence on this would be impossible to find, it may be the case that the proliferation of commercially based harm-reduction programmes – from Coca-Cola through the working-class, doughnut-shop coffee of AA to the new shops that sell a large variety of coffees as if they were vintages – is closely related to a phenomenon that I will in the next chapter call 'the resurrection of the will'. With so many risk-free alternatives available, including glamorized drinks marketed as self-indulgences, people who drink regularly are finding it increasingly difficult to justify their alcoholic habits. If sobriety had continued to be associated with self-denial, it would not have been a very viable programme for our time. But who can resist the siren song of a risk-free pleasure? Who can just say no to substances that promise glamour and flavour but pose no risk to health and safety and cause no harm to the freedom of our beloved will?

# CHAPTER 8

# JUDICIAL DIAGNOSTICS: INTOXICATED AUTOMATISM AND THE RESURRECTION OF THE WILL

The plot of the best-selling Victorian melodrama *The moonstone* turns on the assumption that unwittingly consuming a small amount of opium can produce the condition that in today's legal circles is called 'intoxicated automatism'. In this state, akin to sleepwalking, the hero of the novel gets up in the night, searches for, finds, and then conceals the fabulously valuable oriental stone of the novel's title, but has no memory of this the next day. This narrative device, which seems contrived and implausible to us today, was in its day both plausible and timely. The sleepwalker, now a minor farcical character holding no interest for science, was closely connected to some of the most fundamental tensions in Victorian culture. At a time when the unified, purposeful self of the Puritan ethic was at the height of its pre-Freudian success, the educated as well as the illiterate showed a morbid fascination with psychic phenomena involving split selves and unconscious conduct. From the lowbrow practices of spiritism and amateur hypnotism to the psychiatric diagnoses of hysteria and 'double-consciousness', a whole series of practices, diagnoses, and experiences found in locations as diverse as magic shows, consulting rooms, popular circuses and ladies' parlours challenged the conventional Victorian view of the human soul as ruled by rationality, purposefulness, and volition.[1] Foucault has drawn our attention to the ways in which the identification of a population of mad (later, mentally ill) people served to uphold the dominion of a certain type of rationality. But stories such as *The moonstone*, or for that matter *Dr Jekyll and Mr Hyde*, blurred the line between reason and insanity, raising the possibility that being sane and rational does not always guarantee control over one's actions, or even a singular personality.

In our own day, popular culture continues to be fascinated with phenomena in which the self appears to have fragmented and conduct has become detached from self-awareness, volition, or both. Tabloid stories about people possessed by aliens are the modern-day equivalent of the medieval tales of spirit possession and witchcraft: like witchcraft, alien possession suggests that it is not always easy to tell who or what is *really* responsible for someone's conduct. If popular culture is at ease with the idea that the self is not always unified, expert knowledges, by contrast, generally wish to confine such phenomena to the realm of insanity. Schizophrenia is medically recognized, but one would be hard pressed to find an addiction expert who would today testify in a drug trial in favour of Wilkie Collins' picture of automatism. Today, forensic knowledges are more likely to be deployed to excuse victims (or offenders, like battered women who kill their abusers, who can be re-cast as victims) than to medicalize and/or excuse the archetypal forensic figure, the male violent offender. A reflection on the disappearance of the alcoholic identity and the resurrection of the unfettered, fully responsible free will in today's debates about intoxicated offenders – the substance of this chapter – will simultaneously act as a coda, recalling and bringing together the major themes of the book.

Through a case study of a recent Canadian Supreme Court case regarding the defense of intoxicated automatism in a sexual assault case, this concluding chapter will map some of the most recent developments in the genealogy of the free will. It will be seen that people who, forty years ago, appeared as pitiful alcoholics with weak personality assets are now increasingly regarded as ordinary violent criminals, not only by populist law-and-order advocates but even by experts in addiction. The debates about intoxication and responsibility that have recently taken place in both the United States and Canada have unfolded as if the alcoholic identity had never existed. Even the Canadian Supreme Court justices who bucked popular opinion so far as to not only uphold but even extend the automatism defense (vainly, as it turned out) were not making claims about the relentless determinism of the alcoholic *identity* but, on the contrary, strenuously defending the legal doctrine of *mens rea* or individual subjective culpability. This case study suggests that, at least in the context of crime, the complex arguments about inebriety and alcoholism as diseases of the will that have been documented in this book have been not so much rejected as forgotten.

A closer look at other areas of medico-legal interest, however, suggests that the demise of the alcoholic identity (which is in any case only partial) cannot be read as indicating that the whole tradition of diseases of the will documented in earlier chapters has become irrelevant. This tradition has been not so much forgotten as dispersed. The alcoholic identity may have little or no purchase in the context of the criminal law; but, as documented in chapter 1, if the alcoholic is perhaps an old-fashioned identity confined largely to AA and to self-help lay psychology, there has been a tremendous proliferation of identities loosely based on the model of the addict. The new identities, as Elayne Rapping and others have noted, tend to be feminized,[2] in contrast to the masculinization of alcoholism since World War II. This book's scope does not permit a full analysis of the contrasts and the interactions between alcoholism and more recent identities directly or indirectly rooted in the diseases of the will tradition. But, by way of opening up avenues for future work, the chapter, and hence the book, will conclude with a brief comparison of the demise of intoxicated automatism with the rise of a controversial identity that is both a disease of memory and a disease of the will: multiple personality disorder.

## THE DEATH OF THE WILL?: THE LEGAL DISEASE OF AUTOMATISM

In the controversial 1994 *Daviault* case involving a very drunk man who raped a wheelchair-bound elderly woman, the Supreme Court of Canada maintained and extended the intoxicated automatism defense. The court's decision, weakened from the start by the fact that only four of the seven justices agreed to it, was quickly denounced not only for its political effects – something that one would expect, particularly given the gender organization of the particular case – but also, and less predictably, for its bad science. In contrast to the main trends in forensic psychiatry a century ago, today's experts tend to think that actions performed when intoxicated, when sleepwalking, during an epileptic fit, or in any other temporary state of automatism are rarely purposeful and complex. A noted Toronto pharmacologist working at the Addiction Research Foundation (ARF), Dr Harold Kalant, stated that, contrary to popular and judicial ideas about sleepwalking murderers, what the courts call automatism is really (that is, scientifically) much more prosaic, generally involving "inappropriate behaviour that is usually repetitive and of low complexity . . . There is rarely violence and even more rarely a sufficiently organized pattern of violence to sustain an attack on another person."[3] Dr Kalant and his colleagues at the ARF submitted a brief to the Canadian parliament which ridiculed the judicial diagnosis of automatism by stating that neither drinkers nor sleepwalkers can claim the "defence of automatism in any case where the accused acted in a *non-habitual* manner, or performed actions never done before".[4] The deployment of the unscientific category of habit to draw an artificially sharp distinction separating the harmless somnambulists and epileptics from the violent and legally culpable drunk is in keeping with the general history of addiction discourse, since, as documented earlier in this book, expert debates about where to draw the line between a free act and a medicalized compulsion often rely on the intermediate category of habit. But the ARF submission breaks with the addiction tradition insofar as it manages to avoid even a single mention of either alcoholism or addiction. "Anyone who drinks alcohol assumes the burden of increased risk of harm to themselves and others", the experts write, as if the psychiatric category of dependence did not exist.

A more telling indication that the Euro-American project to turn alcoholism into an identity characterized by the compulsion to drink has failed to dominate expert knowledges could scarcely be found. One hundred years after Dr Norman Kerr made his learned plea in favour of the inebriate identity, his direct descendants at one of the world's most famous addiction research institutions are intervening in legal debates as if the inebriety/alcoholism/addiction project had never existed. Along with the courts, they assume that drinking is always a willed act. This would have been difficult to maintain if the experts involved had been clinicians used to diagnosing addiction/dependence disorders; but the knowledge deployed in ARF's submission was not that of psychiatry or psychology but rather that of pharmacology, a knowledge in which there are no types, just alcohol circulating in bodies.[5] The erasure of identity-based arguments, and indeed of all projects to govern alcohol consumption by governing persons, might have led in other contexts to epidemiological arguments about risk factors dissolving the individual in a sea of statistics. But this was a criminal case concerned with the adjudication of individual responsibility. Therefore, instead of going forward from discipline to risk management, the experts went backward from discipline to sovereignty. In its submission to parliament, the ARF experts stated: "The presence of amnesia in no way demonstrates that the person was incapable of forming a *moral* decision. It is not uncommon for someone to suffer amnesia after heavy drinking, although the person was able to form complex thoughts and make *moral* decisions during the time not remembered [emphasis added]."[6]

The debate about intoxication and responsibility that took place in Canada in 1994 and 1995 was by no means confined to experts and judges. Public opinion was mobilized as if a war had been declared, with women's groups making particularly influential arguments about the need to not excuse rape, arguments converging with the newly developed neo-temperance sentiments of many health-conscious middle-aged Canadians. As has been the case in American jurisdictions in which law-and-order and strict liability arguments are being deployed to reverse traditions considering intoxication and/or alcoholism to be either a defence or a mitigating factor, the public debate across Canada showed an overwhelming belief in the resurrection of the free will. As in the United States, the neoconservative emphasis on individual responsibility converged with a very different trend, one emphasizing that crimes and punishments should be evaluated not from the traditional legal perspective of *mens rea* but rather from the point of view of effects and consequences.[7] The two trends arise from contradictory thought-spaces. While in the world of risk factors there is no volition, only probabilities and effects,[8] neoconservative moralists hold as a central tenet that the individual free will, although weakened to the point of dissolution by the welfare state and psy expertise, can now be resurrected. Nevertheless, despite their opposing positions on the importance of the will, these two powerful forces happily converge on the policy issue of the intoxication defense – as they had converged some years earlier in the formation of the drinking-driving moral panic.[9]

The convergence of epidemiological studies of alcohol and risk, the victims movement's emphasis on harm rather than intention, the rise of neoconservative morality, and the growing influence of feminist concerns about violence against women – supplemented by the unexpected testimony of experts who no longer believe in addiction – resulted in a very powerful movement for law reform. Although the Canadian parliament has often failed to respond to judicial moves, in this case it did not hesitate to defy the court, and quickly passed a law disallowing the intoxication defense not only in sexual assault but in all crimes involving violence. This move was greeted by near-universal acclaim within Canada. It was also very much in keeping with developments south of the border. In the same year, 1995, the California state legislature passed a law disallowing some uses of the intoxication defense. And, in 1996, the US Supreme Court upheld a Montana statute holding intoxicated offenders fully responsible for the consequences.[10]

The justices of the Canadian Supreme Court had not invented the judicial diagnosis of intoxicated automatism. They inherited from the common law a distinction between "insane automatism", which has the effect of acquitting a defendant but placing them under psychiatric surveillance, and "non-insane automatism", which covers conditions such as sleepwalking, behaviour following concussion, and some instances of heavy drinking. As Nigel Walker explains in his discussion of English law on the issue, non-insane automatism is a twentieth century term, but its paradigmatic content is provided by the typically late Victorian phenomena of hysterical fugue (a condition in which people move around without knowing where or why), mesmerism, and somnambulism.[11]

"Alcoholic automatism" or "inebriate trance" was a diagnosis proposed by the late turn-of-the-century inebriety experts discussed in chapters 2 and 3. Dr Norman Kerr, the leader of the medical inebriety movement in the United Kingdom, explained that,

> while in this practically somnambulistic state (which may co-exist with either excessive or moderate drinking, or during a post-inebriate period) anyone so affected may speak, eat, drink, walk, talk, and generally act to all appearance as if he were in the full possession of his senses. Yet all the while he may be a mere automaton . . .[12]

Although in fin-de-siècle France the notion of automatism gained some legal standing, partly because of the greater scientific status of hypnotism and partly because of the unusual influence of psychiatry (in Paris, at least) on noted criminal trials,[13] in the United Kingdom and other common-law jurisdictions the notion of non-insane automatism did not prosper. The influential prison doctor William Sullivan complained in 1904 that the courts were not recognizing this condition, defined by him as involving both a lack of rationality and a deficiency of the will, as a form of insanity.[14] By and large, only delirium tremens was counted as a form of insanity for legal purposes. Evidence of drunkenness was sometimes taken by judges as an aggravating rather than a mitigating factor in sentencing.[15]

By the mid-twentieth century, courts in common-law jurisdictions still generally failed to recognize either extreme acts of intoxication or inebriate identity claims as defenses. But gradually they came to allow some extremely intoxicated offenders to claim that they were acting without any volition and/or reason, and therefore without any culpability. A 1935 Kentucky judicial decision, cited at length in a 1961 pamphlet on criminal responsibility widely distributed among American lawyers, expressed what would become the mid-twentieth century consensus in both American and Canadian courts. This was that intoxication could not be alleged as a defense by most drunken offenders, since "the intoxication must be, in order to be available [as a defense] of that degree and extent as renders the defendant practically an *automaton* with the loss of his rudder of reason . . . [emphasis added]"[16] It should be noted that, in legal discourse, the "rudder of reason" seems to be directly attached to or even indistinguishable from what the psychologists call volition: as we shall see later in the context of the 1995 Canadian law on the intoxication defense, the legal category of criminal intent is a hybrid of cognition and morality, of intellect and the will.

In most common-law jurisdictions, the intoxicated automatism defense has not been available to all very drunk defendants. It has been available only in a category of offenses known as 'specific intent' offenses. These are defined as involving an intent to cause consequences beyond the actual criminal act. Robbery and murder are specific intent offenses, for instance, since they are thought to involve a calculative process by which the criminal act is foreseen to have certain consequences advantageous to the offender. By contrast, other offenses, known as 'general intent' offenses, are thought to involve a lesser amount of volition and calculation.[17] There is still a requirement that a certain amount of criminal intent be present, since intent is the sine qua non of the criminal law, as distinct from civil suits in which one does not have to prove that anybody intended anything. But general intent offenses are thought to require less calculation and a weaker control over the will – a "minimal intent", as Canadian judicial discourse has it. The courts have generally held that drunken offenders are sometimes unable to form the more sophisticated intent associated with specific intent offenses, but that it is well within the powers of drunks to form the minimal intent of such offenses as sexual assault.

The distinction between general and specific intent offenses is usually presented by judges as an ontological distinction etched in the human soul. Occasionally, it is admitted that the distinction is arbitrary; but even judges who admit that the distinction is less than clear and distinct demonstrate a fervent wish to hold on to it. Canadian Supreme Court Justice John Sopinka, in his dissent in *Daviault*, admits that it is difficult to separate the "minimal degree of consciousness" of general intent offenses from the "ulterior intent" of specific intent offenses, but then he happily borrows the language of an English law lord to justify maintaining the doctrine: "Absolute logic in human affairs is an uncertain guide and a very dangerous master."[18]

One therefore needs to look not to the inner logic of law but to the extra-legal field that judges call policy to discover the reasons for the longevity of a judicial distinction so often criticized as arbitrary. The distinction between the two modes of consciousness/volition, it turns out, performs a very useful function: it translates into the lofty language of legal doctrine of commonsense a number of taken-for-granted, everyday views about the effects of alcohol on human conduct. A feature of English-speaking societies is the belief that people who are very drunk cannot form 'higher' thoughts or complex intentions, but that they are capable of, and indeed are particularly susceptible to, more 'impulsive' acts. That drinking is inherently disinhibiting (a belief belied by anthropological research) is held by both experts and lay persons to be an absolute truth. Disinhibition is thought to produce fuzzy thoughts as well as poor self-control. Thus, although drunk people may not be able to think clearly enough to make the calculations associated with specific intent offenses, they not only can but are highly likely to commit the sort of impulsive crime that Euro-American societies have often blamed on alcohol's effects. Such impulsive crimes are blameworthy, but less so than if they were premeditated and committed in cold blood.

These traditional (and ethnocentric) views about the effects of alcohol on the passions and on the moral quality of one's conduct underlie the judicial doctrine of general vs. specific intent offenses. And, as attitudes toward drinking have shifted, the doctrine has come under attack. In the mid-twentieth century, when the doctrine of general vs. specific intent was popularized, attitudes toward drinking were at a historic high point of permissiveness, and the figure of the alcoholic constructed by both alcohol science and popular culture was, as chapter 4 documents, more an object of pity than a source of fear. But in recent years, in North America in particular, people have been drinking less, and heavy drinking, for instance at parties, has become unfashionable. Converging with this shift, a renewed emphasis on the dangers that violent and/or drunken men pose for women has served to further stigmatize heavy drinking by linking it to masculine violence, an association which had been common in the days of the Women's Christian Temperance Union but which had lost its plausibility in the 1940s and 1950s. The intoxicated rapist was thus a convenient lightning rod for several otherwise unrelated trends and fears – about alcohol, about sex, about rationality, about violence, about gender. It is thus not surprising that the judicial doctrine that had originally developed to allow the courts to punish most drunken offenders but allow some room for the argument that 'he didn't really know what he was doing' would begin to crumble.

The Canadian Supreme Court case *Daviault vs. The Queen* was, from the strictly legal point of view, a case about whether the intoxicated automatism defense should be made available not only in specific intent crimes (most notably murder) but also in general intent crimes, namely sexual assault.[19] This presented a problem for judicial legitimacy because, while in a murder case a defendant acquitted of murder can be simultaneously convicted of manslaughter, there is no sexual equivalent of manslaughter (at least, not in Canadian law). And yet, it was not so easy to disallow the intoxication defense. The Charter of Rights, in force in Canada since 1982, holds the courts to a high standard of fairness, equal treatment, and universality; in particular, it authorizes the courts to strike down not only laws but also common-law doctrines that infringe on human rights. Arguments were thus made that the general vs. specific intent distinction, and the related restriction of intoxicated automatism defense to specific intent crimes, fatally clashed with the

Charter of Rights. It was claimed that extremely intoxicated persons could not form even the minimal intent required for a sexual assault conviction, since the only act they truly intended was to drink. The Charter of Rights' concern for fairness, uniformity, and logic, it was argued, made it necessary to overturn the common-law practice of convicting some drunken offenders because they happen to have committed general intent offenses while acquitting other equally drunken offenders who have committed specific intent offenses.

Four of the seven justices hearing the *Daviault* appeal decided to side with the charter's logic of codified, universal rights, declaring the old judicial custom unconstitutional. In doing so, they sided with legal developments in Australia and New Zealand and against both traditional English and recent American law. In an impeccably logical analysis, Justice Cory argued that judicial practice in regard to general intent crimes had been based on the untenable fiction that it was permissible to substitute one intent for another: "The accused's intention to drink is substituted for the intention to commit the prohibited act."[20] Cory finds that, having consumed several beers followed by over 30 fluid ounces (close to one litre) of brandy, Daviault could not have formed even the minimal intent to commit a sexual assault.

Henri Daviault, needless to say, claimed to remember nothing, and so his testimony was of no help in proving whether there was intent. The majority opinion thus relied on expert evidence to establish that the will of the accused was in fact inoperative. At Daviault's original trial, held in Quebec, a pharmacologist had testified that someone consuming such quantities of alcohol would indeed be likely to be in a state of "*amnésie-automatisme*". This very French (and rather nineteenth century) phrase, inaccurately translated by the English-speaking justices as "blackout", was taken to justify allowing the common-law defense of intoxicated automatism.[21] "Blackout" usually means a drunken episode that cannot be remembered later, but few people, including few self-declared alcoholics, would describe their unremembered actions as those of an automaton. As the Addiction Research Foundation pointed out, there is little expert evidence supporting the claim that not remembering something means one had no awareness of it at the time or that no volition was involved. The ARF experts went on to note that there is no such term as "automatism" in the DSM or in medical dictionaries, hence revealing that the judicial diagnosis of intoxicated automatism has very tenuous links to medical science.[22]

Why would judges, not only in Canada but in the United States and in the United Kingdom, have felt obliged to defend the medically unsupported claim that there is such a thing as intoxicated automatism? In the Canadian public debates, the four justices who upheld the notion of "*amnésie-automatisme*" were widely accused of being the stooges of deterministic psychiatric doctrines. This populist accusation, however, failed to understand the fundamental logic of the *Daviault* decision. While indeed pronouncing Daviault's will to be diseased, the general thrust of the majority decision is not to bury the human will, but rather the opposite. It is precisely to preserve the pristine purity of the legal conception of subjective intent that the justices are willing to allow a few extremely intoxicated offenders a quasi-medical defense.

Knowing full well that their decision to expand the scope of the intoxicated automatism defense would meet with near-universal disapproval, the four majority judges bent over backwards to explain why extending the defense is paradoxically necessary to preserve the key legal mechanism for propounding the free will, namely the doctrine of *mens rea*:

> The mental aspect of an offence, or *mens rea*, has long been recognized as an integral part of crime. The concept is fundamental to our criminal law. That element may be minimal in general intent offences; nonetheless, it exists. In this case, the requisite mental element is simply an intention to commit the sexual assault or recklessness as to whether the actions will constitute an assault . . . Given the minimal nature of the mental element required for crimes of general intent, even those who are significantly drunk will usually be able to form the requisite *mens rea* and will be found to have acted voluntarily. [But] neither an insane person nor one in a state of automatism is capable of forming the minimum intent required for a general intent offence.[23]

The automatism defense is here presented not as a humanitarian measure to let a few pitiful alcoholics off the hook, but rather as a necessary measure to preserve the legal doctrine that the criminal is someone who *willed* an action or, at the very least, neglected to exercise the minimal duty of care. The doctrine of individual responsibility would fall into disrepute, the four justices believe, if *mens rea* becomes so watered down as to include people acting randomly and unknowingly.

## THE RESURRECTION OF THE WILL

The three dissenting justices shared their colleagues' faith in individual autonomy and in the necessity of proving a subjective element in crime. But, for them, the ideology of cognitive and moral autonomy inherent in the doctrine of *mens rea* requires that all drunken individuals be held accountable. They may not intend to commit a crime or even know that they are committing it, but they intended to drink, and therefore they can be held accountable. The questionable logic of this argument was subtly ridiculed by Justice Cory, who pointed out in his decision that drinking is "not *yet* a crime".[24] But logically or not, the three judges in the minority chose to defend the legal doctrine of the will not by ejecting those of dubiously valid volition but rather by the opposite route of including even drunks under the banner of the free will.

In keeping with the popular outcry against the judicial majority decision, the law passed by the Canadian parliament in June of 1995 chose the latter route – as laid out by the *Daviault* dissent – to uphold the free will. The law states that free will exists at all times in people who are not insane and that intoxication (which is described as "self-induced", to highlight the volition involved), should not "be used socially and legally to excuse violence, particularly violence against women and children". This view claimed to have support in both popular and expert opinion. In regard to public opinion, the law's preamble states that "the Parliament of Canada shares with Canadians the moral view that people who, while in a state of self-induced intoxiation, violate the physical integrity of others are blameworthy in relation to their harmful conduct", with the phrase "in relation to" acting to blur the difference between being responsible for drinking and being responsible for an assault. At the level of expertise, the preamble also claims that the Parliament of Canada is "aware of scientific evidence that most intoxicants, including alcohol, by themselves, will not cause a person to act involuntarily".

The 1995 law contains some features that are distinctly of our own time, particularly the mention of women and children and the word 'harmful'. But, apart from these contemporary touches, the theory of the human soul that is deployed to undermine the automatism defense repeats the conventional wisdom of the early Victorian period – when the division between the sane and the insane had not yet been blurred by such categories as neurosis, inebriety, neurasthenia, alcoholism, and maladjusted personality.

This legislative move is hardly unique. In other fields (e.g. the American war on drugs), we have also been witnessing a thoroughgoing rejection of many of the principles and practices of therapeutic and welfarist approaches to questions of social disorder. In the war on drugs, the notion of addiction as a disease deserving of treatment has little purchase: politicians and police officers prefer to talk about drug abuse. But it is remarkable that, while judicial authorities are split on whether drinking fatally impairs the will, neither the relatively enlightened Liberal-dominated Canadian parliament nor, even more surprisingly, the experts furnished by the Addiction Research Foundation consider the possibility that an act such as drinking may be itself due to a pre-existing impairment of the will. Indeed, there is no longer much room, in today's discourse on alcohol and crime, for the notion of "diseases of the will". In both the United States and Canada, the furor about drunken offenders of the mid-1990s echoed the words spoken by a Michigan judge in 1870 about those who drink excessively:

> He must be held to have purposely blinded his moral perceptions, and set his will free from the control of reason – to have suppressed the guards and invited the mutiny; and should therefore be held responsible as well for the vicious excess of the will, thus set free, as for the acts done by its prompting.[25]

## THE DISPERSAL OF DISEASES OF THE WILL

If in the field of alcoholism – especially in its relation to crime – we are witnessing a veritable apotheosis of the free will, the free and ever-responsible will is nevertheless not being restored across the whole domain of medico-legal knowledges. The new diseases of food addiction, sex addiction, and codependence propagated by entrepreneurs of self-help have some historical roots in the Victorian medico-moral writings on diseases of the will.[26] Most of these new identities have little or no visibility in the context of the criminal law; but there is one that is very much in evidence in one of the most controversial areas of the criminal law, known as historical child abuse, and that is the diagnosis of multiple personality disorder (MPD).[27] Like Wilkie Collins' sleep-walking and like the judicial diagnosis of non-insane automatism, MPD is medically thought to involve partial amnesia. Although discussions of MPD have largely revolved around issues of *memory*, the North American abuse survivor movement nevertheless claims that volition as well as memory is impaired through trauma and the subsequent personality fragmentation: "alters" do things that the dominant personality has not willed. To that extent, then, the debates about MPD are part of the genealogy of the free will. And yet, despite the fact that MPD has its roots in the same Victorian debates about consciousness and freedom that also gave rise to 'inebriety' and its successors, there has been virtually no traffic between controversies about recovered memory syndrome and multiple personalities, on the one hand, and jurisprudential discussions concerning the uses of the intoxication defense in criminal trials, on the other.

One significant factor that helps to maintain these two areas of medico-legal debate in separate boxes is that the two issues have opposite gender ascriptions and, not at all coincidentally, opposite places in the powerful binary opposition of criminal vs. victim. The automatism debate portrays men as the paradigmatic drinkers and as the universal criminals,[28] while the MPD identity is one claimed by victims who are overwhelmingly female. Despite the many diachronic and synchronic

continuities between the double-consciousness debates and the intoxication defense, then, judicial rulings on MPD and recovered memory are
not regarded as having a bearing on whether defendants can claim that
'I wasn't myself, the booze made me do it'. MPD is something that
feminized (innocent) victims may or may not have; intoxicated automatism is the last refuge of male scoundrels.

The contrast between intoxication and MPD sheds light on the ways
in which the situational roles of victim and criminal have been turned
in the very recent past into essentialized identities, with these identities
being further naturalized by being attached to the gender binary.[29]
These two related binary oppositions could easily be deconstructed if
one were to focus on a case involving an intoxicated *female* offender
accused of committing recklessly violent acts who deployed in her
defense some argument about child/gender abuse. But such stories do
not seem to give rise to judicial precedents or new laws – not
surprisingly, since they give rise to mixed feelings rather than to self-
righteous outcries.

The lack of cross-references between the two areas of forensic debate
is overdetermined in yet another way: historically. Although both
debates are happening simultaneously, nevertheless I would argue that
they are not contemporaneous. While MPD is, as Ian Hacking has
argued, a disease entity upon which many of the fears and hopes of our
particular present have converged, the legal discussions about intoxication have a distinctly Victorian flavour. The feature that most clearly
suggests that the intoxication debates are in a time-warp, re-enacting
mid-Victorian controversies rather than arising from the scientific
studies of alcohol and alcoholism of the mid-twentieth century, is that
the question of whether intoxicated defendants can blame their
drinking on their alcoholic *identities* does not even arise. As seen both in
the Canadian case study and in related debates in the United States,
pharmacologists, judges, law-and-order politicians, feminists concerned
about sexual assault, and mothers against drunk drivers disagree on
many things, but they all assume that drinking is a willed act. The
powerful identity claims that shape not only the abuse survivors' movement but our whole political arena (and which tend to assume that
political agency arises from injury rather than from ideology) have had
little impact on the debates about intoxication and violence.[30]

It may be, then – although to prove this would require another book
– that our present is characterized by a kind of dispersal of the nineteenth century debates on freedom and determinism. The Victorian
debates in which philosophical, religious, and medical authorities
waged major battles about the relationship between consumption,
desire, and freedom have become partial and local struggles whose

political and philosophical stakes are rarely made visible. One can today find earnest discussions that re-enact the Victorian debates in remarkably unchanged form – for example, in Internet lists for metha-done users in which addicts themselves avidly debate the theory of addiction as will-lessness or lack of control. And one can analyze issues such as codependence or recovered memory syndrome/MPD in such a way as to lay bare the deep philosophical questions that continue to trouble ordinary people as they try to deal with the reconfiguration of gender, sex, and familial powers in today's world. One can even document, as has been done here, the perhaps unusual case of the demise of intoxicated automatism – unusual in that it reveals a modern medico-social identity (the alcoholic) disappearing into old-fashioned discrete acts (violent crimes). But these discussions and debates are running along separate tracks, in different sites. If they have anything in common, it is their blissful ignorance about their own preconditions, a sort of total amnesia.

Knowing nothing about the historical roots of the issues at stake, the participants, however intelligent and humane, are unable to make links and connections to groups, issues, and discussions that share some of the same history but have taken that history in a different direction. Uncovering historical connections would be helpful in breaking through vicious circles and avoiding unknowing, forgetful repetitions. As Derrida says in another context, those who do not acknowledge the spectres that arise from the past and actively haunt them in the present are fated to reiterate and repeat the quandaries of the past.[31] As has been noted earlier in this book, the forgetful re-enactment of past debates is a major feature of contemporary debates on alcohol, and more generally of discussions regarding the relation between consump-tion, the passions, and human freedom. In the arena of criminal law, judges and lawyers today debate the merits of the battered wife defense one day and the evils of the intoxication defense the next day, but they do not cross-reference these discussions, even though such cross-referencing would be very valuable not only to scholars but also to those lawyers who themselves deplore the public's tendency to dichotomize victims and criminals.

The disappearance of the alcoholic identity from the domain of the criminal law, then, is not a curious fact in the history of alcohol, or, at least, it is not only that. If placed only in the context of the history of alcoholism, the absence of the alcoholic from intoxication debates might suggest that the history of forensic discussions of inebriety has been completely forgotten. But if one takes a broader perspective, considering the relation between the rise and fall of alcoholism and the very different developments that have resulted in battered wives, abused children, and multiple personalities proliferating in the courts, one might conclude not that the psy knowledges have become irrelevant but rather that the only psychiatry that has any validity in the present is that whose gaze is trained upon the victim.

The absence of an effective history[32] of the relation between addiction and freedom, and the consequent lack of an ability to make connections, is not an exclusive characteristic of legal arenas. Amnesia seems to affect not only those who make pronouncements about others but even those who speak only of their own experiences. Those who define themselves as alcoholics, sex addicts, codependents, or multiple personalities know little about the history of diseases of the will and, in many cases, not much more about each other. They tend to stick to self-help groups for their own identity, rather than participating in broader networks within which the underlying political and philosophical issues might be discussed in something resembling a public sphere. They are separated from each other by their respective identities/diagnoses. And, more importantly, they are separated from the citizenry at large, insofar as the central truth these self-help groups produce is that 'we are different' – we are alcoholics, or sex addicts, or whatever, and as such, not like regular people. Of course, the people for whom this book is ultimately written – those who seek to understand and transform themselves by experimenting with ways of understanding and changing the relation between consumption, desire, and freedom – are hardly to be blamed for the absence of a democratic public sphere. It is in all probability the absence of such a sphere – which is in turn related to the fact that intimate discussions linking experience to theories of freedom seem to take place mostly in the voyeuristic, non-participatory sphere of commercial radio and television – that has in the first place led to the felt need for micro-public spheres encompassing only those affected by a particular condition or injury. And an understanding of history is in this case not directly helpful, given the dearth of historical precedents for democratic and inclusive public spheres.

The idea of a public sphere in which people might be encouraged to speak not only about ideas and values (as the rationalist Habermasians would have it) but also about desires, pleasures, and obsessions, is therefore an inevitable fiction. This is not because speaking of desires, including the desire to consume alcohol, is impossible: on the contrary, the proliferation of twelve-step groups has enabled us to document our own compulsions and unfreedoms in more intimate detail than the psychiatric gaze was ever able to do. But twelve-step groups are divided from one another by the proliferation of distinct addictions regarded as distinct identities, and are often in the business of reproducing rather arbitrary theories (e.g. about the inner child) that are presented as gospel truth rather than as ideas for debate. And yet, despite the dearth of sites conducive to non-evangelistic discussions of our problems and our wishes, only a dogmatic pessimist in the Frankfurt school tradition would claim that law, medicine, and popular culture have jointly and severally corrupted everything irretrievably. The less dogmatic historian of the present will admit that, in everyday conversations, and in some self-help groups on their better days, it is occasionally possible to discuss one's feelings, hopes, and regrets without either rationalizing oneself in the name of the free will or psychologizing oneself in the name of some diagnosis. These inconclusive conversations will never amount to a public sphere, of course; but they may be the only indications we have that the habits and theories about the will and its compulsions that we have inherited were not historically inevitable and are now not unshakeable. The fiction of a public sphere that neither medicalizes our compulsions nor rationalizes our capacity for freedom may be a weak and mostly negative idea with which to conclude. Nevertheless, without turning it into yet another tool for regulating and adjudicating theoretical and ethical alternatives, such an idea may serve to inspire us as we scavenge for useful bits among the ethical and intellectual fragments of our present. Or, at least, it may serve us better than the alternatives: the legal doctrine of the abstract free will, the medicalized quest for underlying psychic determinations, the liquor-licencing project to regulate consumption through purely environmental, objectivist measures, and the twelve-step project that transmutes passions into identities. One thing that can be said with some certainty is that the citizens of this wholly fictional community are different from us in that, in discussing their hopes for freedom and their fears about compulsion, they do not feel compelled to deploy abstractions such as the free will. And that alone would be a blessing.

# THE TWELVE STEPS

1. We admitted that we were powerless over alcohol – that our lives had become unmanageable.
2. Came to believe that a Power greater than ourselves could restore us to sanity.
3. Made a decision to turn our will and our lives over to the care of God *as we understood Him* [emphasis original].
4. Made a searching and fearless moral inventory of ourselves.
5. Admitted to God, to ourselves, and to another human being the exact nature of our wrongs.
6. Were entirely ready to have God remove all these defects of character.
7. Humbly asked him to remove our shortcomings.
8. Made a list of all persons we had harmed and became willing to make amends to them all.
9. Made direct amends to such people wherever possible, except when to do so would injure them or others.
10. Continued to take personal inventory and when we were wrong promptly admitted it.
11. Sought through prayer and meditation to improve our conscious contact with God *as we understood Him* [emphasis original], praying only for knowledge of His will for us and the power to carry that out.
12. Having a spiritual awakening as the result of these Steps, we tried to carry this message to alcoholics and to practice these principles in all our affairs.

# NOTES

## INTRODUCTION

1 For a study of the pleasure/danger dialectic of cigarette smoking, see R. Klein, *Cigarettes are sublime* (Durham, NC, Duke University Press, 1993).

2 B. Rush, *Medical inquiries* (Philadelphia, 1812; reprinted New York, Hefner, 1962), 270.

3 "A la fin du XIXe siècle, la volonté a tout à fait disparu de la psycho-pathologie des psychiatres . . . Jusqu'à aujourd'hui la psychiatrie recusait la volonté." H. Grivois and M. Gourevitch, *Les monomanies instinctives: funestes impulsions* (Paris, Masson, 1990), 9.

4 E.K. Sedgwick, "Epidemics of the will" in *Tendencies* (Durham, NC, Duke University Press, 1993), 133.

5 Sedgwick, "Epidemics of the will", 133.

6 Although I am borrowing the idea of repetition compulsion because the dynamic outlined by Freud helps us to understand the peculiar logic of the genealogy of addiction, I am not thereby importing Freud's ontological assumptions about unconscious causality.

7 M. Valverde, "'Slavery from within': the birth of alcoholism and the dilemmas of freedom in late Victorian Britain" *Social History* vol. 22, no. 3 (1997).

8 Luther Gulick (President of the American Institute of Public Administration), foreword to L. Harrison and E. Laine, *After repeal: a study of liquor control administration* (New York, Harper and Brothers, 1936), xix.

9 For some theoretical elaborations of the study of the relations among different modes of governance, see the special issue of *Economy and Society* co-edited by F. Pearce and M. Valverde, "Conflicts and contradictions in governance", vol. 43, no. 2 (August 1996).

10 *Report of the British Columbia Liquor Inquiry Commission* (Government of British Columbia, 1970), 11.

11 J. Edwards, *Freedom of the will* (c. 1750; reprinted New York, Irvington, 1982).

12 Edwards, *Freedom of the will*, 152. There are a number of other places in the book where Edwards uses habitual drunkenness to explain his synthesis of freedom and determination.

13 N. Kerr, *Inebriety or narcomania: its etiology, pathology, treatment, and juris-prudence* 3rd edn (London, H.K. Lewis, 1894), 17.

14 E. Rapping, *The culture of recovery: making sense of the self-help movement in women's lives* (Boston, Beacon, 1996); see also L. Alcoff and L. Gray, "Survivor discourse: transgression or recuperation?" *Signs* vol. 18, no. 21 (1993), 260–90.

15 J. Bovell, *A plea for inebriate asylums presented to the legislature of the province of Canada* (Toronto, Lovell and Gibson, 1862), 33.

16  Bovell, *A plea* . . . , 34.

17  For a more detailed theorization of the role of the internal control over one's desires in the development of nineteenth century liberalism, see M. Valverde, "'Despotism' and ethical liberal governance" *Economy and Society* vol. 43, no. 2 (August 1996).

18  N. Rose, *Inventing ourselves: psychology, power, and personhood* (Cambridge University Press, 1996), 16. See also N. Rose, *Governing the soul* (London, Routledge, 1990), and *The psychological complex* (London, Routledge and Kegan Paul, 1985).

19  That it is ordinary people, not philosophers, who are most guilty of thinking abstractly was an insight first articulated by the philosopher Hegel but also fundamental to Foucault's methodology, as Paul Veyne has forcefully argued. P. Veyne, "Foucault revolutionizes history" in A. Davidson, ed., *Foucault and his interlocutors* (University of Chicago Press, 1997).

20  R. Room, "Dependence and society" *British J. of Addiction* vol. 80 (1985), 133–39.

21  M. Foucault, The Tanner Lectures, reprinted in L. Kritzman, ed., *Michel Foucault: politics, philosophy, culture* (New York, Routledge, 1988).

22  "Doctors debate Internet addiction: should webaholics seek medical help?" *Globe and Mail* June 15, 1996, A1.

23  See listserv@netcom.com

24  S. Zizek, *Tarrying with the negative: Kant, Hegel, and the critique of ideology* (Durham, NC, Duke University Press, 1993), 236; see also S. Zizek, *For they know not what they do: enjoyment as a political factor* (London, Verso, 1991).

## 1 DISEASE OR HABIT?

1  Questionnaire reprinted in C. Knapp, *Drinking: a love story* (New York, Dial Press, 1996), 111–13.

2  Medicalized models of alcoholism, as Don Cahalan has pointed out, have often replicated the melodramatic narrative structure of temperance tracts. Jellinek's influential 1960 formulation of the disease model of alcoholism, for instance, "is of a piece with Hogarth's famous illustration of a drunkard's progress on the downward path to perdition". D. Cahalan, *Problem drinkers: A national survey* (San Francisco, Jossey-Bass, 1970), 4.

3  Foucault's interview with P. Rabinow and H. Dreyfus, in P. Rabinow, ed., *Michel Foucault: ethics, subjectivity and truth (Volume I of The essential writings of Foucault)* (New York, New Press, 1997), 260–63.

4  E.M. Jellinek, *The disease concept of alcoholism* (New Haven, CT, Hillhouse Press, 1960); and see the entry for "Addiction" in the *Oxford companion to medicine* (New York, Oxford University Press, 1986), 6–17.

5  Pat O'Malley, "Consuming risks", paper given at the Centre of Criminology, University of Toronto, October 1996.

6  American Psychiatric Association, *Diagnostic and statistical manual* IV, 190 (henceforth cited as DSM-IV).

7  For behind-the-scenes accounts of the fortunes and misfortunes of addiction, see the interviews with addiction experts collected in G. Edwards,

ed., *Addictions: personal influences and scientific movements* (New Brunswick, NJ, Transaction, 1991).

8 The DSM-IV often uses driving-related mishaps and arrests as examples of the sorts of behaviours that justify a diagnosis of substance dependence or abuse, although it shrinks from concluding that *not* driving might be a good way to lower one's risk of substance-related disorders.

9 DSM-IV, 178.

10 Outside of the United States the logic of harm reduction has gone further: the International Classification of Diseases that is generally used by European physicians has no category for substance *abuse*, referring rather to *harmful use*, a more ethically neutral choice of terms. For the differences between the American and the European/WHO approaches to addiction, see R. Room, "Alcohol and drug disorders in the International Classification of Diseases: a shifting kaleidoscope" (unpublished paper, Addiction Research Foundation, 1997).

11 N. Rose and P. Miller, "Political power beyond the state: problematics of government" *British J. of Sociology* vol. 43, no. 2 (1992), 190.

12 The amount of alcohol figures prominently in currently available programmes to curtail one's drinking without stopping altogether, programmes which carefully avoid pathologizing the client or otherwise invoking 'alcoholism'. See chapter 7 for a discussion of controlled drinking and harm reduction.

13 Alcoholics Anonymous, *Alcoholics Anonymous* (New York, 1939). I am using the third (1976) edition, which includes all of the 1939 edition plus a number of other texts.

14 The most detailed account of early AA is E. Kurtz, *Not-God: A History of Alcoholics Anonymous* (Center City, Minn., Hazelden, 1979); for the twelve step story, see 70–71.

15 "The pragmatic method . . . is to try to interpret each notion by tracing its respective practical consequences. What difference would it practically make to any one if this notion rather than that notion were true? . . . Mr [Charles] Pierce, after pointing out that our beliefs are really rules for action, said that, to develop a thought's meaning, we need only determine what conduct it is fitted to produce: that conduct is for us its sole significance." W. James, *Pragmatism: a new name for some old ways of thinking* (London, Longmans, Green, and Co., 1907), 45–46.

16 A clever polemic against recovery from the point of view of an enlightened rationalism is found in W. Kaminer, *I'm dysfunctional, you're dysfunctional: the recovery movement and other self-help fashions* (Reading, Mass., Addison-Wesley, 1992).

17 "Co-dependence", "codependence" and "codependency" are used interchangeably in the literature, although the latter appears to be increasingly favoured in the United States, perhaps because of the not coincidental connection to the semi-moral condition of welfare dependency. "Dependence", by contrast, has stronger medical associations connected to withdrawal symptoms and physical addictions. I have chosen to use the term "codependence", somewhat arbitrarily.

18 [no author] *Co-dependency: an emerging issue* (Deerfield Beach, FL, Health Communications, 1984), 2.

19 *Co-dependency*, 1.

20 J.S. Rice, *A disease of one's own: psychotherapy, addiction, and the emergence of codependence* (New Brunswick, NJ, and London, Transaction, 1996), 8.

21 Quoted in Rice, *A disease of one's own*, 9. Rice's study does not show the connections between commercialized US feminism and the institutions and ideas of codependency; for a study of this important link, see E. Rapping, *The culture of recovery: making sense of the self-help movement in women's lives* (Boston, Beacon, 1996).

22 Rapping, *The culture of recovery*.

23 Reconciling the imperative to focus on one's needs with the Christian belief in selflessness that most Americans today claim to hold is rather difficult. For an awkward attempt to marry the focus on the self's needs with mainline Protestantism, see M. Beattie, *Codependent no more: how to stop controlling others and start caring for yourself* (Center City, Minn., Hazelden, 1987 [1992]). This book, one of the bestsellers of codependence, sold over 3 million copies in the first edition.

24 S. Wegscheider-Cruse, *Choicemaking: for co-dependents, adult children, and spirituality seekers* (Deer Beach, FL, Health Communications, 1985), back cover.

25 P. Alasuutari, *Desire and craving: a cultural theory of alcoholism* (Albany, NY, SUNY Press, 1992), 153.

26 B. Cruikshank, "The will to empower: technologies of citizenship and the war on poverty" *Socialist Review* vol. 23, no. 4 (1994), 29–55; B. Cruikshank, "Revolutions within: self-government and self-esteem" *Economy and Society* vol. 22, no. 3 (1993), 327–43.

27 Queen Elizabeth II and other old-fashioned royals were not directly accused of being codependents and control freaks during the worldwide mourning for Diana in the summer of 1997, but the accusations that were made reflected those sentiments.

28 W. James, *The varieties of religious experience: a study in human nature* (New York, Modern Library, 1994). This work is the one text, out of the whole canon of academic philosophy and psychology, that is commonly found in 'recovery' bookstores.

29 W. James, *The principles of psychology* (New York, Dover, 1890), 121.

30 James, *The principles of psychology*, vol. I, 109, 124.

31 J. Dewey, *Human nature and human conduct* (New York, Random House, 1922), 67, 27, 35, 66, 176, 177.

32 C. Hull, *Principles of behaviour: an introduction to behaviour theory* (New York, Appleton-Century, 1943).

33 For this analysis I have drawn significantly upon Bruno Latour's influential work on the binaries of modernity; B. Latour, *We have never been modern* (Cambridge, Mass., Harvard University Press, 1993).

34 Charles Camic has documented the peculiar disinterest of classical sociological theory in habit; C. Camic, "The matter of habit" *American J. of Sociology* vol. 91, no. 5 (1986), 1039–87. Currently, Pierre Bordieu's work has

broken with this traditional contempt; for his theorization of habit, see among other works P. Bordieu, *Distinction: a social critique of the judgement of taste* (Cambridge, Mass., Harvard University Press, 1984).

35  J. Stewart, "Prevention of the development of inherited inebriety" *Proceedings of the British Society for the Scientific Study of Inebriety* [henceforth BSSI], no. 31 (1892), 2.

36  See, for example, F.R. Lees, "On some illogical assumptions and statements regarding inebriety" *Proceedings BSSI* no. 38 (1893), 3. Lees went on to annex a Christian theory to this view of the relation between habit and disease, stating that a concentration or repetition of sins would cause a certain habit (habitual drunkenness) which would, if repeated without reformation, lead to disease. There was less consensus about the sin part of this argument, but a great deal of consensus, in American as well as British circles, about the connection between vicious habits and disease, in the realm of inebriety as in the realm of sexuality.

37  Jellinek, *The disease concept of alcoholism*, 115–19.

38  Quoted in Jellinek, *The disease concept of alcoholism*, 118.

39  E. Sedgwick, "Epidemics of the will" in *Tendencies* (Durham, NC, Duke University Press, 1993), 138–39.


## 2 REPAIRING DISEASED WILLS

1  T. Clouston, "Some of the psychological and clinical aspects of alcohol" *British J. of Inebriety* vol. II, no. 3 (1914), 114.

2  For a thorough review of theories about alcoholism current in the mid-twentieth century (most of which are still current), see E. Jellinek, *The disease concept of alcoholism* (New Haven, CT, Hillhouse Press, 1960). Jellinek lists about twenty different psychological theories that regard alcoholism as a disease and half a dozen that regard it as a symptom (pp. 55–59). This is in addition to a very wide array of non-psychological theories.

3  S. Bacon, "Concepts" in W. Filstead, J. Rossi, and M. Weller, eds, *Alcohol and alcohol problems: new thinking and new directions* (Cambridge, Mass., Ballinger, 1976), 94.

4  R. Straus, "Problem drinking in the perspective of social change, 1940–1973" in Filsted, Rossi, and Weller, *Alcohol and alcohol problems*, 50–51.

5  Bacon, "Concepts", 94.

6  On the scientific appropriation of memory, see I. Hacking, *Rewriting the soul: multiple personality and the sciences of memory* (Princeton University Press, 1996).

7  See, for instance R. Smith, *Trial by medicine: insanity and responsibility in Victorian trials* (Edinburgh University Press, 1981).

8  On Esquirol and the evolution of the monomania diagnosis, see the detailed socio-historical study by J. Goldstein, *Console and classify: the French psychiatric profession in the nineteenth century* (Cambridge University Press, 1987).

9  See J.P. Eigen, "'I answer as a physician': opinion as fact in pre-MacNaughtan insanity trials" in M. Clark and C. Crawford, eds, *Legal medicine in history* (Cambridge University Press, 1994), 184–87.

10 See, for example, the chapter on "mania" in T.S. Clouston, *Mental diseases* (London, Churchill, 1887), 138–60.

11 These three diagnoses were commonly employed in American and British as well as in French asylums. See D. Rothman, *The discovery of the asylum* (Boston, Little, Brown and Company, 1971); A. Scull, *Museums of madness: the social organization of insanity in nineteenth century England* (London and New York, Allen Lane and St Martin's Press, 1979); and Goldstein, *Console and classify.*

12 Other classifications were also popular, such as 'intellect, imagination, emotions', or 'intellect, memory, imagination, passions, volition'. See R.M. Young, *Mind, brain, and adaptation in the nineteenth century* (Oxford University Press, 1970); and R. Smith, *Inhibition* (New Brunswick, NJ, Free Association Books, 1992).

13 E. Esquirol, *Des maladies mentales* (Paris, Baillière, 1838), vol. II, 72–83.

14 Goldstein, *Console and classify*, 170. Goldstein traces the decline of monomania diagnoses in the third quarter of the nineteenth century, and points out that the monomanias of the will were the first to be discredited. However, there seems to be at least some interest today in reviving this particular approach to diseases of the will; see H. Grivois and M. Gourevitch, *Les monomanies instinctives* (Paris, Masson, 1990).

15 E. Esquirol, *Mental maladies: a treatise on insanity* tr. E.K. Hunt (Philadelphia, Lea and Blanchard, 1845), 355.

16 The leading French expert on alcoholism in the late nineteenth century developed his theories through careful studies of dogs fed large quantities of alcohol and later dissected: V. Magnan, *De l'alcoolisme* (Paris, Delahaye, 1874). As late as 1907, alcoholism meant (in the leading scientific site of Yale's psychological laboratory) not a personality type or psychiatric syndrome but the effects of alcohol poisoning: see G. Cutten's Yale doctoral dissertation, *The psychology of alcoholism* (New York, Charles Scribner's Sons, and London, Walter Scott, 1907).

17 For the medicalization of the moral treatment invented by Quakers in Britain, see A. Scull, *Social order/mental disorder* (Berkeley, University of California, 1989), esp. ch. 4. Goldstein demonstrates that moral treatment was not easily medicalized in France, partly because of the persistent use of nuns and monks not only as nurses but to run and administer asylums (Goldstein, *Console and classify*).

18 There is a large literature on moral treatment and various interpretations of its role within psychiatry; see, for example, A. Digby, "Moral treatment at the Retreat, 1796–1846" in W.F. Bynum, R. Porter, and M. Shepherd, eds, *The anatomy of madness: essays in the history of psychiatry* vol. II (London, Tavistock, 1985), 52–72; and A. Scull, *The most solitary of afflictions: madness and society in Britain 1700–1900* (New Haven, Yale University Press, 1993), 188–213, who both stress the origins of moral treatment outside of and against medicine. Medicine, however, was never as unified and monolithic as Digby and Scull portray it.

19 Esquirol, *Mental maladies*, 356.

20 The term 'pastoral' is here borrowed from Foucault's analysis of the political function of Jewish and Christian metaphors of the shepherd in the

lecture entitled "Omnes et singulatim" in L. Kritzman, ed., *Michel Foucault: politics, philosophy, culture* (New York, Routledge, 1988), 57–85. The hybrid term 'pastoral–clinical' is chosen to stress that the pastoral quality of this type of treatment did not replace or exclude the better understood relations of the clinical gaze, but was rather integrated with it, often in an unsystematic and contradictory fashion. For current views on the clinical gaze, see C. Jones and R. Porter, eds, *Reassessing Foucault: power, medicine and the body* (London, Routledge, 1994).

21  Goldstein, *Console and classify*, 265. See also Scull, *Social order/mental disorder*, 66.

22  Entry for "Addiction" in *Oxford companion to medicine* (1986), vol. I, 313–14. An 1892 medical dictionary gives "dipsomania" as a synonym for drink monomania: *The New Sydenham Society's lexicon of medicine and the allied sciences* (London, The New Sydenham Society, 1892), vol. IV, unnumbered.

23  Magnan, *De l'alcoolisme*, 256.

24  A. Peddie, *The necessity for some legalised arrangements for the treatment of dipsomania or the drinking insanity* (Edinburgh, Sutherland and Knox, 1858). See also A. Peddie, *On the pathology of delirium tremens* (Edinburgh, Sutherland and Knox, 1854).

25  A. Peddie, "The Habitual Drunkards Act of 1879" *Proceedings BSSI* no. 7 (1886), 14–15.

26  See G. Johnstone, "From vice to disease? The concepts of dipsomania and inebriety, 1860–1908" *Social and Legal Studies* vol. 5 (1996), 37–56. Johnstone, however, incorrectly states that dipsomania and inebriety were synonymous.

27  *A dictionary of medicine* (London, Longmans, Green and Co., 1890), 381.

28  See, for instance, *Report of the Inspector* of inebriate institutions for 1912, British Parliamentary Papers (P.P.) 1914, xxxvi, 255, where the Inspector states that "inebriate" means "habitual drunkard, chronic alcoholic, or dipsomaniac".

29  T. Clouston, "Diseased cravings and paralysed control: dipsomania, morphinomania, choralism, cocainism" *Edinburgh Medical J.* vol. 35 (1889–90), 697, 998. On Dr Clouston (who was knighted in 1912, much to his competitor Henry Maudsley's chagrin), see M. Thompson, "The wages of sin: the problem of alcoholism and general paralysis in 19th century Edinburgh" in W.F. Bynum, R. Porter, and M. Shepherd, eds, *The anatomy of madness: essays in the history of psychiatry* vol. III (London, Routledge, 1988), 316–40.

30  R. Castel, *The regulation of madness: the origins of incarceration in France* (Berkeley, University of California, 1988).

31  See the anonymous article "Oinomania: or the mental pathology of intemperance" in *The Journal of Pathological Medicine and Mental Pathology* [London], vol. VIII (April 1, 1855), 175–207. The author states that oinomania (a term which he claims to have invented, although it appeared in Peddie's 1854 work as a term in use) is a type of monomania characterized by "a desire for pleasurable excitement and little power of the will" (p. 177). A. Peddie, *On the pathology* . . .

32  See, inter alia, A. Paredes, "The history of the concept of alcoholism" in R. Tarter and A. Sugerman, *Alcoholism: interdisciplinary approaches to an enduring problem* (Reading, Mass., Addison-Wesley, 1976).

33  See, for instance, Scull, *The most solitary of afflictions.*

34  J. Ordronaux, "Is habitual drunkenness a disease?" *American J. of Insanity* (April 1874), 439.

35  N. Kerr, "The relation of alcoholism to inebriety" [lecture to the British Medical Association], *Proceedings BSSI* no. 14 (1887), 14–15.

36  T.D. Crothers, "Alcoholism and inebriety: an etiological study" *British J. of Inebriety* vol. 2, no. 2 (1904), 70–5.

37  "We must not seek a formula in every case, but in some cases we must grasp the point by analogy" (*Metaphysics* 1048a).

38  This is how 'inebriety' appears in the *Quarterly J. of Studies on Alcohol*, insofar as it appears at all, which is rarely.

39  There is a vast literature on degeneration theory and its successor, eugenics. Most useful for my purposes have been D. Pick, *Faces of degeneration: a European disorder, 1818–1918* (Cambridge University Press, 1989); and N. Rose, *The psychological complex* (London, Routledge and Kegan Paul, 1985), chs 3 and 4.

40  The *Journal of the American Medical Association* (JAMA) published countless articles from 1900 to 1914 on whether alcohol was a "food" and a possible therapeutic aid or whether it was always "toxic". The journal's editors gave space to both views and occasionally took a position somewhere in between these two, obviously not wanting to alienate either 'wets' or 'drys'.

41  Caleb Saleeby stated that the first International Eugenics Congress definitively proved that "alcohol is a racial poison"; Saleeby in *British J. of Inebriety* vol. 10, no. 2 (1912), 59. For the European debates, see W.F. Bynum, "Alcoholism and degeneration in 19th century European medicine and psychiatry" *British J. of Addiction* 79 (1984), 59–70.

42  Like other French male intellectuals, Zola was primarily concerned with depopulation, not bad mothering; see R. Fuchs, *Poor and pregnant in Paris: strategies for survival in the 19th century* (New Brunswick, NJ, Rutgers University Press, 1992), esp. 56–57.

43  R.P. Hobson, *Alcohol and the human race* (New York and Chicago, Fleming Revell Company, 1919), 113. For more on social purity, see M. Valverde, *The age of light, soap, and water: moral reform in English Canada 1880s–1920s* (Toronto, McClelland and Stewart, 1991).

44  H.A. Moody, "Preventive medicine" *JAMA* (Nov. 14, 1903), 1200.

45  A. Sparks, "Alcoholism in women" *Medical News* 83, no. 1 (1903), 159.

46  A. Davin, "Imperialism and motherhood" *History Workshop* 5 (1978), 9–57; L. Zedner, *Women, crime and custody in Victorian England* (Oxford, Clarendon Press, 1991); L. Bland, *Banishing the beast: English feminism and sexual morality 1885–1914* (Penguin, 1995), ch. 6. It is worth noting that the *Proceedings* of the British Society for the Scientific Study of Inebriety did not begin to speak about race or about mothers until 1889, when these two topics suddenly gained prominence.

47  D.W. Gutzke, "'The cry of the children': the Edwardian medical campaign against maternal drinking" *British J. of Addiction* 79 (1984), 71–84.

48  L. Zedner, *Women, crime and custody*, ch. 6.

49  N. Kerr, *Inebriety or narcomania* (London, H.K. Lewis, 1894), 142.

50 Charles Booth was convinced that the drinking habits of the poor were responsible for much of their poverty. See C. Booth [et al.], *Life and labour of the people of London* (London, Williams and Margate, 1902), 17 vols; especially vol. 8, 59–75.

51 M. Scharlieb, "Alcohol and the children of the nation" *British J. of Inebriety* vol. 4, no. 2 (1907), 65. Similar views were expressed in a lecture at Oxford University by W. McAdam Eccles, "The relation of alcohol to physical deterioration and national efficiency" *British J. of Inebriety* vol. 5, no. 4 (1908); and by E. Sloan Chesser, "Inebriety among women" *British J. of Inebriety* vol. 6, no. 3 (1909), 186–89.

52 M. Scharlieb, presidential address, *British J. of Inebriety* vol. 10, no. 2 (1912), 57.

53 M. Valverde, "'When the mother of the race is free': race in the sexual and reproductive politics of first-wave feminism" in F. Iacovetta and M. Valverde, eds, *Gender conflicts: new essays in women's history* (University of Toronto Press, 1992).

54 K. Pearson and E. Elderton, *A second study of the influence of parental alcoholism on the physique and ability of the offspring* (Cambridge University Press, 1910).

55 W.F. Bynum, "Alcoholism and degeneration", 67–68.

56 For an overview of the public health programmes directed at the population of urban poor mothers, see E. Ross, *Love and toil in outcast London* (New York, Oxford University Press, 1995); C. Steedman, *Childhood, culture and class in Britain, Margaret McMillan 1860–1931* (New Brunswick, NJ, Rutgers University Press, 1990).

57 H. Campbell, "Principles of heredity: a review" *British J. of Inebriety* vol. 3, no. 1 (1905), 34. See also G.A. Reid, "The pathology of chronic alcoholism: a reply", same number, 16–30; this reply goes back to a debate between Reid and Dr Ford Roberts in 1903 and 1904 (vols 1 to 3, *British J. of Inebriety*).

58 W.C. Sullivan, "The children of the female inebriate", *Quarterly J. of Inebriety* vol. 22, no. 2 (1900), 129–38. This was also published as "The children of the female drunkard" *Proceedings BSSI* no. 63 (1900), 1–8.

59 One early article reporting scientific studies of alcohol's effect on fetuses was published in the *Journal of the American Medical Association* in 1901: anonymous note, "Congenital alcoholism" *JAMA* (March 30, 1901), 1214–15). Many others followed in the next few years.

60 W. Sullivan, *Alcoholism: a chapter in social pathology* (London, James Nisbet, 1906).

61 *Report of the Inspector* for 1909, British P.P. 1911, xxix, part 1, 13ff.

62 See D. Gutzke, *Protecting the pub* (London, Royal Historical Society, 1989), 244; and D. Gutzke, "'The cry of the children'", 71–84.

63 There were in the early twentieth century very few women doctors in Britain, and it is perhaps difficult to generalize. But women physicians elsewhere certainly shared the general medical enthusiasm for eugenics; for a study of English Canada, see A. MacLaren, *Our own master race: eugenics in Canada* (Toronto, McClelland and Stewart, 1991).

64 M. Gordon, "Female inebriates" *British J. of Inebriety* vol. 12, no. 2 (1914), 98–101. See also her reports for 1913 and 1914, included with the (male) Inspector's reports.

65 *Report of the Inspector* for 1905, British P.P. 1906, vol. xvi, 9; there, Branthwaite claims that only 37 per cent of inebriates are of average mental capacity. See also his 1906 *Report*, British P.P. 1907, x, 604ff. This research was published in the *British J. of Inebriety* vol. 5, no. 3 (1908), 112–19.

66 For example, F.W. Mott, "Alcohol and insanity" *British J. of Inebriety* vol. 9, no. 1 (1911), 19.

67 L. Zedner, *Women, crime and custody in Victorian England*, 295.

68 On the Mental Deficiency Act of 1913, see N. Rose, *The psychological complex* (London, Routledge and Kegan Paul, 1985), chs 3 and 4; D. Garland, *Punishment and welfare* (London, Gower, 1985), ch. 3; and J. Harris, *Private lives, public spirit: Britain 1870–1914* (Harmondsworth, Penguin, 1993), 29–30, 208.

69 On Maudsley, see A. Scull, C. Mackenzie, and N. Hervey, *Masters of Bedlam: the transformation of the mad-doctoring trade* (Princeton University Press, 1996), ch. 8.

70 H. Maudsley, *Body and will* (New York, Appleton, 1884). See also H. Maudsley, *The physiology of mind* (London, Macmillan, 1876).

71 Maudsley, *Body and will*, 27, 29, 191, 192.

72 For example, see S.E.D. Shortt, *Victorian lunacy: Richard M. Bucke and the practice of late nineteenth century psychiatry* (Cambridge University Press, 1986).

73 Hobson, *Alcohol and the human race*, 83.

74 Maudsley, *Body and will*, 273.

75 On Ribot's construction of a science of the diseases of memory, see Hacking, *Rewriting the soul*, 165ff. Ribot's work *The diseases of the will* went through many editions in both French and English from 1894 onward; I have used the fourth, enlarged English edition (Chicago, Open Court, 1915).

76 Ribot, *The diseases of the will*, 61.

77 T. Ribot, *Heredity* (New York, Appleton, 1889), esp. 335–46.

78 W.J. Collins, "An address on the institutional treatment of inebriety" *British J. of Inebriety* vol. 1, no. 1 (1903), 110–11.

79 C. Palmer, *Inebriety: its source, prevention, and cure* (New York, Fleming Revell, 1898). By the third edition this little book had sold 7,000 copies, according to an insert in the copy I used.

80 Cutten, *The psychology of alcoholism*, 125.

81 T. Wright, "The special influences of alcohol – the morals" *Proceedings BSSI* no. 38 (1893), 14.

82 The last quote is from an Ovaltine advertisement appearing regularly in the *British J. of Inebriety*, 1908–10. In the first decade of the twentieth century, Coca-Cola (which then contained small amounts of coca) was also marketed as a remedy for tiredness, headache, and "brain fag" (The World of Coca-Cola museum, Atlanta, Georgia).

83 See, for example, the recipe for drunkenness tonic in *JAMA* (Nov. 9, 1901), 1271; *JAMA* (April 27, 1901), 338; *JAMA* (August 11, 1900), 337–38; and *JAMA* (May 26, 1900), 1329. In an anticipation of the Antabuse treatment popular in the 1950s, one physician wrote in with his recipe (which included both nitroglycerine and strychnine) "to create a distaste for drink", *JAMA* (July 21, 1900), 160.

84 See, for example, the article summarized in *JAMA* (Nov. 16, 1901), 1351, which advocates the use of drugs to help break the physical habit, but emphasizes that the doctor must "get the patient's consent and cooperation" and support him in his resolution.

85 "Hypnotism in alcoholism" *JAMA* (July 2 (?) 1903), 1680; "Dipsomania and its treatment by suggestion" *JAMA* (August 18, 1900), 456.

86 F. Hare, "The medical treatment of inebriety" *British J. of Inebriety* vol. 3, no. 4 (1906), 201.

87 Kerr, *Inebriety*, 197, 17. As one would suspect from this rhetoric, Dr Kerr was a member of the Church of England Temperance Society as well as a physician.

88 An ex-patient, "The psychoanalysis of an inebriate: a record of experiences and reflections" *British J. of Inebriety* vol. 12, no. 1 (1914), 22–27.

89 In *the birth of the clinic*, Foucault discusses the concern of early clinical medicine for individual features (which is in contrast to the impersonal taxonomies of biopower). But many alcoholism treatments seem to have exceeded or disrupted the clinical gaze, which is why I have used the term 'pastoral–clinical'. M. Foucault, *Birth of the clinic: an archaeology of medical perception* (London, Tavistock, 1973).

90 G.H.R. Dobbs, "Fluid alternatives" *British J. of Inebriety* vol. 2, no. 1 (1904), 37–38.

91 Goldstein emphasizes that moral treatment was not medicalized in France particularly effectively: against Foucault's and Castel's exaggerated claims about the victory of discipline, her work documents a religious tradition of consoling the mentally afflicted that lasted – even in lunatic asylums – until the very end of the nineteenth century (Goldstein, *Console and classify*).

92 For these case studies or stories, see Kerr, *Inebriety*, 6, 9, 44–50, 58.

93 For a discussion of the Rev. Willis' treatment of King George III, the situation that popularized moral treatment, see Goldstein, *Console and classify*, 86–87; and Scull, *Social order/mental disorder*, 66.

94 Goldstein, *Console and classify*, 265.

95 R. Castel, *The regulation of madness*, 75. This transfusion of the will was said by Pinel to be particularly effective for cases of mania.

96 A similar point could be made in regard to hypnotism, a treatment often associated with omnipotence on the part of the practitioner, but which was often thought to work only on those who wanted to be hypnotized.

97 N. Rose, *Governing the soul* (London, Routledge, 1990).

## 3 THE FRAGMENTATION OF INEBRIETY

1 A. Oakley Hall, "American legislation for the inebriate" *Proceedings BSSI* no. 2 (1884), 1–8. The mixed-economy technique of providing public funding for philanthropic institutions was widely used in both the US and Canada: M. Valverde, "The mixed social economy as a Canadian tradition" *Studies in Political Economy* 47 (1995). In the UK the existence of the Poor Law meant that public funding for social services was monopolized by fully public institutions.

2 J. Baumohl, "Inebriate institutions in North America, 1840–1920" in C. Warsh, ed., *Drink in Canada: historical essays* (Montreal, McGill-Queen's Press, 1993), 92–114.

3 *Proceedings* of the American Society for the Study and Cure of Inebriety, 1870–1875 (reprinted New York, Arno Press, 1981).

4 A substantial majority of the articles on inebriety published in American medical journals, including the influential *JAMA*, from 1900 to 1914, were authored by Dr Crothers, and were often reprints from his own specialist *Quarterly Journal of Inebriety*.

5 R. Harris, *Murders and madness: medicine, law and society in the fin de siecle* (Oxford, Clarendon Press, 1989), ch. 7.

6 Dr D.G. Dodge, "Restraint as a remedy in the treatment of inebriety" *Proceedings* of the American Society for the Study and Cure of Inebriety for 1870 [New York, Arno Reprints, 1981], 53, 55.

7 [T.D. Crothers], *The disease of inebriety* (American Society for the Study and Cure of Inebriety, 1893), 215–16. Patient rebellions, not at all common in lunatic asylums, seemed a regular feature of inebriate asylums: the Massachusetts state hospital for dipsomaniacs and inebriates, opened in 1893, was soon closed partly because of patient uprisings (J. Baumhol, "Inebriate institutions", 112).

8 [T.D. Crothers] *The disease of inebriety*, 22–24. A similar account of the failure of this institution is found in C.J. Douglas, "Historical notes on the sanatorium treatment of alcoholism" *Medical Record* 57 (1900), 410.

9 T.D. Crothers, "The Norman Kerr Memorial Lecture" *British J.of Inebriety* vol. 3, no. 3 (1906), 122–24.

10 See, for instance, "Minnesota law for treatment of inebriates invalid", anonymous note in *JAMA* (Dec. 22, 1900), 1655.

11 Crothers, "The Norman Kerr Memorial Lecture", 124.

12 J. Baumohl, "Inebriate institutions in North America"; and J. Baumohl, "Dashaways and doctors: the treatment of habitual drunkards in San Francisco from the Gold Rush to Prohibition" (DSW thesis, University of California at Berkeley, 1986). On temperance and respectability, see the classic work by J. Gusfield, *Symbolic crusade: status politics and the American temperance movement* (Urbana, University of Illinois Press, 1963); and R. Bordin, *Woman and temperance: the quest for power and liberty 1873–1900* (New Brunswick, NJ, Rutgers University Press, 1990).

13 To medicalize excessive drinking, Crothers used an eclectic mixture of the fashionable discourse of degeneration and earlier medical views about the role of such traumas as railway accidents, grief, and sunstroke in causing inebriety and other forms of madness. See, for instance, Crothers, "Dementia preceding and following inebriety" *JAMA* (Feb. 1, 1902), 307–10.

14 At least one alcohol specialist believed that Keeley did not give patients gold chloride, but rather hypnotized them. This speculation is consistent with the belief that no drug cures would ever be found, since alcoholism was not a physiological condition but a disease of the will. See G. Cutten, *The psychology of alcoholism* (New York, Charles Scribner's Sons, and London, Walter Scott, 1907), 322–24.

15 G.M. Beard, "Chronic alcoholism" *Proceedings* of the American Society for the Study and Cure of Inebriety (1874), 47 [New York, Arno Reprints, 1981]. On Beard and neurasthenia, see F. Gosling, *Before Freud: neurasthenia and the American medical community* (Urbana, University of Illinois Press, 1987); and A. Rabinach, *The human motor* (New York, Basic Books, 1990), 153–73. In the United States, neurasthenia became a rich source of both cultural and financial capital for the emerging profession of psychology; but in Britain, where psychology around 1900 tended to be more akin to neurology and physiology than to psychiatry, neurasthenia seems to have been diagnosed by the same physicians who dealt with the legally insane, that is, those we would call psychiatrists, at least until the emergence of the shellshock diagnosis during World War I. See, among others, M. Stone, "Shellshock and the psychologists" in W.F. Bynum, R. Porter, and M. Shepherd, eds, *The anatomy of madness: essays in the history of psychiatry*, vol. II (London, Tavistock, 1985), 242–71.

16 J. Collins, "The law and the inebriate: with remarks on the treatment of inebriety" *New York Medical Journal* vol. 73 (May 4, 1901), 765.

17 C.J. Douglas, "Historical notes on the sanatorium treatment of alcoholism" *Medical Record* vol. 57 (1900), 410.

18 S. Garton, "'Once a drunkard, always a drunkard': social reform and the problem of 'habitual drunkenness' in Australia, 1880–1914" *Labor History* no. 53 (1987), 38–53.

19 For an interesting early plea for inebriate legislation, see J. Bovell, *A plea for inebriate asylums presented to the legislature of the province of Canada* (Toronto, Lovell and Gibson, 1862). Bovell was a professor of theology at the high-Anglican Trinity College and a medical doctor.

20 Baumohl, "Inebriate institutions", 107–108. For the funding of asylums, see S.E.D. Shortt, *Victorian lunacy: Richard M. Bucke and the practice of late nineteenth century psychiatry* (Cambridge University Press, 1986), 33–34. In 1893 Ontario asylums received just over half a million dollars, out of a total provincial expenditure of less than four million. In 1900 the Ontario legislature was considering yet another inebriate bill; see anonymous note in *JAMA* vol. 34 (1900), 1572.

21 Gallup Poll of Canada, May 30, 1953.

22 The negative and fatalistic attitudes of public hospital physicians are documented in R. Straus, "Problem drinking in the perspective of social change, 1940–1973" in W. Filstead, J. Rossi, and M. Keller, eds, *Alcohol and alcohol problems: new thinking and new directions* (Cambridge, Mass., Ballinger, 1976). The optimistic exception to this general trend was the network of federally funded alcoholism centres set up under the 1970 alcoholism law. See D. Armor, M. Polich, and H. Stambul, *Alcoholism and treatment* (New York, John Wiley, 1978).

23 L. Zedner, *Women, crime and custody in Victorian England* (Oxford, Clarendon Press, 1991), ch. 6; G. Hunt, J. Mellor, and J. Turner, "Wretched, hatless and miserably clad: women and the inebriate reformatories from 1900–1913" *British J. of Sociology* vol. 40, no. 2 (1989), 244–70; and G. Johnstone, "From vice to disease? The concepts of dipsomania and inebriety, 1860–1908" *Social and Legal Studies* vol. 5, no. 1 (1996), 37–56.

24 An Act to Provide for the Treatment of Habitual Inebriates, 12 August 1898, 62 Vict.

25 *Report of the Inspector* for 1906, British P.P. 1907, x, 594. The 80 per cent figure is not an artefact of a one-off sweep on mothers; that same percentage obtains for the first five years of the Acts' operation.

26 A. Peddie, "The Habitual Drunkards Act, 1879" *Proceedings BSSI* no. 7 (1886), 7. See also B. Price, "Legislation and the care and control of the inebriate" *British J. of Inebriety* vol. 10, no. 1 (1912), 25–34; and the 1908 *Report of the Departmental Committee* . . . British P.P. 1908, xii, 817ff, which contains a brief history of the legislation.

27 Definition quoted in the *Report of the Departmental Committee* British P.P. 1908, xii, 3.

28 *Report of the Inspector* for 1901, British P.P. 1902, xii, 47.

29 *Report of the Inspector* for 1912, British P.P. 1914, xxxvi, 263.

30 By 1912, close to the end of the Acts, 4,403 patients had been admitted to retreats under the Acts, 5,504 privately; and of course many other private patients sought help in homes not licenced under the Acts at all. *Report of the Inspector* for 1912, British P.P. 1914, xxxvi, 270.

31 "Annual Report of Licencee of Newmains Retreat for the Year 1907" in the *Report* of the Inspector of Inebriates for Scotland for 1907, British P.P. 1908, xii, 13. (Scottish institutions had their own inspector.) Scotland had been a popular site for establishments catering to the nervous middle classes, partly because it was out of reach of the English Lunacy Commissioners; that legal consideration would not apply to inebriates, but undoubtedly some existing private establishments in Scotland sought to expand their clientele by seeking out legal inebriates.

32 *Report of the Inspector* for 1896, British P.P. 1897, xvii, 691–95. The Salvation Army later reported running a home for inebriate women, called The Grove, so the administration of this institution may have changed hands.

33 Lady Somerset's Duxhurst project included a "farm colony" for working-class women and what she called a "Manor House" on the same grounds but in a different building; the surplus income from the Manor House paying patients was used to provide for the poor women in the farm colony. See, for example, *Report of the Inspector* for 1901, British P.P. 1902, xii, 617.

34 Lady H. Somerset, "The female inebriate" *British J. of Inebriety* vol. 12, no. 1 (July 1914), 8.

35 Information compiled from the annual *Reports of the Inspector*; see also N. Kerr, "President's address" *Proceedings BSSI* no. 8 (1886), 1–8.

36 Dr Hogg's report, reproduced in *British J. of Inebriety* vol. 9 (1911), 48–50.

37 Advertisement for the Invernith Lodge Retreat in Colinsburgh, Scotland, in the back of the *British J. of Inebriety*, numerous issues (e.g. 1908, 1909, 1910). The licencee for this institution was firmly opposed to drug cures advertised by non-licenced establishments; see, for example, his report included in the *Report of the Inspector* for Scotland, British P.P. 1908, xiii, 1258.

38 Advertisement for "Plas-Yn-Dinas", back pages of *British J. of Inebriety*, 1910–14.

39 Robert Parr, director of the NSPCC, justified this gender-specific policy at length in his "Alcoholism and cruelty to children" *British J. of Inebriety* vol. 6, no. 2 (1908), 77–81.

40 D. Garland, *Punishment and welfare* (London, Gower, 1985); R. Nye, *Crime, madness and politics in modern France* (Princeton University Press, 1984); R. Harris, *Murders and madness.*

41 J. Sturrock, "The criminal inebriate woman" *British J. of Inebriety* vol. 10, no. 2 (1911), 203–4. In much of the contemporary literature on female working-class inebriates, the names used to designate typical cases are often Irish.

42 *Report of the Inspector* for 1909, British P.P. 1911, xxix, part 1, 45.

43 *Report of the Inspector* for 1903, British P.P. 1905, xi, 136; *Report of the Inspector* for 1906, British P.P. 1907, x, 608.

44 On the radical shift in alcohol management that took place in 1914, see J. Woiak, "'A medical Cromwell to depose King Alcohol': medical scientists, temperance reformers, and the alcohol problem in Britain" *Social History/Histoire Sociale* vol. 27, no. 54 (1994), 360–61.

45 L. Radcinowicz and R. Hood, *A history of English criminal law* vol. 5 (London, Stevens and Sons, 1986), 35.

46 Garland, *Punishment and welfare*, 218.

47 Mental Deficiency Act, 15 August 1913, 4 Geo. 5; on the children of inebriates, see Garland, *Punishment and welfare*, 222–23.

48 R. Smith, *Inhibition* (New Brunswick, NJ, Free Association Books, 1992).

49 R. Castel, *The regulation of madness* (Berkeley, University of California, 1988), 217.

50 T. Osborne, "Medicine and epistemology: Michel Foucault and the liberality of clinical reason" *History of the Human Sciences* vol. 5, no. 2 (1992), 63–93.

51 J. Fairbank, *Booth's boots: social service beginnings in the Salvation Army* (London, Salvation Army, 1983); L. Marks, "Hallelujah lasses" in F. Iacovetta and M. Valverde, eds, *Gender conflicts: new essays in women's history* (University of Toronto Press, 1992); M. Valverde, *The age of light, soap, and water* (Toronto, McClelland and Stewart, 1991), ch. 5.

52 Anonymous, "The experiences of a dipsomaniac" *Social Gazette* [London] (June 9, 1900), 1–2.

53 The records of the British Salvation Army were largely destroyed when their London headquarters was bombed during World War II, but there are printed publications that survive and have been consulted. In addition, the weekly newspaper (*War Cry*) and the annual social-work reports of the Canadian Salvation Army, which I have consulted at the Army's archives in Toronto, carry many reports of the Army's work around the world, especially in Britain. For present purposes I am making no distinctions among the different national branches of the Salvation Army.

54 "One of love's triumphs" *Love did it* [annual report of Canadian Salvation Army's social work] (Toronto, Salvation Army Heritage Centre, 1897), 8.

55 Mrs Gen. Booth, "Problems of social work in their legal aspect" *International Social Council of 1921* (Toronto, Salvation Army Heritage Centre), 143.

56 C. Bramwell-Booth, *Catherine Booth: the story of her loves* (London, Hodder and Stoughton, 1970), 247.

57 Mrs Bramwell Booth, "The management of the inebriate woman" *The Deliverer*, Nov. 1911 (Toronto, Salvation Army Heritage Centre), 164.

58 *Report of the Departmental Committee* British P.P. 1908, xii, 820.

59 *Report of the Departmental Committee* British P.P. 1908, xii, 5–6.

60 The exception to this general rule is behaviourist psychology, which was at its height aimed exclusively at measuring habits and finding ways to mechanically alter them. The behaviourist understanding of habit, aimed at scientifically colonizing the realm of ethics, defeats itself precisely by eliminating the ethical. Behaviourism dispenses completely with the notion of a *character* that one works on – there is no care of self in behaviourism, only mechanical responses. When people other than behaviourist psychologists speak of habits they refer not to *behaviour* but rather to *conduct* that may not be consciously willed but is nevertheless not devoid of subjective significance and intentionality. Psychological programmes today have gone back to something closer to the Victorian understanding of habit, restoring the human or subjective dimension in everything from labour relations in auto plants to schooling techniques.

61 M. Foucault, *The use of pleasure: volume 2 of the history of sexuality* (New York, Vintage Books, 1985).

## 4 ENLIGHTENED HEDONISM

1 A tolerant attitude toward drunken sprees is evident in two articles written by US military officers: F. Harrison, "The alcohol problem in the navy" *Quarterly J. of Studies on Alcohol* [henceforth *QJSA*] vol. 5 (1944–45), 413–25; and I. Berlien, "Alcohol and the soldier" *QJSA* vol. 5 (1944–45), 405–12. In both of these articles, the alcohol problem is reduced to the problem of a small number of alcoholics who drink constantly and whose ability to function while on duty is severely impaired.

2 A. Myerson, "Alcohol: a study of social ambivalence" *QJSA* vol. 1 (1940–41), 13–20.

3 S. Bacon, "The classic temperance movement of the USA", *British J. of Addiction* vol. 62 (1967), 5–18. Bacon prided himself on being a member of the noted Yankee Bacon family and a descendant of Francis Bacon, a position which distinguished him from the other early alcohologists, many of whom were Central European immigrants.

4 The British Society for the Study of Addiction did concern itself periodically with para-medical issues, such as drinking and driving. But its capacity to govern the circulation of alcohol throughout society – as opposed to governing the medical entities of inebriety and addiction – was severely hampered by the fact that only physicians were allowed to be full members and to speak at meetings; anybody else with experience in alcohol issues was relegated to associate status.

5 P. Miller and N. Rose, "Mobilizing the consumer: assembling the subject of consumption" *Theory, Culture, and Society* vol. 14, no. 1 (1997), 1–36, a study of the Tavistock's work with advertising issues; and P. Miller and N. Rose,

"The Tavistock programme: governing subjectivity and social life" *Sociology* 22 (1988), 171–92.

6  The administration at Yale University, never an enthusiastic supporter of the centre, became positively hostile to it in the 1950s. Jellinek moved away to work for the World Health Organization, and it was left to Selden Bacon – a member of the New Haven elite – to defend the centre, but eventually, in 1960, the Yale Corporation voted "that the administration should help the Center for Alcohol Studies to find a more appropiate home". Interview with M. Keller, in G. Edwards, ed., *Addictions: personal influences and scientific movements* (New Brunswick, NJ, 1991), 62. The other interviews with Yale personnel in this anthology generally support Keller's account.

7  The World League Against Alcoholism, active in the 1920s, was a Protestant temperance organization, although, like all moral reform movements of the 1920s in the English-speaking world, it was interested in scientific research. See, for instance, the programme of the International Convention against alcoholism held in Toronto in November 1922 (Griffin-Greenland Collection, Archives of Canadian psychiatry, Queen Street Mental Health Centre, Toronto).

8  AMA statement quoted in T. Plaut, *Alcohol problems: a report to the nation* (New York, Oxford University Press, 1967), 191–92; see also 27.

9  Antabuse was invented in Denmark in the mid-1950s and quickly became popular in European and American hospitals and in private practice. The drug, if combined with alcohol, produces extreme nausea and other ill effects; but, as physicians quickly realized, it was no easier to convince alcoholics to take Antabuse every day than to persuade them to stop drinking in the first place.

10  R. Roizen, "The American discovery of alcoholism, 1933–1939" (PhD thesis, University of California at Berkeley, 1991), viii, 276, and passim. See also R. Room, "Governing images of alcohol and drug problems: the structure, sources and sequels of the conceptualizations of intractable problems" (PhD thesis, University of California at Berkeley, 1978).

11  R. Roizen, "How does the nation's 'alcohol problem' change from era to era? Stalking the social logic of problem-definition transformations since repeal", paper to conference on historical perspectives on alcohol and drug use in American society, Philadelphia, May 1997.

12  The phrase 'problem drinkers' seems to have acted as a switchpoint between the older, more medicalized alcoholism studies and the newer, more sociological interest in alcohol problems. See, for instance, D. Cahalan, *Problem drinkers* (San Francisco, Jossey-Bass, 1970). For an analysis of this and other historical shifts in American alcohology, see Room, "Governing images of alcohol".

13  "Interview with Mark Keller" in Edwards, *Addictions*, 61. Keller himself, a Central European immigrant like several other American alcohol scientists, came into alcohol studies via physiological research, but he was not a physician. See also the interview with Selden Bacon in the same volume.

14  The text of the summer school lectures was published by the Yale Center for Alcohol Studies under the title *Alcohol, science, and society* (Yale University,

1945). The lecturers at this school included four MDs, but they were heavily outnumbered by a combination of sociologists, psychologists, social workers, clergymen, and assorted others, including a judge and a traffic expert.

15 E.M. Jellinek, in Yale Center for Alcohol Studies, *Alcohol, science, and society*, 111.

16 An article proving that children of alcoholics adopted by non-alcoholics did *not* become alcoholics in disproportionate numbers opened with the following statement: "Innumerable reports have pointed out that among the offspring of alcoholics infant mortality is high, and epilepsy, idiocy, psychosis and excessive drinking are common. Many of these studies have been interpreted as indicative of physical or chemical germ damage. The present consensus is that this does *not* occur." A. Roe, "The adult adjustment of children of alcoholic parents raised in foster homes" *QJSA* vol. 5 (1944–45), 378.

17 I owe this point to a discussion at the Toronto History of the Present group; special thanks to Steve Katz and Lorna Weir.

18 Dr Dent, a major figure in the society, relentlessly pursued somatic explanations and physical cures throughout the 1950s; the society also built up a research fund that was specifically earmarked for biological research into neurological function.

19 There was one major exception to the marginalization of psychiatry within alcoholism treatment, and that was the publicly funded network of veterans hospitals; but even in those hospitals the actual treatment of alcoholics tended to be left to psychologists (Robin Room, personal communication).

20 The sociologist was David Pittman, and the unit opened in 1961 in the Washington University Medical Center, St Louis, Missouri. See D. Pittman, ed., *Alcoholism* (New York, Harper and Row, 1967), especially his own article; and D. Pittman and C. Snyder, eds, *Society, culture and drinking patterns* (New York, John Wiley and Sons, 1962).

21 S. Bacon, "Concepts" in W. Filstead, J. Rossi, and M. Weller, eds, *Alcohol and alcohol problems: new thinking and new directions* (Cambridge, Mass., Ballinger, 1976), 121.

22 Bacon, "Concepts", 95.

23 Veyne explains that Foucault's method was not so much to map general historical shifts as to provide the tools to analyze the changing "objectivizations" through which governing practices are carried out. P. Veyne, "Foucault revolutionizes history" in A. Davidson, ed., *Foucault and his interlocutors* (University of Chicago Press, 1997), 154, 155.

24 The publications of Toronto's Addiction Research Foundation – which began life as the Alcoholism Research Foundation of Ontario, then changing its name to the Alcoholism and Drug Addiction Research Foundation, until alcohol was finally erased completely from its title – are a case in point. The Finnish Foundation for Alcohol Studies in Helsinki is an exception to this general trend to eliminate alcohol's specificity under the broader label of addiction.

25 R. Room, "Alcohol and drug disorders in the International Classification of Diseases: a shifting kaleidoscope", paper prepared for 23rd annual alcohol epidemiology symposium, Reykjavik, June 1997; see also R. Room et al.,

"WHO cross-cultural applicability research on diagnosis and assessment of substance use disorders: an overview of methods and selected results" *Addiction* vol. 91, no. 2 (1996), 199–200.

26  J. Thomas, "Alcoholism and mental disorder" *British J. of Inebriety* vol. 37, no. 2 (1939), 76.

27  S. Bacon, "The administration of alcoholism rehabilitation programs" *QJSA* vol. 10 (1949), 5–6.

28  M. Chafetz, "Practical and theoretical considerations in the psychotherapy of alcoholism" *QJSA* vol. 20 (1959), 281. See also D. Odlum, "Alcoholism and drug addiction in relation to mental health" *British J. of Inebriety* vol. 34, no. 2 (1936), 55–60; and D.K. Henderson, "Alcoholism and psychiatry" *British J. of Inebriety* vol. 34 no. 3 (1937), 99–123.

29  C. Landis, "Theories of the alcoholic personality" in Yale Center for Alcohol Studies, *Alcohol, science, and society*, 130.

30  N. Lewis, "Personality factors in alcoholic addiction" *QJSA* vol. 1 (1940–41), 23–24.

31  Bacon, "The administration of alcoholism rehabilitation programs", 3.

32  E.M. Jellinek, "Phases in the drinking history of alcoholics" *QJSA* vol. 7 (1946–47), 1–87.

33  The most comprehensive and rigorous compilation of alcohology around 1960 was Pittman and Snyder, eds, *Society, culture, and drinking patterns*, a massive interdisciplinary volume characterized by sophisticated methods of social inquiry and a certain skepticism about the notion of alcoholism.

34  M. Glatt, "Group therapy in alcoholism" *British J. of Addiction* vol. 54, no. 2 (1957), 143.

35  T. Plaut, *Alcohol problems*, 74.

36  Bacon, "Concepts", 92–93. In the United Kingdom, Dr Glatt's group therapy at Warlingham Park Hospital included referral to AA groups, although the psychotherapy work in the hospital itself was done by physicians.

37  D. Stafford-Clark, *Psychiatry today* (Harmondsworth, Penguin, 1963 [1952]), 132. Like other British physicians, Stafford-Clark tends to emphasize biological factors and inheritance more than American alcohologists do.

38  The discussions of the British Society for the Scientific Study of Inebriety in the 1940s and 1950s contain repeated self-congratulatory remarks about the gradual disappearance of the population of female habitual inebriates that had, at the turn of the century, been the prime target of the Habitual Inebriates Acts. Although this topic received no special study, the offhand remarks suggest that the physicians believed that rising standards of living and more middle-class patterns of heterosocial leisure had made the urban fallen woman an anachronism.

39  The German psychoanalyst Wilhelm Stekel had put this theory forward in the 1920s: "Drunkards suffer from serious paraphilias (sadism, necrophilia, pedophilia, zoophilia, etc); nearly all of them are latent homosexuals . . ." W. Stekel, *Peculiarities of behaviour* (London, Williams and Norgate, 1925), vol. 1, 202. Karl Abraham is also quoted as stating that "every drinking bout is tinged with homosexuality", by N. Lewis, "Personality factors in alcoholic addiction", (p. 30), but Lewis himself cites this only to disagree with it.

40 Commenting on the movie version of *The lost weekend*, Selden Bacon complained that the film showed hospital treatment facilities in a very bad light. He further complained that the portrayal of the Manhattan bar in which much of the action takes place suggests that the sheer availability of alcohol produces alcoholics. In Bacon's somewhat skewed view, the film covertly supported the temperance movement's view that alcohol was inherently bad. "Current notes" [signed S.D.B.], *QJSA* vol. 6, no. 3 (1945), 402–5.

41 C. Jackson, *The lost weekend* (New York, Farrar and Rinehart, 1994; London, John Lane, 1945).

42 F. Halpern, "Studies of compulsive drinkers: psychological test results" *QJSA* vol. 6, no. 4 (1946), 477.

43 H. Blane, *The personality of the alcoholic: guises of dependency* (New York, Harper and Row, 1969), 14.

44 The typographical instability of Blane's text is likely rooted in the fact that, in medical circles, addiction is regarded as a matter of physical *dependence*, while broader public discussions of issues such as welfare often use the spelling 'dependency'. As noted in chapter 1, today's discussions about codependency show the same typographical instability, with much the same effects.

45 E. O'Neill, *The iceman cometh* (New York, Vintage, 1946). Although published in 1946, the play was copyrighted in 1940.

46 For an interesting account of the sharp differences between female and male alcoholics in Hollywood films of this time, see M. Kanner, "Drinking themselves to life, or the body in the bottle" in C.B. Burroughs and J.D. Ehrenreich, eds, *Reading the social body* (University of Iowa Press, 1993), 156–70.

47 R. Straus and S. Bacon, "Alcoholism and social stability" *QJSA* vol. 12 (1951), 260. Straus and Bacon overtly stated that women alcoholics were, like social drifters, not worth helping.

48 R. Straus, "Problem drinking in the perspective of social change, 1940–1973" in Filstead et al., *Alcohol and alcohol problems*, 47.

49 D. Courtwright, *Dark paradise: opium addiction in America before 1940* (Cambridge, Mass., Harvard University Press, 1982).

50 S. Bacon interview in Edwards, *Addictions*, 69.

51 Interview with R. Straus, in Edwards, *Addictions*, 87.

52 The results of the small-scale AA survey were published as Jellinek, "Phases in the drinking history of alcoholics", 1–88. The theory of the phases contained in that article was popularized by Jellinek himself in the Yale summer courses on alcohol issues. He later modified the questionnaire and administered it to a much larger population of 2,000; those results were published under the auspices of the World Health Organization's alcoholism subcommittee and reprinted as E.M. Jellinek, "Phases of alcohol addiction" *QJSA* vol. 13 (1952), 673–84.

53 H. Trice and R. Wahl, "A rank order analysis of the symptoms of alcoholism" in Pittman and Snyder, *Society, culture and drinking patterns*, 361–81.

54 E.M. Jellinek, *The disease concept of alcoholism* (New Haven, CT, Hillhouse Press, 1960), 36.

55 Jellinek, *The disease concept of alcoholism*, 37–38. There are also "delta" alcoholics, but this type seems more of a grab-bag for people who do not fit the other types than a distinct type.

56 Jellinek, "Phases of alcohol addiction", 673.

57 One work that would become highly influential, not so much in alcohology but in the growing field of social problems research, was J. Gusfield, *Symbolic crusade: status politics and the American temperance movement* (Urbana, University of Illinois, 1963). Gusfield was not at Yale, but he worked in collaboration with the younger leaders of alcohology, Harry Levine and Robin Room, and was associated with the Berkeley Alcohol Research Group.

58 Jellinek, *The disease concept of alcoholism*, 35. Emphasis in original.

59 Reflecting his eclecticism, Jellinek changed his terminology several times during these years in quite fundamental ways ('addiction', for instance, was in favour at first, then out of favour, then back in), but discussion of this has been omitted here for the sake of clarity.

60 Jellinek, "Phases of alcohol addiction", 680–81.

61 Jellinek, *The disease concept of alcoholism*, 12.

62 In this regard, a key anthropological text developing the hedonism side of postwar alcohology and explicitly refusing epidemiology's premise that alcohol was a real social problem is the collection edited by M. Douglas, *Constructive drinking* Cambridge University Press, 1987).

63 Plaut, *Alcohol problems*, 129.

64 Plaut, *Alcohol problems*, 135.

65 Typically, people of Chinese descent are underrepresented in American statistics on alcoholism treatment and drinking-driving offences. Some alcohologists explained this biologically by claiming that "Orientals" tended to experience physical distress if they drank too much (the so-called "Oriental flush"). Most alcohol studies, however, paid no attention to Chinese drinking.

66 R. Bales, "Cultural differences in rates of alcoholism" *QJSA* vol. 6, no. 4 (1946), 480–99.

67 C. Snyder, *Alcohol and the Jews* (Yale Center for Alcohol Studies and the Free Press, 1958).

68 Snyder, *Alcohol and the Jews*, 10.

69 A later study of ethnic differences in mental dysfunction and drinking problems among US Army recruits apparently also showed that "since psychiatric illness among Jews is at least as high as among non-Jews of comparable social class and educational levels, the low rates of problem drinking cannot be understood in terms of generally lower frequency of psychological disorders. Thus it is probable that attitudes and practices regarding drinking are responsible for the lower rates of problem drinking." Plaut, *Alcohol problems*, 125–26.

70 Bales, "Cultural differences", 484. Bales claims that this attachment to the mother was documented in his own psychological testing of eighty Irish-American alcoholic men, but this testing had no control group.

71 The Irish drunk stereotype was challenged – from the standpoint of ethnic sociology, not alcohology – in R. Stivers, *A hair of the dog: Irish drinking and American stereotypes* (Philadelphia, Pennsylvania University Press, 1976).

72 C. MacAndrew and R.B. Edgerton, *Drunken comportment: a social explanation* (Chicago, Aldine, 1969).

73 On this shift, see R. Smart and C. Ogborne, *Northern spirits: a social history of alcohol in Canada* (Toronto, Addiction Research Foundation, 1997), 173–75, and R. Room, "Sociological aspects of the disease concept of alcoholism" in *Research advances in alcohol and drug problems* vol. 7 (1983), 47–91.

## 5 THE POWER OF POWERLESSNESS

1 See, for instance, K. Plummer, *Telling sexual stories: power, change and social worlds* (London, Routledge, 1995).

2 Tradition 10 states: "No AA group or member should ever, in such a way as to implicate AA, express any opinion on outside controversial issues – particularly those of politics, alcohol reform, or sectarian religion. The Alcoholics Anonymous groups oppose no one" (*Alcoholics Anonymous* [The Big Book], 3rd edn, 567).

3 A. Collins, "The pathological gambler and the government of gambling" *History of the Human Sciences* vol. 9, no. 3 (1996), 69–100.

4 This is not to say that either AA or alcohol science caused rising levels of alcohol consumption; the rising level of aggregate consumption that occurred in most industrialized countries in the period 1945–75 was part of a general shift in both the economics and the culture of consumption.

5 Challenging the monopoly of doctors over diagnosis does not necessarily challenge medicine as such, since, as Nikolas Rose has observed, the history of medical authority is not coterminous with the history of the profession. There are various assemblages, including AA, in which medical techniques are deployed for a number of ends. See N. Rose, "Medicine, history, and the present" in C. Jones and R. Porter, *Reassessing Foucault: power, medicine and the body* (London, Routledge, 1994).

6 Alcoholics Anonymous, 1996 Membership Survey, no pagination.

7 Interview no. 9, 1997.

8 Some AA texts prefer the term 'illness' to 'disease', precisely because it sounds less medical.

9 This was the definition given to me by a man chairing a small AA group (group no. 2); it is closely based on the text of the Big Book.

10 P. Antze, "Symbolic action in Alcoholics Anonymous" in Mary Douglas, ed., *Constructive drinking* (Cambridge University Press, 1987), 149–81.

11 For an interpretation of the clinical gaze that differentiates clinical judgement from the disciplinary logic of science, see T. Osborne, "Medicine and epistemology: Michel Foucault and the liberality of clinical reason" *History of the Human Sciences* vol. 5, no. 2 (1992), 63–93.

12 The distinction between rationalities and techniques of government is drawn from N. Rose and P. Miller, "Political power beyond the state: problematics of government" *British J. of Sociology* vol. 43, no. 2 (1992), 173–205.

13 The term "hybridity" is borrowed from Bruno Latour's work on science and modernity, *We have never been modern* (Princeton University Press, 1993).

14  R. Smith, *Inhibition: history and meaning in the sciences of the brain* (London, Transaction, 1992).

15  AA's survey findings are consistent with the group observation studies carried out by myself and my research assistant, Kimberley White-Mair. It is quite common to hear people at AA meetings declare that they have been sober for ten, fifteen, or even twenty years.

16  The text of the twelve steps is reproduced in the Appendix.

17  A long-term member of AA married to a wine connoisseur described at length her ultimately successful struggles to allow and even support her husband's interest in good wines (interview no. 17).

18  "Spiritual awakening" was the phrase used by AA's founder, Bill W., to refer to a significant spiritual experience he had some time after he had stopped drinking. AA's other founder, Dr Bob, never had such an evangelical experience.

19  M. Mann, *New primer on alcoholism* 2nd edn (New York, Holt, Rinehart and Winston, 1958 [1st edn 1950]).

20  Quoted in J.S. Rice, *A disease of one's own: psychotherapy, addiction, and the emergence of codependence* (New Brunswick, NJ, and London, Transaction 1996), 149.

21  In contrast to AA's emphasis on individual responsibility for one's drinking, groups such as Adult Children of Alcoholics and Codependents Anonymous tend to encourage the blaming of parents, and sometimes of social institutions, always on the assumption that "the inner child" is corrupted from the outside.

22  A useful analysis of the bootstrap culture of self-improvement is the collection edited by R. Keat and N. Abercrombie, *Enterprise culture* (London, Routledge, 1991). Further evidence that, in AA, ambition is not valued in the way it is in the rest of American society is found in Makela et al., *Alcoholics Anonymous: a study of mutual help in six societies* (Madison, University of Wisconsin Press, 1996), 129.

23  Hamilton B., *Getting started in AA* (Center City, Minn., Hazelden, 1995), 53.

24  From interview no. 14.

25  Hamilton B., *Getting started in AA*, 96.

26  In North America, most AA self-help books today are not published by AA itself but by the commercially run Hazelden organization. AA official publications are always anonymous, although it is acknowledged that Bill Wilson, AA's founder, wrote most of the original Big Book (and received the royalties from it, an exceptional practice that was never repeated).

27  N. Robertson, *Getting better: inside Alcoholics Anonymous* (New York, William Morrow, 1988), 100. As Robertson and others point out, AA is highly unusual among philanthropic organizations in that, instead of fundraising, it prevents its members from giving large donations: no member may donate more than $1,000 per year, and no estate gifts of more than $1,000 are allowed.

28  Makela et al., *Alcoholics Anonymous*, 94. See also E. Kurtz, *Not-God: A history of Alcoholics Anonymous* (Center City, Minn., Hazelden, 1991).

29 The term "drunkalogues" is from interview no. 17.

30 'Oldtimers' are sometimes granted a certain privilege to make instant judgements about newcomers, but the oldtimers' cross-talk is often followed by a reminder that "we cannot take inventory for others" (a reference to steps 5–8).

31 The Makela et al. study repeats the conventional wisdom about AA being largely middle-class (*Alcoholics Anonymous*, 104); but our group observation would suggest the opposite, namely that AA, at least in Toronto, is largely working class, not only numerically but also in terms of the communicative practices used in group meetings. A meeting held in the cafeteria of a major bank head office (group no. 1) was remarkable in that less than a quarter of the men present were wearing ties, and those remained uniformly silent; the women who spoke also seemed to be blue-collar rather than white-collar workers.

32 Hamilton B., *Getting started*, 67.

33 Group meetings do not provide any insights into the workings of sponsorship, but there is a detailed discussion of AA members' mixed feelings about becoming sponsors, in G. Hettelhack, *Second-year sobriety* (San Francisco, Harper, 1992).

34 Anonymous AA member, quoted in K. Davis, *Primero Dios: Alcoholics Anonymous and the Hispanic community* (Selingsgrove, Susquehanna University Press, 1995), 24.

35 Interview no. 12.

36 Several individuals interviewed indicated that they had been victims of child sexual abuse, but the struggle for sobriety was always the main plot line – a narrative tactic completely at odds with the general perception of child sexual abuse as that which trumps all other issues.

37 *Alcoholics Anonymous*, ch. 4, "We agnostics".

38 Group no. 1.

39 Hamilton B., *Getting started in AA*, 29.

40 P. Antze, "Symbolic action in Alcoholics Anonymous", 162. This is confirmed by several of our interviews, in which AA members spoke of their Higher Power in maternal/loving terms.

41 Nevertheless, AA is still a Protestant organization in many respects. Many groups close each meeting with the Protestant version of the Lord's Prayer. Some group business meetings in the Toronto area have debated the question of the Lord's Prayer almost as vehemently as they have argued the most divisive question in AA today, namely whether smoking should be allowed at meetings (interview no. 17).

42 Interview no. 14, 1997.

43 Davis, *Primero Dios*, 29.

44 Indeed, AA meetings are conspicuously lacking in computer-generated images, transparencies, videos, and other paraphernalia of modernity. The only objects that circulate regularly among AA members, other than the dull-looking pamphlets produced by the organization, are audiotapes (copied from other tapes rather than commercially sold) of AA members' statements and discussions at conventions.

45 Hettelhack, *Second-year sobriety*, 10.

46 M. Foucault, "Writing the self" in A. Davidson, ed., *Foucault and his interlocutors* (University of Chicago Press, 1997), 237.

47 Sometimes these bits of wisdom are neither anonymous nor collective – the fame of Kahlil Gibran's *The prophet* will attest to this – but AA has done a remarkable job of collecting, circulating, and distributing anonymous *hupomnemata* that generate no royalties.

48 One could also mention early homosexual activists in this context. As AA did, people like Dr Magnus Hirschfeld built hybrid assemblages for the self-governance of deviant populations through techniques that were partly borrowed from the psy and medical sciences and partly developed in experience-based self-help contexts. But the hybrid knowledge of the homosexual identity that existed in the 1930s did not proliferate into other realms until our own times.

49 W. Brown, *States of injury: power and freedom in late modernity* (Princeton University Press, 1995).

50 W. James, *The varieties of religious experience* (New York, Random House, 1994 [1902]), 561.

51 J. Dewey, *Human nature and human conduct* (New York, Random House, 1922), part I.

52 People in AA and AA texts spend very little time analyzing the drinking of non-alcoholics, since they do not believe that alcoholics can learn from normal drinkers to drink moderately; therefore, the comments here and elsewhere on AA's perception of normal drinkers rely mostly on the implicit contrast that helps AA to define alcoholism not in terms of an amount of alcohol consumed but in terms of a specific identity.

53 P. Hadot, *Philosophy as a way of life: spiritual exercises from Socrates to Foucault* (Oxford, Blackwell, 1995).

54 A lengthy account of her own life by Angie D., a Mexican-American member active in AA for twenty years, describes one marriage as an integral part of her sobriety, but also recounts a long period of sobriety in which she made a promise to herself to "not get married, one day at a time" (Angie D., audiotape distributed by AA members, 1984).

55 See, for example, C. Knapp, *Drinking: a love story* (New York, Dial Press, 1996).

## 6 THE LIQUOR OF GOVERNMENT

1 'Governing through persons' is William Walters' phrase (personal communication).

2 A. Hunt, *The governance of consumption: a history of sumptuary laws* (London, Macmillan, 1995).

3 For a critical analysis of the notion of 'culture', see J. Clifford, *The predicament of culture* (Cambridge, Mass., Harvard University Press, 1988).

4 There are several close ethnographic studies of drinking in southern European contexts in D. Gefou-Madianou, ed., *Alcohol, gender and culture* (London, Routledge, 1992).

5 Some useful anthropological studies are: M. Douglas, ed., *Constructive drinking: perspectives on drink from anthropology* (Cambridge University Press,

1987); C. MacAndrew and R.B. Edgerton, *Drunken comportment: a social explanation* (Chicago, Aldine, 1969); E. Akyeampong, *Drink, power,and cultural change: a social history of alcohol in Ghana* (Portsmouth, NH, Heinemann, 1996); M. Marshall, ed., *Beliefs, behaviours, and alcoholic beverages* (Ann Arbor, University of Michigan, 1979).

6 The concept of 'institutional habits' developed in conversation with Pat O'Malley.

7 [No author], *Alcohol, society and the state* (Toronto, Addiction Research Foundation, 1981, 2 vols); M. Moore and D.R. Gerstein, eds, *Alcohol and public policy: beyond the shadow of prohibition* (Washington, National Academy Press, 1981); B. Harrison, *Drink and the Victorians* (London, Faber and Faber, 1971); D. Gutzke, *Protecting the pub: brewers and publicans against temperance* (London, Royal Historical Society, 1989); Mass Observation, *The pub and the people* (London, Victor Gollancz, 1943); E. Malcolm, *Ireland sober, Ireland free: drink and temperance in nineteenth century Ireland* (Dublin, Gill and Macmillan, 1986); M. Ajzenstadt, "The medical-moral economy of regulations: alcohol legislation in British Columbia, 1871–1925" (PhD thesis, Simon Fraser University, 1983); R. Campbell, *Demon rum or easy money: government control of liquor in British Columbia from prohibition to privatization* (Ottawa, Carleton University Press, 1991); L. Harrison and E. Laine, *After repeal: a study of liquor control administration* (New York, Harper and Brothers, 1936); J. Gusfield, *Contested meanings: the construction of alcohol problems* (Madison, University of Wisconsin Press, 1996); E. Single and T. Storm, eds, *Public drinking and public policy* (Toronto, Addiction Research Foundation, 1985).

8 Harrison and Laine, *After repeal*, 68–69.

9 There are many studies on Finland's post-prohibition state alcohol monopoly; a good overview is D. Beauchamp, "The paradox of alcohol policy: the case of the 1969 Alcohol Act in Finland" in Moore and Gerstein, *Alcohol and public policy*.

10 Hon. W.F. Nickle, address in reply to the speech from the throne, February 17, 1925 (Archives of Ontario, MS 1695, R.G. 3-6-0, 778ff). This speech came toward the end of Ontario's prohibition period; Nickle's main point was that American university studies showed that one could not possibly get drunk on 2.5 per cent alcohol beer.

11 Single and Storm, *Public drinking and public policy*; R. Smart and A. Ogborne, *Northern spirits: a social history of alcohol in Canada* (Toronto, Addiction Research Foundation, 1997), esp. 140–43.

12 M. de Certeau, *The practice of everyday life* (Berkeley, University of California Press, 1984).

13 In 1984 the alcohol expert Robin Room argued that public health experts ought to take a strong interest in the operation of state alcohol control and licencing systems, but his call was not particularly successful, as far as I can determine. R. Room, "Alcohol control and public health" *Am. Rev. of Public Health* 5 (1984), 293–317.

14 The sale of alcoholic drinks has also been a historic source of vast fiscal resources for various states, an interesting subject that remains beyond the scope of this study.

15 I. Baird, "'A privilege to enjoy': liquor licencing and inspection in Toronto, 1926–1946" (MA research paper, Centre of Criminology, 1996). Information on the nature of KGB files is from Lynne Viola (personal communication).

16 M. Foucault, *Discipline and punish* (New York, Random House, 1977), 195–230.

17 In the United States, early liquor laws often prohibited screens and anything else that might obstruct the view of passersby looking into taverns. This organization of the moral gaze "has made law enforcement easier", Harrison and Laine argued, and "has curtailed the feeling of abandon on the part of the patrons which the sense of privacy generates". Harrison and Laine, *After repeal*, 67.

18 *Report of the British Columbia Liquor Inquiry Commission* (Government of British Columbia, 1970), 43.

19 Individual liquor permits were issued in a number of post-prohibition repeal jurisdictions. For Finland, see K. Makela et al., "Drink in Finland: increasing alcohol availability in a monopoly state" in [no editor], *Alcohol, society and the state* vol. 2, 45. For Ontario, see E. Single et al., "The alcohol policy debate in Ontario in the post-war era", also in *Alcohol, society and the state* vol. 2, 153. For British Columbia, see R. Campbell, *Demon rum*, 43.

20 Harrison, *Drink and the Victorians*, 45–85.

21 Baird, "'A privilege to enjoy'".

22 Baird, "'A privilege to enjoy'", 19.

23 I have not been able to determine when the "ladies and escorts" rule was abolished in the province in which I live, Ontario, but when I was an undergraduate, from 1972 to 1976, it was still in operation in the downtown working-class bars, though not in the university student pub.

24 Moore and Gerstein, *Alcohol and public policy*, 13.

25 There is a vast literature on the shift from discipline to risk, in the sociology of medicine, in criminology, and in other fields. Three sources that have been important for me are R. Castel, "From dangerousness to risk" in G. Burchell, C. Gordon, and P. Miller, eds, *The Foucault effect: studies in governmentality* (University of Chicago Press, 1991); J. Simon, "The ideological effects of actuarial practices" *Law and Society Review* vol. 22, no. 4 (1988), 772–800; P. O'Malley, "Risk, power and crime prevention" *Economy and Society* vol. 21, no. 3 (1993) 252–75.

26 Memorandum from the School of Graduate Studies to M. Valverde, December 17, 1996.

27 This repeal was general, not total: specific prohibitions, most notably applying to aboriginal peoples, were unaffected by the legislation repealing general prohibition.

28 R. Rosenzweig, *Eight hours for what we will* (Cambridge University Press, 1983).

29 Gusfield, *Contested meanings*, 91.

30 L. Gulick, in Harrison and Laine, *After repeal*, xi.

31 Harrison and Laine, *After repeal*, 65.

32 M. Douglas, *Purity and danger* (New York, Praeger, 1966).

33 Baird, "'A privilege to enjoy'".

34 Campbell, *Demon rum*, 54, 119.
35 The same dialectic of temperance measures creating drunkenness is found in Australia and New Zealand. There, as in the United Kingdom, the preferred target of regulation was, historically, time rather than food or space, and so the effort to get working-class men out of the bars and into the home for dinner was operationalized in six o'clock closing, a technique widely criticized for creating a uniform time for drunkenness, the "six o'clock swill". J. Bradbury, "The implementation and enforcement of liquor legislation in hotels and taverns in New Zealand" in Single and Storm, eds, *Public drinking and public policy*, 153–60.
36 Harrison and Laine, *After repeal*, 237. An appendix to *After Repeal* provides a very comprehensive list of liquor regulations throughout the United States in force in 1936.
37 Campbell, *Demon rum*, 54.
38 E.T. May, *Homeward bound: American families in the Cold War era* (New York, Basic Books, 1988); J. Parr, ed., *A diversity of women: Ontario 1945–1970* (University of Toronto Press, 1995).
39 Campbell, *Demon rum*, 118–19. See also Government of British Columbia, *Report*, 43–44.
40 The same drunkenness effect was noted in South Africa when municipal (white) governments set up beer halls – where anything but beer drinking was forbidden – to undercut home brewing, generate tax revenue, and exercise surveillance on (black) drinkers; P. la Hausse, *Brewers, beerhalls and boycotts: a history of liquor in South Africa* (Johannesburg, Ravan Press, 1988).
41 On actuarialism, see J. Simon, "The ideological effects of actuarial practices" *Law and Society Review* vol. 22, no. 3 (1988), 771–800.
42 M. Douglas, *Risk and blame: essays in cultural theory* (New York, Routledge, 1992).
43 This finding, from an Ontario 1991 study, is reported in Smart and Ogborne, *Northern spirits*, 118.
44 As Ian Baird's study shows, the Ontario liquor authorities put the proprietors in an impossible position. The burly waiters at Toronto's Parkdale Hotel sometimes threw drunken customers out, among other things to protect the licence, but this prompted the board to chastise the proprietor for "manhandling" customers (Baird, 'A privilege to enjoy', 51). This concern for the rights of drunken patrons reinforces the point that the board disciplined the proprietors, not the patrons.
45 Jefferson quoted in W. Unrau, *White man's wicked water: the alcohol trade and prohibition in Indian country, 1802–1892* (Lawrence, University of Kansas Press, 1996), 15.
46 W. Lauzun-Brown, "The toleration of alcoholic liquors" *Proceedings* of the British Society for the Scientific Study of Inebriety 65 (1900), 10–14.
47 T.D. Crothers, *The disease of inebriety from alcohol, opium, and other drugs* (American Society for the Study and Cure of Inebriety, 1893), 124.
48 Anonymous, *Journal of the American Medical Association* (*JAMA*), vol. 34 (1900), 614; Anonymous, *JAMA* vol. 34 (1900), 1137.

49  T. Clouston, "Some of the psychological and clinical aspects of alcohol" *British J. of Inebriety* vol. 11, no. 3 (1914), 110. See also C. Harford, "The drinking habits of uncivilized and semi-civilized races", *British J. of Inebriety* vol. 2, no. 3 (1905), 92–103.
50  Akyeampong, *Drink, power and cultural change*, 67, 84–94. South Africa was exempted from this general policy.
51  la Hausse, *Brewers, beerhalls and boycotts.*
52  Quoted in Akyeampong, *Drink, power and cultural change*, 109. The speech was given in 1933.
53  For an account of the WCTU's struggle to change British imperial policy in the direction of temperance and/or prohibition, see I. Tyrrell, *Woman's world/woman's empire: the WCTU in international perspective* (Chapel Hill, University of North Carolina Press, 1991).
54  In the mid-nineteenth century, annuities paid to Indian tribes in exchange for land concessions quickly found their way into the hands of poor white settlers who got the federal money back into white hands by selling liquor in contravention of the law or by using the many loopholes in the law. Nineteenth century observers seemed as struck by the Indians' refusal to save money as they were by their purported tendency to drink until all the liquor was gone. Unrau, *White man's wicked water*, 48–55.
55  In early twentieth century New Hebrides, for example, the British liked to blame the French, specifically the ne'er-do-well beachcomber types, for corrupting the morals of aboriginals through drink. M. Lindstrom, "*Grog Blong Yumi*: alcohol and kava on Tanna, Vanuatu" in M. Marshall, ed., *Through a glass darkly: beer and modernization in Papua New Guinea* (Boroko, Institute of Applied Social and Economic Research, 1982), 425–26.
56  Indian Act, Revised Statutes of Canada, 1906, c.43, s.137.
57  *R. vs. Verdi* (1914) 23 C.C.C., 47–48.
58  Archives of Ontario, LCBO files, 1927, Circular 63.
59  A documentary on aboriginals in the Canadian Army interviewed an aboriginal veteran from British Columbia who reported that the Mounted Police would patrol small-town bars and ask anybody who looked Indian for proof of their enfranchisement, since if they had officially given up Indian status they were allowed to drink. "The Journal", CBC television, Nov. 11, 1996.
60  Archives of Ontario, LCBO files, Circular 526, Nov. 1, 1928.
61  *R. vs. Drybones* (1967) 61 W.W.R., 370.
62  *R. vs. Whiteman* (1971) 2 W.W.R., 216; confirmed in *R. v. Lonethunder* (1979) 4 C.N.L.R., 109.
63  *R. vs. Mellon* (1900), Territories Law Reports, vol. V, 301–2. See also *R. vs. Hughes* (1906), B.C. Reports, vol. XII, 290.
64  The judicial decisions upholding the validity of the intoxicant sections of the Indian Act never fail to mention that the Act was passed to *protect*, not discriminate against, Indian people.
65  Aboriginal veteran from British Columbia interviewed on CBC television's 'The Journal', Nov. 11, 1996. In rural British Columbia, Legion halls and other licenced establishments also functioned as places to find out about job opportunities for blue-collar men.

66 For what follows, I am relying on Unrau, *White man's wicked water.*
67 Quoted in Unrau, *White man's wicked water,* 111.

## 7 REDUCING RISKS, REPLACING FLUIDS

1 There is a large body of literature showing that the effect of alcohol on behaviour is largely a product of cultural expectations. The most influential source in this literature is C. MacAndrew and R.B. Edgerton, *Drunken comportment: a social explanation* (Chicago, Aldine, 1969); see also M. Marshall, ed., *Beliefs, behaviours, and alcoholic beverages: a cross-cultural survey* (Ann Arbor, University of Michigan, 1979).
2 J. Simon, "In the place of the parent: risk management and the government of campus life" *Social and Legal Studies* vol. 3 (1994), 32.
3 M. Sanchez-Craig and A. Wilkinson, "Guidelines for advising on the goal of treatment: abstinence or moderation" in B. Howard, S. Harrison, V. Carver, and L. Lightfoot, eds, *Alcohol and drug problems* (Toronto, Addiction Research Foundation, 1993), 133.
4 In the addiction research community in North America, numerous stories circulate orally about the ways in which members of AA either succeeded in stopping, or threatened to stop, funding for controlled drinking programmes or even research on controlled drinking. For an account of one such struggle, see R. Roizen, "The great controlled drinking controversy" in M. Galanter, ed., *Recent developments in alcoholism* vol. 5 (New York, Plenum, 1987), 245–79.
5 See, for example, F. Duckert, "'Controlled drinking': a complicated and contradictory field" in Nordic Council for Alcohol and Drug Research, *Perspectives on controlled drinking* (Helsinki, NAD publication no. 17, 1989).
6 T. Osborne, "Of health and statecraft" in A. Petersen and R. Bunton, eds, *Foucault, health and medicine* (London, Routledge, 1997), 185. See also A. Petersen, "Risk, governance, and the new public health", in the same volume.
7 *Alcohol,* pamphlet published by the Addiction Research Foundation, 1991.
8 Pat O'Malley has suggested that, in the drug field, harm-reduction programmes not only teach people how to consume drugs wisely and with fewer risks, but even how to consume risks themselves. See P. O'Malley, "Consuming risks", paper presented at the Centre of Criminology, University of Toronto, October 1996.
9 S. Ronnberg, "Issues in the self-monitoring of alcohol problems" in Nordic Council, *Perspectives on controlled drinking.*
10 D.M. Gorman, "Alcohol misuse and the predisposing environment" *British Medical Bulletin* vol. 50, *Alcohol and alcohol problems* (1994), 37. It should be pointed out that the author of this article is located at the Rutgers Center for Alcohol Studies in the United States, which may explain the pro-temperance views; but, in general, studies published in Britain, though usually more biologically and medically oriented than American ones, do not show much interest in the findings of epidemiology.
11 Royal College of General Practitioners, *Alcohol – a balanced view* (Reports from general practice, 1986), 24.

12 Sanchez-Craig and Wilkinson, "Guidelines . . .", 137. This is in sharp contrast to the harm-reduction programme of methadone maintenance: heroin users are not told that they need to be completely clean for three weeks *before* they go on methadone, undoubtedly because heroin is thought to be truly addictive, while even advocates of the disease model of alcoholism tend to believe that if one really tries one can simply quit.

13 M. Valverde, "Judging speech: sex and harm in Canadian obscenity law" in A. Hutchinson and K. Petersen, eds, *Censorship in Canada today* (University of Toronto Press, forthcoming).

14 "How alcohol affects you" poster (Toronto, Addiction Research Foundation, 1996).

15 *Facts about alcohol* (Toronto, Addiction Research Foundation, 1991). A full-colour pamphlet for pregnant women on drugs and alcohol states: "'Safe' level is not known; consider avoiding alcohol entirely." (*Is it safe for my baby?* Toronto, Addiction Research Foundation, 1991.)

16 Even very young inner-city women are well informed about fetal alcohol; see M. Cornelius, H. Lebow, and N. Day, "Attitudes and knowledge about drinking: relationships with drinking behaviour among pregnant teenagers" *J. Drug Education* vol. 27, no. 3 (1997), 321–43.

17 C. Shammas, "Changes in English and Anglo-American consumption from 1550 to 1800" in J. Brewer and R. Porter, eds, *Consumption and the world of goods* (London, Routledge, 1993), 183–85; see also article by S. Mintz, "The changing roles of food in the study of consumption" in the same anthology, esp. 265.

18 B. Harrison, *Drink and the Victorians* (London, Faber and Faber, 1971), 302.

19 Gladstone quoted in G. Wilson, "The liquor problem in England and Wales: a survey from 1860 to 1935" *British J. of Inebriety* vol. 38, no. 4 (1941), 157.

20 Harrison, *Drink and the Victorians*, 296–305.

21 For example: "Cocoa and chocolate are undoubtedly among the most palatable and nutritious of beverages, especially for winter days . . . Messrs Fry and Sons, Ltd, of Bristol, have long enjoyed a great reputation for the purity and all-round excellence of their products . . .", editorial notes, *British J. of Inebriety* vol. 12, no. 3 (1915), 185. George Cadbury, not coincidentally, was among a small number of non-physicians who joined the British Society for the Scientific Study of Inebriety as associate members.

22 N. Robertson, *Getting better: inside Alcoholics Anonymous* (New York, William Morrow, 1988), 22. Coffee was and still is used as a hangover remedy, probably because of its psychological effect (coffee in fact exacerbates the dehydration of hangovers).

23 This is borne out by the observation of AA groups carried out by myself and a research assistant. Every AA group we attended, however small, had a coffee urn in a prominent place, and members often drank from it the way chain smokers smoke.

24 Anonymous, "The nursing of alcoholic patients" *British J. of Addiction* vol. 44, no. 2 (1947), 78.

25 The World of Coca-Cola museum, Atlanta, Georgia.

26 E.J. Kahn, *The big drink: the story of Coca Cola* (New York, Random House, 1960), 57.

27 Reproduced as a postcard available from the Coca-Cola museum.

28 Coca-Cola was, in the early and mid-twentieth century, rather expensive. Children and youths tended to drink cheaper substitutes, such as Pepsi.

29 Opium and cocaine were not unusual ingredients in health drinks, particularly those sold to cure inebriety and/or neurasthenia and debility. Coca-Cola contained a small amount of cocaine in the first decade of its existence (a fact carefully suppressed in the Coca-Cola museum's vast displays). See Kahn, *The big drink*.

30 Kahn, *The big drink*, 14–15; and W.D. Wrynn, *Coke goes to war* (Missoula, MT, Pictorial Histories Publishing Co., 1996).

31 While not featuring children or youth in its ads, in the 1920s Coke developed major Christmas-time campaigns featuring a particular image of Santa Claus that has since proliferated throughout North America and even beyond. The ads usually had Santa Claus himself drinking, not the children, but the implications seemed to be that, on the special occasion in which even temperate families would bring out a bottle, it was possible to enjoy the pleasures of family and gift-giving without alcohol. (See the Christmas-related displays and ads in the Coca-Cola museum.)

32 In Toronto, the cappuccino chain The Second Cup (which is very similar to the American Starbucks) has subway ads promoting the "hot, steamy romance" of cappuccino.

## 8 JUDICIAL DIAGNOSTICS

1 For popular interest in spiritism in late Victorian England, see J. Walkowitz, *City of dreadful delight: narratives of sexual danger in late-Victorian London* (University of Chicago Press, 1992), ch. 6; for expert knowledges of 'double consciousness', see I. Hacking, *Rewriting the soul: multiple personality and the sciences of memory* (Princeton University Press, 1995).

2 E. Rapping, *The culture of recovery: making sense of the self-help movement in women's lives* (Boston, Beacon, 1996); P. Ewick, "Corporate cures: the commodification of social control" *Studies in Law, Politics and Society* vol. 13 (1993), 137–57.

3 H. Kalant, "Intoxicated automatism: legal concept vs. scientific evidence" *Contemporary Drug Problems* 23 (Winter 1996), 637. Kalant then admits that "dissociative disorders" can involve complex aggressive acts, but he quickly states that these descendants of the old category of hysteria belong fully to the psychiatric province of mental disorder, and are therefore separate from the situation of non-insane persons who claim to have been acting in a state of automatism.

4 Addiction Research Foundation, *Response to consultation paper on options to reform the Criminal Code of Canada* (January 1995), 8.

5 Pharmacologists and epidemiologists, for whom alcoholism is invisible, are not the only or even the main type of researcher at the Addiction Research Foundation (ARF): there are plenty of psychiatrists, psychologists, and social workers among its 600 or so staff members. Nevertheless, psychiatric

perspectives were not included in ARF's submission to parliament on the intoxication defense.

6  Addiction Research Foundation, *Response* . . . , 7.

7  See M. Keiter, "Just say no excuse: the rise and fall of the intoxication defence" *J. of Criminal Law and Criminology* vol. 87, no. 2 (1997), 482–519. This article provides a comprehensive survey of recent American legislative bans on the intoxication defense.

8  For an analysis of the differences between disciplinary techniques aimed at individuals and the newer risk-based techniques associated with what Foucault called government by security, see R. Castel, "From dangerousness to risk" in G. Burchell, C. Gordon, and P. Miller, eds, *The Foucault effect* (University of Chicago Press, 1991). My analysis differs from Castel's, however, in that both the study of liquor control in chapter 6 and the present study of the intoxication defense show that risk management does not necessarily rely on numerical calculations by experts.

9  J. Gusfield, *Contested meanings: the construction of alcohol problems* (Madison, University of Wisconsin Press, 1996), ch. 13.

10  Keiter, "Just say no excuse", 482.

11  N. Walker, *Crime and insanity in England* (Edinburgh University Press, 1968), ch. 10 ("Automatism and drunkenness"). See also R. Smith, *Trial by medicine: insanity and responsibility in Victorian trials* (Edinburgh University Press, 1981).

12  N. Kerr, *Inebriety or narcomania* (London, H.K. Lewis, 1894), 500.

13  R. Harris, *Murders, madness, and medicine: law and society in the fin-de-siecle* (Oxford, Clarendon Press, 1989).

14  W. Sullivan, "The criminal responsibility of the alcoholic" *British J. of Inebriety* vol. 2, no. 2 (1904), 50.

15  See, for instance, S. Atkinson, "The forensic psychology of inebriety" *British J. of Inebriety* vol. 2, no. 1 (1904), esp. 17–19.

16  Cited in Joint Committee on Continuing Legal Education of the American Law Institute and the American Bar Association, *The problem of intoxication as a defense* (1961).

17  S. Hopwood and K. Milner (physicians at Broadmoor), "Some observations on the relation of alcohol to criminal insanity" *British J. of Inebriety* vol. 38, no. 2 (1940), 52–70; Walker, *Crime and insanity in England* vol. 1, ch. 10; and Joint Committee . . . *The problem of intoxication*, 26.

18  Sopinka J., in *Daviault vs. The Queen* [1994], Supreme Court Reports, 3, 125.

19  *Daviault*, 63–132. See also R. Room, "Drinking, violence, gender and causal attribution: a Canadian case study in science, law and policy" *Contemporary Drug Problems* 23 (Winter 1996), 649–86.

20  Cory J., in *Daviault*, 79.

21  Because it is a federal and officially bilingual institution, the Supreme Court cannot take official notice of the very different histories of anglophone vs. francophone expert knowledges within Canada, particularly in the case of the criminal law, which unlike in the United States is the same throughout the nation-state (Quebec maintains a separate legal system for civil law).

22 *Response to consultation paper on options to reform the Criminal Code of Canada* (Addiction Research Foundation, January 10, 1995).

23 Cory J., in *Daviault*, 90, 99–100.

24 Cory J., in *Daviault*, 92.

25 Cited in Joint Committee . . . *The problem of intoxication as a defence*, 7.

26 Medical and temperance literatures are of course not the only antecedents of contemporary self-help discourse on addiction; there is also a separate but converging influence deriving from the power of positive thinking and other commercial, non-medical approaches to improving and maximizing the self.

27 Hacking, *Rewriting the soul.*

28 The law enacted by the Canadian parliament in 1995 in direct opposition to the Supreme Court's earlier ruling on the intoxication defense has a very lengthy preamble whose second paragraph runs as follows: "Whereas the Parliament of Canada recognizes that violence has a particularly disadvantaging impact on the equal participation of women and children in society and on the rights of women and children to security of the person . . ." (1995, 42-43-44 Elizabeth II, ch. 32). Such language makes it seem as if drunken men never hit or kill other men, and perpetuates the image of women as essentially victimized.

29 Criminality and violence are explicitly gendered masculine only in feminist discourse, but in the more dominant discourses that classify criminality as essentially connected to race and to youth there is nevertheless an implicit gendering of the criminal.

30 For an analysis of the contemporary utilization of victimized identities as sources of political capital, see W. Brown, *States of injury* (Princeton University Press, 1995).

31 J. Derrida, *Spectres of Marx* (New York, Routledge, 1994).

32 "Effective history" is Michel Foucault's phrase; see M. Dean, *Critical and effective histories* (London, Routledge, 1995). Unlike Dean, however, I take Foucault's "effective history" to have an affinity with Walter Benjamin. Unlike either nostalgic nationalist history writing or the empiricist recounting of facts, Benjamin's history is an embodied history evoking a particular set of events in the concrete context of a particular crisis in the present. Effective history is always someone's history – for Benjamin, the history of a particular oppressed group – and it always addresses a contemporary dilemma. See W. Benjamin, "Theses on the philosophy of history", in *Illuminations* (New York, Schoken, 1968), 253–65.

# INDEX

Authors of secondary sources are listed in the index only when their work is cited in the text. Readers are therefore encouraged to consult the notes for information on both primary and secondary sources.

pre-WWII approach 179
risk-management programme
about 179
second-hand smoke warnings 181
statistical vacuum 181
syndrome 179
zero tolerance policy 180–1
Foucault, Michel
act vs. identity opposition,
deconstruction of 139
*hupomnemata,* observation on 136
identity-based governance 140
madness and rationality 190
nineteenth century clinical/
disciplinary techniques 124
pastoralism 19
surveillance 149
systematic self-observation 175
free will
consumption problems and 3
determinism vs. 3, 16
'epidemic of' 3
existence of 4–5
habit and 14–15
historical workings of 19
necessity and 15
Victorian science and 59–62
*see also* intoxicated automatism
freedom
addiction and 32–3
belief in, necessity of 21
genealogy of modern 17
goal of recovery, as 32, 35
governance, as primary
programme of 17–18
habit and 36, 37
necessity and, opposition between
35–42
self-control, defined as 17
treatment and 32, 62–4, 66–7
Freud
compulsion to repeat dilemmas 5
pleasure principle of 97

gambling 121
Garland, David 83, 86
gender
cocktail lounge segregation 158–9
intoxicated automatism and 202
Gladstone, William 182
Gordon, Dr Mary 58, 90

government sales regulation *see*
liquor regulation
Grove Retreat for Inebriate Women
79
Gulick, Luther 154, 155
Gusfield, Joseph 118, 154

habit
Alcoholics Anonymous and 140–2
alcoholism and 39–40
behaviourism and 38
conservative nature of 35–6
determinism and 38
Dewey, John, views of 23, 37–8, 40,
139, 140
eating and drinking 62–4
education and 37
free will and 14–15
freedom and 36, 37
genealogy of the will and 41
inebriety and 93
James, William, views of 35–7
limitations of analysis of 41–2
modern scientific treatment of 40
natural determinism and 38
pragmatist approach to 36, 38
rejection of by European
philosophers 38
science of 38
second nature, as 37
habit forming drugs 39–40
Habitual Drunkards–Inebriates Acts
(UK)
administrative problems 85–6
aftermath of 87
demise of 86
Drunkards Act (1879), proponent
of 77
failure of 86–7
free patients vs. coerced criminals
85–6
groups governed by 76
habitual drunkard, definition of
77
Inebriates Act (1898) 76–8
local government resistance to 85,
86
medical testimony, no
requirement for 76, 77
middle/upper class inebriates 76
research studies on inebriates 86

liquor control/licencing (*cont.*)
objective of 145, 161–2
officials, non-expert qualifications
of 148
Ontario: beer alcohol level debate
147; licence holders,
disciplining of 150; Liquor
Control Board 12, 151; liquor
inspectors, detailed records of
149
opening hours strategy 147
post-repeal 159, 160
premises *see* saloons
prostitution 151
pub licencing vs. individual permit
system 150
public administration, as subject
of 9
rationale, lack of clear 147
regulatory anarchy, as 10
risk factors as rationale 152–3, 161
social effects of 169–70
space of public drinking, focus on
12, 147
Spain, attitude in 145
specific drinks, debates about 147
state monopoly vs. private
enterprise 148
subcontracting of governing
function, as 151–2
time vs. space control 146–7
United Kingdom, licencing in
146–7, 150–1
United States, licencing debate in
147
variety in regulatory strategies 146
visibility issue 149–50
*see also* aboriginal peoples; saloons
liquor regulation
disorder purpose 144
generally 143–5
prohibition, general vs. specific
144–5
purpose of 144
risk factor purpose 144
taxation policy, through 1, 144
*see also* liquor control/licencing
Locke, John 14

Magnan, Valentin 48
Manchester Women's Christian
Temperance Association 79

mania 45–9
Maudsley, Henry 59–61
medicalization *see* inebriety;
inebriate asylums
men
alcoholism as disorder of
masculine identity 106–9
degeneration theory and 52
saloons and working class culture
154, 159
*see also* gender
Mental Deficiency Act (UK),
reclassified female inebriates
under 58, 87
moderate drinking *see* harm
reduction
monomania 2, 45, 46, 48
*moonstone, The* 190
Morel, B.A. 48
multiple personality disorder
gender ascription of 201–2
generally 192
historical child abuse 201
intoxication defence, failure to
cross-reference to 201–2
recovered memory syndrome 201
victim focus 203–4
Victorian roots of 201, 202–3
Myerson, Dr Abraham 97

National Society for the Prevention
of Cruelty to Children (NSPCC)
53, 76
neurasthenia 11, 72
Nye, Robert 83

oinomaniacs 48
O'Neill, Eugene 108
Ordronaux, John 50
Osborne, Thomas 174

pastoral care
pastoral-clinical care 47
Roman Catholic orders and 88
treatment and 19, 62–7
*see also* Salvation Army
patriotism, as strategy for moderate
drinking 98
Pearson, Karl 56, 58
Peddie, Dr Alexander 48, 77
Pierce, Charles 35
pleasure principle 97

pragmatism
  AA and 137–42
  philosophy of: habit and 36;
    postmodern 20–1
pregnancy *see* degeneration theory;
  fetal alcohol
prohibition
  demise of 96
  general vs. specific 144–5
  post-repeal regulation 159–60
  World War I, during 96
  *see also* aboriginal peoples
Protestant
  ethic 34
  influence on AA 125
psychiatry
  alcoholism, view of 11, 49, 106
  marginalizing of by Yale Center
    100–1
  sexual problems and 102
  theories about alcoholism 98
  *see also* alcohology

*Quarterly Journal of Studies on Alcohol*
  100, 105

Rapping, Elayne 192
recovered memory syndrome 201
recovery
  AA meaning of 125–6
  addiction recovery: literature 16;
    networks 12
  codependence, from 34–5
  freedom and 32–3
  movement, ideological orientation
    of 21
  private treatment facilities 75
  technologies of 28
  World Wide Web homepages 4, 14
  *see also* treatment; twelve steps
reformatories *see* inebriate
  reformatories
regulation *see* liquor regulation
replacement fluids
  AA coffee 183
  Cadbury's 183
  chocolate 183
  Coca-Cola: ads for, evolution of
    184–6; alcohol replacement
    marketing 186, 188;
    Americanization of 186;
    competition to 187;

connection to alcoholic
    pleasure 186;
    internationalization of 187;
    study of 13; success of 184;
    youth marketing 186
  cocoa 183
  coffee 183, 187
  cold drinks 182
  commercial habits, reshaping of
    through 187
  Fry's 183
  health promotion 187, 189
  mineral waters 183–4
  Ovaltine 183
  philanthropic organizations, role
    of 182
  problematization of alcohol and
    187
  Rowntree 183
  Schweppes 182
  soft drinks 184
  tea 182
retreats *see* inebriate retreats
Ribot, Theodule 3, 60–1
Rice, John Steadman 30–1
risk management
  controlled drinking techniques
    177
  fetal alcohol and 179
  liquor licencing strategies and
    144, 160, 161
  *see also* harm
Room, Robin 18
Rose, Nikolas 17
Rush, Dr Benjamin 2, 4, 13, 39
Rutgers Center for Alcohol Studies
  98

saloons
  abolition of word 154
  bars 157
  censorship of names 155
  cocktail lounges 158–60
  contemporary variations 159
  food regulation 156–7
  gender segregation in 158
  immorality associations and 154
  synonyms invented for 154–5
  table service rules 157
  wet vs. dry discussions about 154
  working-class male culture and
    154, 159

249

US National Council on Alcoholism,
    questionnaire on alcoholism
    24–5

Walker, Nigel 194
will, the
    diseased, repairing 43–67
    lesions of 34, 45, 47
    nineteenth century medical
        practices and 45–67
    pastoral medicine and 62–7
    philosophy and, contemporary 3
    psychology, abandonment of by 3
    resurrection of *see* intoxicated
        automatism
    tension between desire and 33–4
    *see also* diseases of the will; free will
Wilson, Bill 29
women
    degeneration theory and 52, 56–8
    doctors 53–4
    drinking by 53–5, 160
    drunk driving warnings to 180
    feeble-minded 58
    intoxicated automatism and 194,
        200

maternal drinking *see*
    degeneration theory
Mental Deficiency Act (UK) and
    58, 87
violence against 194
*see also* gender
Women's Christian Temperance
    Union 53, 80
World Health Organization 39, 119
World War I, prohibition during 96
World War II
    alcohol socialization after 40, 121,
        159–60
    unrestricted alcohol sales 96
World Wide Web
    Interneters Anonymous 20
    recovery home pages 4, 14
    self-help groups on 4

Yale Center for Alcohol Studies 98,
    100–1

Zizek, Slavoj 21

Printed in the United States
43323LVS00005B/46-54